CRtasdul fuh
May 86

British Politics

D1826122

Philip Gabriel
and
Andrew Maslen

MAIDSTONE GRAMMAR SCHOOL
FOR GIRLS
LIBRARY

MGGS Library

R21667J3622

LONGMAN GROUP LIMITED
Longman House,
Burnt Mill, Harlow, Essex CM20, 2JE, England
and Associated Companies throughout the World

© Longman Group Limited 1986

All rights reserved. No part of this publication
may be reproduced, stored in a retrieval system,
or transmitted in any form or by any means, electronic,
mechanical, photocopying, recording or otherwise,
without the prior written permission of the copyright
owner.

First published 1986

ISBN 0582 33136 6

**Printed in Great Britain by
Scotprint Ltd., Musselburgh.**

Contents

MAIDSTONE GRAMMAR SCHOOL
FOR GIRLS
LIBRARY

Acknowledgements

We are grateful to the following for permission to reproduce photographs:

Aerofilms, page 210; BBC Hulton Picture Library, pages 4 *Brady*, 8 and 17; British Telecom, page 185; Camera Press, pages 251 (below) and 256; J. Allan Cash, pages 30, 182 and 250 (below); Central Office of Information, pages 69 and 106; City Syndication, pages 37 and 46; Collector's Photographs, pages 14 and 263; Mary Evans Picture Library, page 196 (above); Imperial War Museum, page 250 (above); Independent Television News Ltd, page 161; Jaguar, page 187; Network Photographers, pages 9 *John Sturrock*, 21 *Judah Passow*, 47 *John Sturrock*, 76 *Judah Passow*, 103 *Judah Passow*, 142 *Chris Davies*, 145 *John Sturrock*, 167 *Mike Abrahams*, 173 *John Sturrock*, 174 *Mike Abrahams*, 192 *John Sturrock*, 193 *Laurie Sparham*, 196 (below) *John Sturrock* and 240 *Katalin Arkell*; The Photo Source, pages 13, 23, 39, 41, 42, 74, 78, 83, 153 and 251 (above); Press Association, pages 11, 24, 51, 61, 140 and 158; Scottish Home and Health Department reproduced by permission of the Controller of Her Majesty's Stationery Office, page 45; Janine Wiedel, page 34.

Cover: Camera Press (above), Network Photographers *Chris Davies* (below)

We are indebted to the following for permission to reproduce copyright material:

The Controller of Her Majesty's Stationary Office for an extract from *Hansard* Vol 969 C 49 (25/6/79); Lambeth County Council for extracts from Council records (29/11/79); Staffordshire Sentinel Newspapers Ltd for two letters from the *Evening Sentinel* (3/3/82).

Part One: BACKGROUND TO BRITISH POLITICS

1   What is politics?

To ask the question 'What is politics?' may, at first sight, seem rather strange. Television, the press, and radio, pour out a stream of information about political events and the activities of politicians.

New laws, speeches in parliament, interviews, conferences, tours around the country by ministers, meetings with political leaders from other countries, are just some examples of the political world presented to us. But such activity does not, in itself, explain what politics is, and it can produce feelings of irritation and frustration about both politicians and politics itself. Why can't 'they' stop arguing, sink their differences, and work together for a change? Why do 'they' break the promises made during the elections? Even worse, why do 'they' make promises which they know can't be kept? Are 'they' in politics just to feather their own nests? Is politics just a dirty game?

It is not the purpose of this book to paint a false picture of politics and maintain that politicians are some breed of super-heroes of outstanding virtue. They are not. But some of the most common criticisms levelled at politicians, and the way politics is conducted, can be based on a misunderstanding of politics and of the problems which lie at the heart of politics. Before we look at over-argumentative and self-seeking politicians, it might be useful to look at ourselves first.

Politics and conflict

If everyone behaved in exactly the same way, and believed in exactly the same things, politics would not exist. Nor would human beings as we know them. People are different, with different *beliefs* and different *interests*, and this creates conflict. Politics exist because of that conflict.

What are these interests which we might have to protect? A plan to build a new car factory, for example, is bound to create a clash of interests. Building firms, car unions, unemployed people living in the area, would support it. But farmers who would lose land, householders faced with a factory at the bottom of their gardens, people living on roads which would carry extra traffic, are all likely to oppose the plan.

It is not just different interests which create conflict. People hold different beliefs as well. In politics the views of many people will be influenced by a belief, however vague, in socialism or conservatism. Others may hold strong religious beliefs which affect their attitudes towards such issues as abortion, or spending money on armaments.

Conflict and groups

Just as the existence of conflicting interests and beliefs is normal and natural in people, so is membership of different kinds of groups. Some groups to which we belong are fairly small, such as the family, a school or college class, or a youth club. Others, trade unions for example, are very large and each member can only get to know a few others personally. The two imaginary individuals below illustrate these differences:

Smith and Jones (see Fig 1.1) clearly have conflicting interests and beliefs: their support of different political parties may well reflect both of these things. Smith, for example, may feel that it is in his interests to work for a Labour government and that the policies of such a government are close to his deeply-held beliefs about society as a whole. For Jones the same would be true of the Conservative Party.

They could also find, however, that there is conflict *between* the groups to which they belong. For example, Jones' engineering firm might be criticised by his Conservative friends for polluting a river.

In the same way there may be conflict *within* the groups. Smith may be in conflict with other members of his trade union about wage demands or he may disagree with some aspects of Labour Party policy.

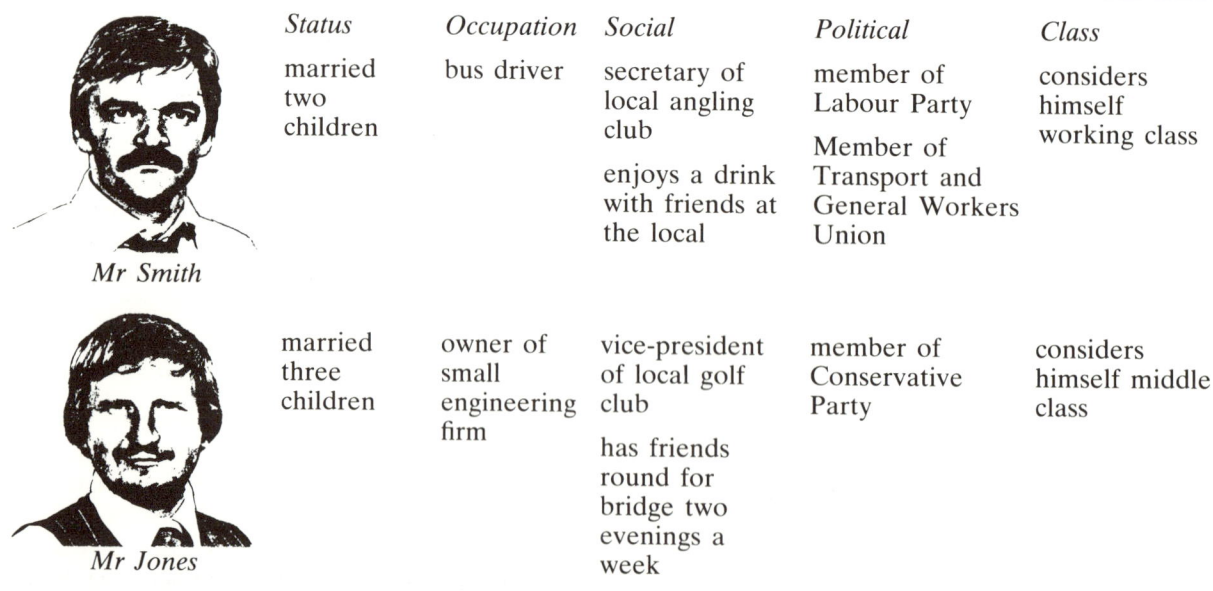

	Status	Occupation	Social	Political	Class
Mr Smith	married two children	bus driver	secretary of local angling club enjoys a drink with friends at the local	member of Labour Party Member of Transport and General Workers Union	considers himself working class
Mr Jones	married three children	owner of small engineering firm	vice-president of local golf club has friends round for bridge two evenings a week	member of Conservative Party	considers himself middle class

Figure 1.1 *Everyday influences help to mould political opinion.*

Conflict and decisions

So far we have seen that conflict, based on clashes of interest and belief, involves all of us, both as individuals and as members of different groups. Disagreement and argument is not just limited to politicians. Such conflict lies at the heart of politics because it presents us with a vitally important problem. Given the fact that people can have such different views on what ought to be done, how is anything done at all? Arguing, debating with each other is healthy enough. But there comes a time when decisions have to be made.

Groups involved in decision-making are not all the same. Some of them, such as families, friends at the pub or at the bridge table, are informal. They may have rules, standards, or shared ways of doing things, but these are not laid down in any precise way. On the other hand, groups such as the golf and angling clubs, the church, the trade union, are highly organised. They have formal rules about selecting officers, the rights and duties of members, *and* about how decisions should be made. These rules are often written down in the form of a **constitution**. However, even when rules are written down, certain customs, habits, or unwritten rules usually develop alongside them. For example in Smith's angling club it might be that, according to the constitution, the president is elected annually, but it is the custom for the president to be returned unopposed if he is willing to stand again. In politics we call this kind of custom or habit a **convention**.

With these formal groups a way has to be found to cope with, or *manage* conflict so that decisions can be made without the group breaking up in disarray. Figure 1.2 shows a system for dealing with differences of opinion, and reaching a decision.

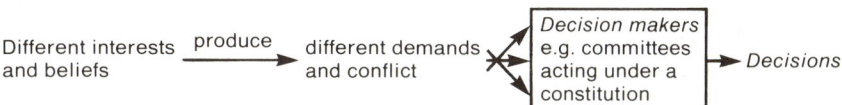

Figure 1.2 Decisions in a formal group.

The existence of rules and agreements about how such groups should run their affairs does not mean that conflict is avoided. But it does mean that different points of view can be channelled, or managed, so that members of a tennis club for example, who disagree with certain decisions, can work within the club rules to try and change these decisions – they don't have to walk out, or blow up the clubhouse.

Politics in a national setting

Politics can be seen as originating in conflict and being concerned with how this conflict is managed peacefully. But the difficulties of doing this are vastly increased if we look at politics in a country as a whole. There

The ultimate conflict in a society is civil war. In the United States, between 1861 and 1865, civil war cost well over a million lives.

are so many individuals and groups, each wanting different things, that government becomes a complex business. Above all, given that groups and individuals who disagree must find ways of working together if society is not to break down, how can this be achieved on a national scale?

One way of solving the problem might be to use force so that people have little choice in the matter. Another solution is to try and work out ways of making decisions which most groups can accept as fair – even when inevitably some can't get their own way. Getting such agreement, or consent, depends on a number of factors – not least whether there has been an opportunity to take part in the political debate so that all opinions have been heard.

Participation and representation

In some of the small groups we belong to it may be possible for decisions to be taken by all the members but, for the nation as a whole, this is not very practical. We are more used to electing people to *represent* us – for example as local councillors or members of parliament. In electing representatives we are, as a result, more likely to accept their decisions even though the person, or the party we support, loses. We also need to have a real choice in elections so that we have some chance of voting according to our interests and beliefs. Choice means that we can dismiss our representatives as well. It follows that politicians who want to gain power, or keep it, must take into account the views of those who elect them. Of course governments are always telling us that unpopular policies are in our own interests, that their medicine sometimes tastes terrible. This may be acceptable if it produces the right results. However, the voters had better be feeling well by election time or a new doctor may be called for!

Participation, however, can mean more than voting in elections. You might be a member of a group such as a trade union, or become interested in a local issue and write letters to newspapers and MPs; however, one of the most direct ways of taking part is by joining a political party.

It follows that the actions of a government become more acceptable if, before making a decision, they consult those who are likely to be most affected. No one likes the thought of a motorway or a coalmine near their home and those who oppose such proposals may take extreme action. Without any chance to have their arguments heard, people can develop a bitter resentment which could spill over into violence.

Linked to this is another key issue. In any form of participation and consultation *information* is a vital first step. It is not enough to rely on the government to tell us all we 'need' to know. Governments are not always happy to release information, and the more information we have, the greater the opportunity for proper debate on the issues which face us. If we suspect that something is being held back we are not so likely to accept government decisions. In this, the television, radio, and the press have an important part to play in investigating issues and criticising the government.

However, open and public disagreements can only work if *all* the conflicting groups share a certain characteristic – toleration. We can all get on with people we agree with. Toleration is based on the idea that we accept the right of others to be different. So long as this basic toleration exists a society has a chance of peaceful government despite clashes of interest and belief between various groups within it.

The political system

In the end it is necessary to channel or manage conflict so that decisions can be taken. The whole process, starting with the wishes or demands of individuals and groups, to arriving at decisions, we can call a **political system**.

Figure 1.3 is partly a summary of what the rest of this book is about. It breaks down the political system into four stages: demands; a method of sorting out these demands into decisions; the decisions themselves; and how they are applied and enforced. You can see that

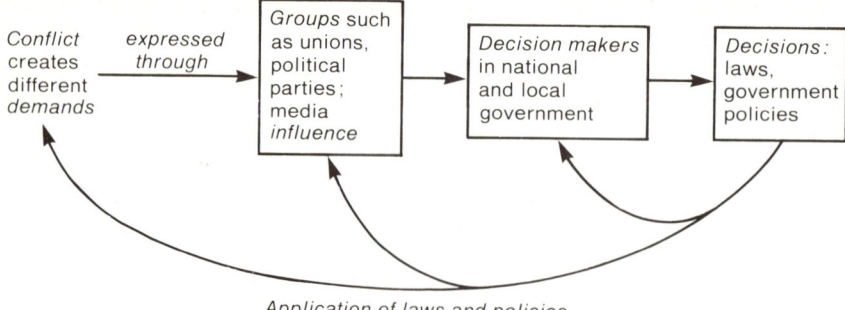

Figure 1.3 Model of a political system.

politics is not just concerned with the actions of the national government, the work of the prime minister, the cabinet, local government, and so on. We must look at the way in which individuals and groups fit into the system – how we fit in – at the kind of decisions which are made, and who carries them out. Naturally each stage raises a number of problems and questions.

Are we all equally important?

If we look at the first stage it is obvious that some individuals and groups are much more powerful than others and are likely to be much more successful in influencing those who make the decisions. Trade unions carry more weight than housewives or pensioners because they are highly organised and have weapons to use, such as strikes. More attention will be paid to those groups which are useful to those in power and, whether out of self-interest or belief, those in power are more likely to reward their political allies.

What kind of government?

The second stage in the diagram is concerned with those with the power to make decisions in government at national and local level. In any modern, industrialised country like Britain there are a vast range of decisions which have to be made, and many of them are enormously complicated. For this we rely on two groups of people – our elected representatives, and appointed officials who advise and help them to frame decisions and put them into operation. Elected politicians cannot be experts in all the matters about which they make decisions, but they can call on expert advice from non-elected officials. The task of politicians in government is to put into practice those policies they presented to us when elected, and to tackle new issues which emerge.

Some might argue that our problems are so complex that they should be left to the experts themselves. Apart from the fact that 'experts' can be found on both sides of any argument, this completely ignores the vital political point that policy can be right in theory but useless if it is not in tune with what people can accept. It is the job of politicians to understand, and respond to, this human dimension. Politics is, in part, the art of the possible, and politicians are there to 'carry the can' if their policies prove to be impossible or plain unpopular.

However, it would be naive to pretend that those in power merely listen to what people want and then do what they ask. They have their own interests and beliefs and sometimes act in a way that does not reflect the views of those who elected them. The issue of capital punishment is an example of this. The House of Commons has refused to bring back capital punishment although, according to opinion polls, there is a clear majority in the country in favour of it.

But if ministers and MPs were incapable of making their own decisions, and unwilling to use their own judgement, this would also produce howls of protest. What we really expect then, is a balance between representing our wishes and leadership.

Laws and freedom

The third stage in the diagram is concerned with the decisions themselves and the fourth with how they are applied.

A frequently-heard complaint is that our lives are too much surrounded by laws and other restrictions. In a sense, every law limits our freedom, but this is not as sinister as it sounds. If people were free to do anything they liked, there would be no peace and security. Laws which take away the 'freedom' to murder, steal or swindle, actually increase our real freedom. Traffic laws which, for example, force us to drive on the left-hand side of the road and punish people who speed or drive when they are drunk, create the freedom to use the roads in safety.

Such laws are designed to prevent undesirable behaviour, but others are more positive – such as those giving free education and sickness benefits. These services cost money which means that taxes have to be imposed. Does taxation limit our freedom by stopping us from spending our money as we would like? In one sense this is true but, without taxes, there could be no 'positive' laws which help to free people *from* poverty, ignorance and sickness.

Why do people obey laws? Partly they are afraid of being caught breaking them and then punished but, to a large extent, laws are obeyed because most people accept that they are for the benefit of society – for everyone. This in turn means that laws must be seen to be necessary and fair. More people will usually respect the law if it reflects their basic attitudes and values. In the end, the real strength behind the law is public opinion.

The British constitution

But where in all this are these written rules? Where is the British constitution? Unlike most countries, Britain does not have a single document which we can call 'the constitution'. The written constitutions of other countries state the powers which each of the different

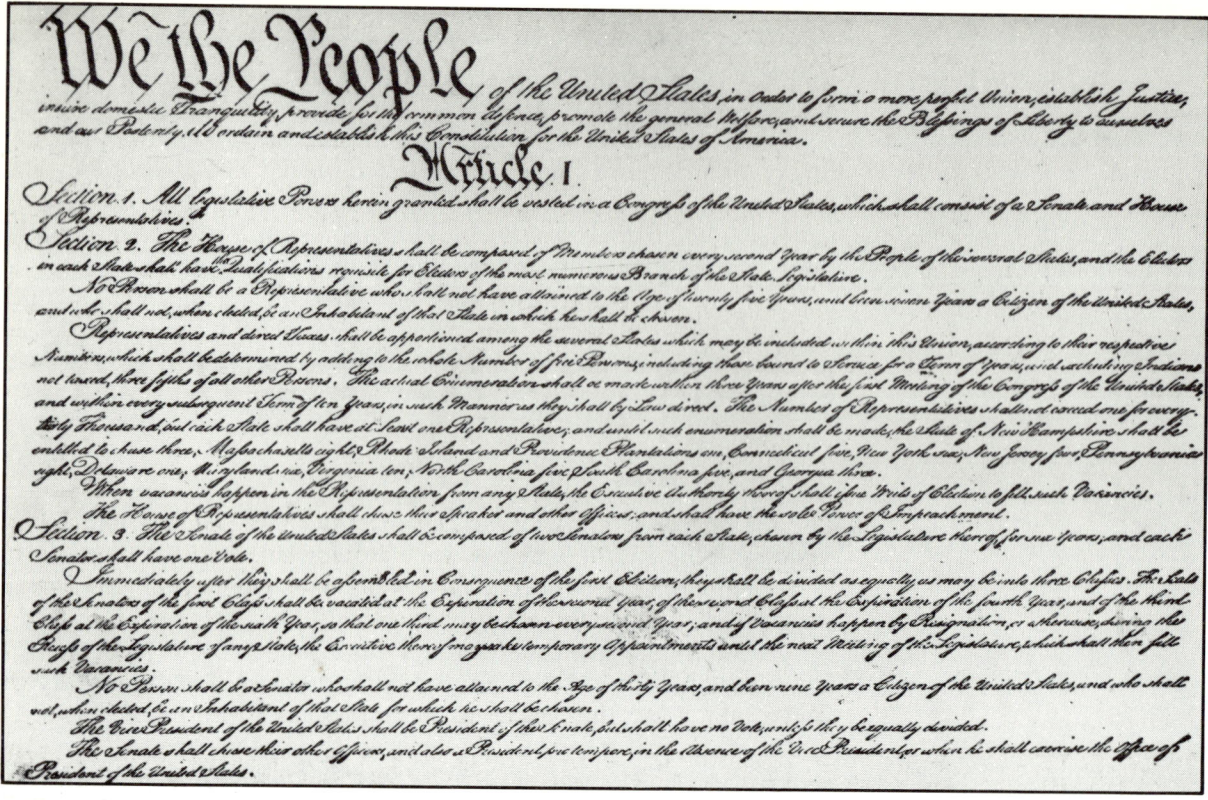

The beginning of the Constitution of the United States drawn up in 1787. Britain does not have such a source for its political system.

parts of government have, how people are to be elected to office, the rights of individuals and so on.

However, a constitution does not have to be written down in one document. The same issues are laid down in Britain but in a variety of ways and places. Part of the British constitution lies in the *laws passed by parliament*. These cover such matters as who can vote, the organisation of local government, and the punishment for breaking the laws of the land. *Decisions by judges* form another part of the constitution. The task of judges is to decide how laws should be applied to individual cases and their decisions are heavily influenced by precedent, that is, how judges have decided similar cases in the past. As a result a body of 'case law' has built up which covers a range of issues. Legal decisions, for example, have helped to establish the extent of our individual rights and have affected other areas such as the freedom to publish. While judges can interpret the law of the land, parliament can pass legislation to change these laws if it wishes. The Conservative government after 1979, for example, altered the law governing trade unions. As a result judges had to apply the new law to cases which came before them.

A third part of the constitution consists of *conventions*. Conventions are more than customs which have been built up over time. The most important of them now have the same strength behind them as laws themselves and, if they were broken, could produce a political crisis. For example, it is a convention that the prime minister must be a member of the House of Commons. Prime ministers in the past were sometimes members of the House of Lords and there is no law against this happening today – only convention. The position of the Crown in British politics is decided by convention as well. On paper the monarch has considerable powers, but these have been taken over gradually by the prime minister and the government. In effect, conventions have come to reflect changes in society itself. As our political system has become one involving greater participation, power has shifted away from the monarch to the elected government.

Political power

Those who are responsible for managing the affairs of society need the power to make their decisions effective. Politics is bound to be concerned with the power some people have over others, the form it takes, and the uses to which it is put.

The arrest of a miner during the coal strike in 1984. A visible example of the 'power' of the state.

It is around the issue of power that we can see a fundamental difference between politics in a national setting and the politics of many formal groups in Britain. Although we can talk about the 'politics' of a golf club it does not have the power to impose its decisions on its members in the same way as national and local government. If we dislike the way a golf club operates we can join another one fairly easily. We could leave Britain if we disliked the way a government was using its power but that is a very much greater, and more difficult, step. Governments, and those who administer laws, such as judges, have considerable coercive power over our lives – they can force us to obey their decisions and punish us if we do not. Without this power, government would be impossible. Where power lies, and how it is exercised, are two issues which will continually appear in this book.

Discussions and essay questions

1. What different interests and beliefs can you identify in the groups to which you belong? Taking each group in turn, describe its method or methods of making decisions.

2. Some of the groups that Smith and Jones belong to are regularly in conflict. But what basic beliefs are they likely to share?

3. How do you find out about politics (a) nationally, (b) locally? Do you think that any of these sources of information are biased?

4. In what sense do laws increase freedom?

5. Are there any political issues which you think should be decided by experts?

6. 'People dislike politicians because when they look at them they see themselves.' Discuss

7. If a majority of people are in favour of bringing back hanging, do you think this is a good enough reason for doing so?

2 The evolution of the British system of government

In Chapter 1 we saw how politics arise out of conflicting interests and beliefs of individuals and groups. A political system is a way of channelling or managing this conflict so that decisions can be made and then acted upon.

All countries face this same political problem even though their solutions can take different forms. Some countries are monarchies, although the monarch usually has little or no political power. Others are republics. Some countries have powerful presidents, such as the United States and France; in others the chief political figure is the

London 1984. The meeting of two political leaders, Mrs Thatcher and President Reagan. In Britain the prime minister is our political leader but the monarch is head of state. The US president is both.

prime minister. Most countries have ways of electing representatives to some kind of assembly or parliament but the power of these representatives can vary considerably and elections may only offer a limited choice of people or parties to vote for, or even no choice at all as in many one-party states. The ways in which countries run their political system may differ, but in every case they need **political institutions** to form the basic framework of government. In Britain these include the two Houses of Parliament, the method of choosing a government, the prime minister and cabinet, the civil service, and the legal system.

Describing our political institutions in this way does not explain how we got them nor why they should take the form they do. Why, for example, should Britain still have a monarchy? Why don't we have a written constitution? To answer such questions we must dig more deeply and examine the way that political institutions, and the whole political system itself, have been influenced by the changes and events which have helped to shape modern Britain. As society changes so do the institutions themselves. In Britain's case there are two characteristics which can be recognised in its national history – continuity and flexibility.

The British experience

Continuity

In modern times, Britain has avoided two experiences which in other countries have frequently led to new forms of government. Firstly, it has not been defeated in a major war since 1783 and, linked to this, it has not suffered from foreign invasion and occupation.

In the nineteenth century, most of the wars fought by Britain were colonial, and although defeat might have embarrassed the government of the day, it could not threaten Britain herself. On the other hand, France suffered invasion, defeat, and humiliation at the hands of Germany in 1870, and again in 1940; at the end of each of these wars, new French constitutions were drawn up. In this century, Germany found itself defeated and occupied in 1918 and 1945; it also broke with the past and changed its system of government. The same was true of Japan after the Second World War ended in 1945.

Secondly, Britain has not experienced a revolution, nor any serious attempt at revolution, since the seventeenth century. Political conflict has never reached the point where the violent overthrow of a government has received significant backing. There has always been enough support for the way our political system works. Or, it might be argued, there has never been enough active hostility towards it for revolution to occur.

Revolutions frequently have their origins in a deep discontent of the people. They might be caused by loss and disillusion as a result of war, by a serious decline in economic well-being, by vast inequalities between the wealthy few and the poor majority, or even by economic

Iranian students protesting about the visit of the Shah of Iran to London in 1978. Hostility to the Shah's rule reached a climax in 1979 when he was forced to leave Iran. Why were the students wearing masks?

and social conditions improving slightly and thus giving a glimmer of what life could be like.

Britain in the nineteenth and early twentieth centuries was not always free of such tensions. Although the condition of many people was often one of hopeless poverty, revolution did not occur because the political system proved capable of responding, however slowly, to new demands and changing conditions. In other words, the political system was able to contain the conflicts of interest which existed within it.

Flexibility

Although Britain did not experience the abrupt, often violent, change in political direction found in the history of many other countries, considerable changes did occur and the political system was flexible enough to adapt to them.

In the mid-eighteenth century Britain was a rural nation with the vast majority of people living in villages or small market towns, although London, as the commercial and government centre, was a big city by the standards of the times.

By 1900 a massive transformation had taken place. The development of industries such as coal, iron and steel, textiles, shipbuilding stimulated the growth of new towns and cities. The population became

A factory in the early twentieth century. Conditions could be very harsh and one response was the formation of trade unions to protect workers.

overwhelmingly urban and, as the birth rate rose and the death rate fell, grew considerably.

These economic and social changes had major political significance. To begin with, two new and powerful groups emerged: the middle-class made wealthy by ownership of factories, mines and railways; and an urban-based working-class providing the labour for the new industry. The old political system, where power had rested in the hands of a landowning nobility, gradually altered under pressure from these two groups. There were four important developments. Firstly, the right to vote – **the franchise** – was extended to the middle-class and later to the working-class population. This was a vital step in the process of making sure that most people remained loyal to the way in which they were governed. Extending the franchise meant that politicians, in order to win power, now had to listen and respond to the wishes and expectations of these new voters. The voters themselves could feel that they had a stake in, were more a part of, the system itself. Political parties also became aware of the need to *organise* their supporters if they were to gain power. Modern political parties with a national following began to develop. Secondly, the old boundaries of constituencies were altered, so that the House of Commons came to reflect, much more

The right to vote

Today almost everyone over eighteen in the UK is entitled to vote in elections. The few exceptions include peers and inmates of prisons and mental homes – hence the graph does not reach 100%. But it was only in the twentieth century that the vast majority of people achieved this right.

The steps to universal franchise

Each extension of the franchise needed an Act of Parliament and, although these can be said to illustrate the way the system responded to new demands, they also show how slow this response could be.

Act of Parliament	People allowed to vote under Act	Effect on population or a whole
1832 Reform Act	The new middle class – included a property qualification.	The working class excluded, in spite of much agitation and, to them, it was the 'Great Betrayal'. Doubled franchise but only 5% to 10%.
1867 Reform Act	All householders and lodgers paying £10 a year in rent. Both in towns only.	A property qualification was retained but it did enable most of the urban working class men to vote.
1884 Reform Act	The same provisions of 1867 were now extended to the countryside.	Agricultural labourers now had the vote.
1918 Representation of the People Act	All men over 21 and women over 30.	For the first time women could vote in parliamentary elections
1928 Equal Franchise Act	All women over 21.	Lingering prejudice about women, which had been reflected in the 1918 Act only giving the vote to those over 30, now, at least formally, disappeared.
1969 Representation of the People Act	Voting age lowered to 18	

Votes for Women!

Women were first able to vote in 1869 but only in local elections (County and County Borough). In 1907 they were allowed to become councillors but they had no vote, nor could they stand in parliamentary elections. To remedy this the Women's Social and Political Union was founded in 1903 with the aim of winning equal suffrage for women. Its supporters were soon known as suffragettes.

The campaign met with little success and from peaceful demonstrations and petitions the battle for women's suffrage moved towards more dramatic ways of expressing their views. Women chained themselves to railings outside the houses of politicans, smashed shop windows, and some, when arrested, went on hunger strike and endured the pain and humiliation of being forcibly fed.

Nothing had been achieved by the outbreak of the First World War (1914–1918) but, large numbers of women were employed during the war in essential industries and this released men for the forces. It also helped to strengthen women's claim for the right to vote.

Figure 2.1 The right to vote.

accurately than before, the new balance of population, and interests, in the country.

Thirdly, the party system changed with the emergence of a new political party – the Labour Party. In 1900 trade unions and other groups formed a Labour Representation Committee to work for the election of MPs who would represent working people in parliament independent of the other parties. In 1906, when it won twenty-nine seats in the House of Commons, it was renamed the Labour Party. Less than twenty years later it replaced the Liberal Party as the main opposition to the Conservatives and, in 1924, the first Labour government came to power.

Fourthly, new pressure groups developed to protect the interests of their members. The most important of these were the trade unions. Industrialisation brought workers together in large numbers and they soon realised that any attempt to press for improved conditions were much more likely to succeed if they acted together. Then, as now, the trade union belief was that strength lies in unity, whether facing employers or governments. All these developments led to a shift in the balance of power of British politics towards the mass of the people, and those in power in successive governments responded to this. In particular, ideas about the proper work of the government changed. In the middle of the nineteenth century it was generally assumed that the government should concentrate on a limited range of activities largely concerned with law and order, defence, and foreign affairs. The more positive freedoms, mentioned (see in Chapter 1) were not seen as the government's responsibility. The right to be educated, proper health care, security against illness or unemployment, protection for the old, and so on, which we can now sum up in the phrase, 'the welfare state', were accepted slowly in the twentieth century, but are now seen as a major part of the government's work and responsibility.

As Britain became industrialised she became a very wealthy country and gradually that wealth became more evenly distributed through taxation and the welfare state; if it had not, great tensions could have emerged. This tradition of continuity, the absence of any sudden break with the past, and this ability to absorb change, help to explain many features of British politics today. We have not experienced the circumstances where a complete re-think of the way we organise our political system has been necessary – hence the rather haphazard way in which the different powers of government are defined, and the absence of a written constitution covering these powers in a single document.

Traditionalism

There is another side as well. Continuity can also mean the existence of lingering, outdated traditions and a complacency about the need for change in the future. Some might argue that a complete re-examination of our political institutions is long overdue. For example, the hereditary element in the membership of the House of Lords means that a voice, and vote, in Parliament is still decided by an accident of birth.

Drawing old age pensions for the first time in 1908 – a painting by A. Forestier. Such benefits are now seen as a normal part of the 'welfare state'.

Changes in the political system were often difficult to achieve. Bitter political battles were fought over many of the rights which we now take for granted: the campaign for women's suffrage was often violent; acceptance of trade unions was a slow process and only achieved after great sacrifices, often against the complete hostility of many employers and politicians.

Where does this leave us today? No society stands still. New strains and tensions emerge, or old ones re-surface, and the flexibility of the political system is being continually tested. It would be a dangerous mistake to assume that we do not face similar problems of adjustment today.

The climate of modern politics

Unitary government

Britain can be described as having a **unitary system** of government. That is to say political power is heavily concentrated in the hands of the central government in London. We have a local government system as well but it does not have any independent existence. For example, if the central government wishes to change the boundaries of counties or districts, or even abolish them, then it has the power to do so. Other countries, such as the United States or Canada, have a **federal system** where political power is divided between central and individual state governments, the powers of both being defined and protected in a written constitution.

Our unitary system is based, in constitutional terms, on the supremacy of parliament. Parliament is the supreme law maker over the whole of the country and there is no other political institution which can challenge it – at least in Britain. (Membership of the European Community has meant that 'Community laws' take precedence over ours – see Chapter 21.) Indeed parliament even has the power, for example, to postpone general elections and did so each year during the Second World War.

Britain may be a unitary state constitutionally but there is a wider sense in which the term may be used as well. Britain is a small country geographically with a well developed communication system. National rather than local issues dominate, and this tendency is reinforced by a national press and national radio and television networks. In many countries national politics can seem remote and the media are much more locally biased. People in Britain share a common language and have many customs and traditions in common, unlike some countries where there are very large minority groups which pride themselves on being different – such as French Canadians.

Society in Britain is mainly urban with over 80 per cent of the population living in towns and cities, so the problems, and hopes, of most people can be understood and shared. Many of the issues facing Glasgow, for example, are not substantially different from those facing Birmingham. These common interests are reflected in the range of organisations which have a national rather than a regional base, such as trade unions, political parties, consumer groups, employers' associations, and so on. And for many of these groups the main focus of activity is likely to be London.

Unity is also seen in the sharing of certain values and attitudes, and British people like to regard themselves as tolerant and fair-minded. Political groups of all kinds are able to exist and seek support – unless they engage in violence. There is a great emphasis on freedom – freedom of speech, freedom of movement, freedom to be different. At the same time there is a general respect for the laws of the country – while we may not agree with all the decisions that govern our lives, there *is* general agreement about the way they are made. In other words we accept the right of our government to exercise power over us – largely because elections put them there.

Symbols such as the monarchy and reminders of a common history and past glories – or even defeats, such as Dunkirk strengthen these unifying forces. Emphasis on unity does not mean that divisions are missing. Some of these divisions illustrate the kind of problems which the political system will have to manage in the future.

The rise of nationalism

Until 1966 the nationalist parties in Scotland (Scottish National Party – SNP) and Wales (Plaid Cymru – PC) made very little impact in politics. Neither could attract enough support to elect MPs to the House of Commons although the SNP had one MP briefly in 1945 and they could only expect a small percentage of votes in general elections. In both cases two dramatic by-election results signalled a change in fortune. Plaid Cymru won Carmarthen in 1966 and the SNP won Hamilton in 1967. As Figure 2.2 shows, support for the SNP increased so rapidly that in the general election of October 1974 they received nearly a third of all Scottish votes and, although the rise of PC was less spectacular, they too had become much more influential in their own country. Even though support for both of them fell in the 1979 and 1983 general elections their position was much stronger than in 1966.

		% of vote in Scotland	Candidates	Seats won
1966	128,474	5.0	23	0
1970	306,802	11.4	65	1
(Feb) 1974	633,180	21.9	70	7
(Oct) 1974	839,617	30.4	71	11
1979	504,259	18.4	71	2
1983	332,045	11.8	72	2

Figure 2.2 SNP general election results.

The stated aim of the nationalist parties is clear enough. They want complete independence for Scotland and Wales and, although neither of them can claim majority support in their countries, their success is a useful reminder that Britain is not just England. Scotland and Wales were formally joined to England by Acts of Union – Scotland in 1709 and Wales in 1536. But both have retained a strong sense of nationality arising from their own special history and traditions developed before, and since, the Union. As small countries linked to a powerful neighbour, they share a natural desire to preserve their identity.

One response to the rise of nationalism was a proposal in the late 1970s that Scotland and Wales should have their own assemblies with limited powers over such matters as education and health (see Figure

	In Favour	*Against*
Scotland	1,230,937	1,153,502
Wales	243,048	956,330

In July 1978 the Labour government managed to get its devolution proposals through parliament. But it had agreed to hold a referendum in each country before setting up the assemblies. Against its wishes parliament insisted that there would have to be both a majority in favour and that those in favour must be, in total, more than 40 percent of those entitled to vote. Wales rejected the proposals but, although a majority of Scots voted in favour (51.6 percent to 48.8 percent of those who voted) the majority only represented 32.5 percent of those entitled to vote. Shortly after, the general election was held, and the new Conservative government was, in any case, opposed to devolution.

Figure 2.3 Referendum results on devolution in Scotland and Wales, March 1979.

2.3). This devolution of power was not intended to create any kind of federal structure in Britain, because parliament would still have retained its ultimate supremacy, but the plan failed. Nationalism may or may not have reached its peak in the mid 1970s but the issues which were a major cause of its success still remain.

Regional imbalance

Both the 1979 and 1983 general elections produced Conservative governments with large majorities, but with marked differences in voting between the South and the Midlands, and the rest of the country (see Figure 2.4). In effect the more prosperous an area, the more likely it was to vote Conservative, and economic prosperity in Britain tends to decline the further north and west people live. Does this matter?

	England (South and Midlands)	England (North)	Scotland	Wales
Conservative	281	81	21	14
Labour	41	107	41	20
Alliance	7	6	8	2

Figure 2.4 MPs returned after the 1983 election.

These regional variations in party support have been growing more noticeable over the last twenty-five years and in Scotland's case the Conservatives have been a minority party since 1964. If parties become too strongly identified with specific regions of Britain, their claim to speak with a national voice must be weakened. When this is linked to the marked differences in economic prosperity, reflected for example, in unemployment figures, then national unity is weakened further by the interests of prosperous areas being different from the rest.

Northern Ireland

Until 1922 the whole of Ireland was part of the United Kingdom. But in that year, after decades of argument and tension over how much independence Ireland should be given and a bloody civil war, the bulk of Ireland formed the new state of Eire. However, six counties stayed within the United Kingdom and became the province of Northern Ireland. The British government set up a parliament at Stormont in Belfast so that Northern Ireland could decide many of its own domestic issues, but it retained its overall control and Northern Ireland sent MPs to Westminster. This division of Ireland was based on the apparently unbridgeable differences between the majority of Irish people, mainly Catholic, who wanted independence, and a minority of 'Loyalists', mainly Protestant, who wanted to remain part of the United Kingdom and who were concentrated in the northern province of Ulster. Of course, as far as Northern Ireland was concerned, the Loyalists formed a majority.

Catholic youths in the Ardoyne sector of Belfast shelter behind a burnt-out car during an exchange of bricks and rubber bullets with an RUC patrol at the top of the road. Any political agreement about the future of Northern Ireland is made virtually impossible by the deep divisions between the two communities.

It is extremely difficult to understand and disentangle the problems and disagreements about Northern Ireland but it does illustrate two important political problems – firstly, how hard it is to arrive at political agreement when there are two separate communities. The economic and social problems of Northern Ireland, especially poor housing and high unemployment, which affect both communities, might appear to be the kind of issues which would bring them closer together. But differences in religion and cultural traditions, and loyalty either to a united Ireland or to Britain, produced quite different political divisions. They are symbolised by each community being almost self-contained. People go to different schools and different churches, they live in separate areas and have separate social lives. In this kind of climate, political compromise becomes difficult and can easily be seen as political surrender.

The second problem is the relationship between the majority and the minority. At all levels of politics we place great emphasis on making decisions by finding out the wishes of the majority. Decisions taken this way can usually be accepted, if not liked, by everyone. And those in the minority can console themselves with the thought that, one day, they might be the majority. We accept that, although people have a right to be different and that minority opinion should not be trampled on, in the end the majority should decide. In Northern Ireland the majority is permanent and the Catholic minority have been discriminated against on sensitive issues such as housing and allocation of seats on local councils for Catholic areas. Many Catholics feel that, given their minority status, there should be some way for them to take part in making decisions rather than being continually excluded.

These problems are just some which the political system now faces. There are others to which we will return later. Britain is now a member of the European Community and its position as a world power with a vast overseas empire has gone. A painful adjustment of attitudes has been needed. Since 1945 new groups of people have come to live in Britain and we are now a multi-racial society. But are we a sufficiently tolerant society? The dangers which can develop when minorities do not feel a real part of the community, and are discriminated against, is one lesson of Northern Ireland. Can the political system prove as responsive to change in the future as it was in the past?

Case study of continuity and change: the monarchy

The British monarchy is a perfect example of the way in which political institutions can be transformed while remaining outwardly the same. For many hundreds of years the 'government' of Britain was the monarch. He (or she) was the centre of political power and authority, which passed on through inheritance – although conflicting claims

The Royal Wedding in 1981. Why was this watched by thousands of people in London and by millions on television?

about who was the rightful monarch often led to bitter conflict and even civil war.

Today, in spite of the considerable changes in British life and politics we still have a monarchy and, on paper at least, it still has far-reaching powers. The Queen has the right to reject Bills passed by parliament, to declare war, to pardon criminals and so on. But in practice, by constitutional convention, these powers have passed to the elected government and are exercised on behalf of the Queen. The central convention applying to the monarchy is quite clear: that the Queen acts only on the advice of the prime minister and government.

Why has the monarchy survived?

It was once said that, in time, Europe would have only five kings – hearts, clubs, diamonds, spades and England. Certainly since 1900, the number of European monarchies has fallen dramatically. Yet in Britain the monarchy has, if anything, increased in popularity as its power has declined. This loss of political power is one of the reasons for its survival. The monarchy has become separated from party politics and the day-to-day business of government. Its popularity is unaffected by the failures, or successes, of governments.

Another reason for its survival is that successive monarchs have obviously worked very hard in the more limited role they now have. Royal tours around the country and abroad, the interest shown in a whole range of individual and community achievements, are indications that modern monarchs have been conscientious in what they do and anxious to cement relations with people from all backgrounds.

On top of this, it can be argued that the pageantry and ceremony surrounding the Royal Family provides the fairytale touch of glamour which many find very satisfying, especially because it reflects national identity and tradition. Colourful parades and ceremonies have a place in every society – whether it is the May Day parades in the Soviet Union, Bastille Day in France, or the inauguration of American presidents – they give a certain dignity to the affairs of government.

The non-political head of state

The political function of the monarchy has been replaced by a different role – that of non-political head of state. All countries have some kind of official head of state. Republics, for example, have presidents who fall into two main groups. Some are highly political and are elected into office, as in the United States or France, and have the problem of separating political duties from the role of representing the nation as a whole. Others are more ceremonial figures as in Italy and West Germany, where there is a political head of government as well.

The monarchy in Britain is near to the second group. As non-political head of state the Queen, for example, has a vast range of

The Queen arrives in Kenya, a member of the Commonwealth, in 1983. Visits like these emphasise the Queen's position as 'Head of the Commonwealth' as well as British Head of State.

duties from touring the country to entertaining foreign visitors, especially other heads of state. Equally important is the task of representing Britain abroad on state visits. Again the Queen is seen to symbolise Britain as a whole. A more formal part of her duties abroad is linked to the Commonwealth. Although many members of the Commonwealth are republics, the Queen is given the title of 'Head of the Commonwealth'. Again this is a symbolic role, but at meetings of Commonwealth heads of government, the Queen will meet and entertain these national leaders. Some Commonwealth countries, such as Australia and New Zealand also recognise the Queen as their own non-political head of state.

Opinion polls show that support for the monarchy is found in well over 90 per cent of the population in Britain. Republican feeling was probably stronger a hundred years ago than it is today. But should the British monarchy follow the more casual style of, for example, Scandinavian countries where there appears to be less distance between the people and the Royal Family? To some extent this has already happened. The 'walkabout' has become a familiar enough picture on royal visits, films have been made to show the Royal Family 'at home', and members of the Royal Family have become identified with activities such as encouraging exports, developing facilities for young people, or protecting the environment. But the pageantry – and the differences in life style from most people – still remains. On top of this, the monarchy helps to reinforce conservative values such as privilege, hereditary status and the conferring of titles. Is the monarchy today, as out of step with a modern democracy as the present House of Lords? Or is it simply that it suits us?

Discussion and essay questions

1. How does the recent history of Britain explain: the existence of constitutional conventions; the absence of a written constitution; the survival of the monarchy?

2. What is meant by (a) federalism (b) a unitary system of government? What advantages/disadvantages can you think of for each system?

3. Discuss how far the term *United* Kingdom is accurate.

4. Discuss the various ways in which the people have been drawn more closely into politics over the last 150 years.

5. If Scotland and Wales were to have a greater say over their own affairs, should the same power be given to England?

6. Can violence ever be justified politically?

7. 'The Queen reigns but does not rule.' In what ways does this sum up the position of the monarchy in British politics?

8. 'If Britain was a republic we would still need someone to perform most of the duties carried out by the Queen.' Discuss.

Part Two: THE PARTY SYSTEM

3   Political parties

Political parties lie at the centre of our political system. Sometimes the emphasis given to the battles between (and within) them is so great that *party* politics and politics itself can even appear to be the same.

However, political activity is not just confined to political parties. People belong to a range of organisations which put forward their political views and express their political demands – for example trade unions, employers organisations, or the Campaign for Nuclear Disarmament. But, unlike other organisations, political parties have *political power* as their central objective. They, and their leaders, aim to win power through elections either alone or in co-operation with other parties, and it is through the party system that we decide who will form the national government.

This search for power has one major result. In order to get the largest possible support, a political party has to bring together the different views of its members. In Britain a party must win a majority of seats in the House of Commons to be certain of forming a government. To do this, it must attract support from millions of voters, because it will never achieve power unless it is able to fight elections on a national scale. This means that individuals and groups who may have different views on particular issues have got to be prepared to work together in general agreement under the same party label. The Labour Party, for example, contains some groups who disagree considerably on what a future Labour government should do. But if each *group* fought elections under different *party* labels – and in doing so fought each other – then a Labour government would never achieve power.

There is therefore an all-important practical reason for a party to maintain its unity. However, members of a party also feel a bond by sharing common values as well. We will look at terms such as 'conservatism' later, but members of a party are drawn together by a belief in, say, Conservative or Labour party principles. Of course, there may be disagreements within parties about their real meaning and especially how they ought to be applied to issues and policies and, in practical terms, a balance needs to be struck between principles and what is acceptable to the voting public.

A two-party system?

	1945	88.1
	1950	89.6
	1951	96.1
	1959	93.2
	1964	87.5
	1966	89.8
(Feb)	1974	73.4
(Oct)	1974	75.1
	1979	80.8
	1983	71.8

Figure 3.1 Percentage of voters supporting the two main parties, 1945–83.

	1945	34
	1950	12
	1951	9
	1955	8
	1959	7
	1964	9
	1966	14
	1970	13
(Feb)	1974	38
(Oct)	1974	40
	1979	28
	1983	42

(Total no. of MPs 1984: 650)

Figure 3.2 MPs from minority parties in the House of Commons, 1945–1983.

It has been usual to describe Britain as having a two-party system and there is evidence to support this view. Since 1945 only the Conservative and Labour parties have formed governments – each winning six general elections. The majority of people vote for one or other of these parties, and they have dominated the House of Commons. Political choice, whether in local or national government, has been largely defined by them.

However Figure 3.1 demonstrates that the two-party emphasis has become weaker in recent years. Look first at the total percentage of people voting for each party in recent elections. In the early 1950s almost 97 per cent voted either Conservative or Labour but in more recent elections this overall percentage has dropped (to less than 72 per cent in 1983). We can now see that nearly 30 per cent of British votes in 1983 were supporting one of the 'minority' parties. But Figure 3.2 shows that only 42 MPs voted into the House of Commons that year were from 'minority' parties – less than 7 per cent of the Commons total membership. Why is this so?

In Britain we have a 'first past the post' system of voting. The country is divided up into constituencies and each one elects an MP. The winner is simply the person with more votes than anyone else. In the October 1983 election, for example, this was the result in the City of Durham:

		% of vote
M. Hughes (Lab)	18,163	36.5
D. Stoker (Alliance)	16,190	32.5
M. Lavis (Con)	15,438	31.0
Labour majority	1973	

This is an extreme example of what can happen: 63.5 per cent of the voters in Durham voted *against*, the winner with the votes of the other party candidates being 'wasted'. Normally it is the smaller parties who suffer the most under this system. It is quite possible for a party to attract millions of voters but only win a few seats. In 1983 the Liberal/Social Democrat Alliance gained 26.1 per cent of the votes in Britain (excluding Northern Ireland) yet only 3.6 per cent of the seats in Parliament. Their problem was that Alliance support was quite thinly spread throughout the country. It only 'peaked' in a very few constituencies which put them first past the post. (The present electoral system, and possible reforms, are looked at in more detail in Chapter 4.)

Increased support for the Liberal Party in the 1970s, and in 1983 for the Alliance, is nevertheless one sign of a decline in the two-party system. The nationalist vote is another: in 1983 Plaid Cymru and the Scottish National Party obtained roughly one in ten of the votes cast in their respective countries (although both fell back from their peaks in the mid 1970s). The SNP took 11.8 per cent of the Scottish vote though this resulted in less than 2 per cent SNP MPs out of the Scottish Commons total. On top of this there have been substantial changes in party politics in Northern Ireland. The old Ulster Unionist Party, which supported the Conservatives in Westminster, has been challenged by new parties such as the Democratic Unionist Party of the Reverend Ian Paisley. So, even under the present electoral system which makes it difficult for them to win seats there is still an important minority party presence in the House of Commons.

A further reason for supposing that the two-party system is no longer so strong is in the change in the depth of support for the two main parties. Research carried out has shown that **partisanship**, the extent to which people feel a strong commitment to a party, has fallen. For both the Conservative and Labour parties the number of people who identify 'very strongly' with their party has declined over the last thirty years. Both main parties have also suffered from a decline in membership. Neither party publishes very reliable figures but it appears that since the early 1950s Conservative Party membership has fallen from 2.8 million to 1.5 million and Labour Party individual membership (excluding unions) from 1 million to less than 300,000.

The Conservative Party

The nature of conservatism

In Chapter 2 you could see how Britain has managed to avoid the kind of major and often violent upheavals which have been the experience of most other European countries over the last two hundred years. The political system has adjusted to change, relatively peacefully.

We have had a continuity of political development which, perhaps inevitably, reinforces the importance of tradition, and a respect for things as they are. It is in this view of society that **conservatism** is firmly rooted. To be a Conservative is not necessarily to believe that all forms of change are undesirable, but rather that change must be built on what we know. If it can be shown that something works then it is foolish to take a leap in the dark hoping that a change will make matters better. There is a distrust of the unknown and the untried. One result of this view is, of course, that existing social arrangements are defended partly because they have the stamp of tradition.

Conservatism is not, however, just a negative attitude. There is a belief that society is essentially a unity rather than being divided by class hostility. Britain is seen as 'one nation' which is often artificially broken up by those who talk in terms of class warfare. Conservatism puts a considerable emphasis on the importance of the nation and, consequently, its values and achievements.

This view of the nation, and the need to preserve its unity, helps to explain the way in which conservatism is able to respond to change. Change needs to be cautious but conservatism has never been so inflexible that it is completely unacceptable. A good example was its reaction to the changes brought about by the Labour government of 1945–1951 which nationalised a large number of industries, introduced the National Health Service, gave independence to India, Pakistan, Burma and Ceylon. The Conservative Party either opposed a number of these policies, or the way in which they were introduced. In 1951, however, when they came back to power there was no massive programme of putting nationalised industries back into private hands, the National Health Service remained and the process of giving independence to colonies was continued.

The real strength of the Conservative Party has always been that it recognises the danger, at least eventually, of not taking into account changes in national attitudes. Failure to recognise such changes may well lead to tension and conflict in society. Of course the danger is that recognition may take some time in coming.

Conservatism also encourages and maintains the principles of free enterprise, profit and competition. It regards individuals as essentially unequal in ability and considers it both fair, and in the wider interest of society, to help the talented to reach the top through competition. Rewards must be given in accordance with differences in ability, and the acquisition of wealth should not, as a result, be discouraged. This emphasis on free enterprise makes modern conservatism far removed from the idea that the state either can or should be the main way of achieving improvements in society. The state has a part to play in some areas of life, for example in education or welfare services, but, as far as possible, it must not be allowed to discourage individual initiative, competition and choice. To Conservatives, for example, the existence of private schools and private medicine is essential because it gives people the right to spend their money as they want.

The Conservative Party has been the great survivor in party politics because of its appeal to tradition and continuity and its ability to recognise when change needs to be accepted. But, when Mrs Thatcher became prime minister in 1979, it became associated with a form of conservatism which does not quite fit in with this pattern. In some ways, of course, Mrs Thatcher carried on in a traditional fashion by emphasising free enterprise and the virtues of competition. But in other areas her government deliberately set out, as she saw it, to change the whole course of government as we had known it since 1945. Massive cuts, in public expenditure for example, were needed to 'roll back the state'. British industry, according to the government, had to be shaken out of its complacency and inefficiency if it was going to compete and survive. For thirty years, under *all* governments, the country had spent too much and earned too little. The discomfort and hardship in following such new policies were bound to be considerable but Mrs Thatcher claimed it was the only course of action.

Staff and boys on their way to early morning chapel at Marlborough College, a public school. Private education – the freedom to choose, or the purchase of privilege? Conservatives see schools like this as representing both educational excellence and freedom of choice. The Conservative government of Mrs Thatcher has, in addition, enabled talented pupils from less well off families to gain places in public schools by helping to pay the cost.

In part, these policies could be regarded as an attempt to return to old Conservative principles. But there is no doubt that they also contained an element of experimentation and break with the past which seems to go against traditional conservatism.

There was a clear conflict between the 'experiment' conducted by Mrs Thatcher plus her supporters in the party, and the views of other Conservatives who wished to slow down the speed of change and feared that some of the policies were likely to create social and political unrest.

The structure of the Conservative Party

The extension of the franchise in the nineteenth century meant that the existing political parties now needed to organise themselves nationally. The Conservative Party had been based only in parliament and there was a 'downward' development of party organisation to the constituencies, seeking to build up popular support. But real power in the Conservative Party stayed essentially with the parliamentary leadership and this remains true today.

The leader of the party is chosen by a secret ballot of Conservative MPs and, whether in government as prime minister or as leader of the opposition, has considerable power. All prime ministers have the right to decide who shall be members of their government and a Conservative opposition leader chooses the 'shadow cabinet' as well. The policies of the party must be finally agreed by the leader and even the national headquarters, Conservative Central Office, comes under his or her control. For example, the leader chooses the Chairman of the Conservative Party, who is responsible for national organisation, and other key officials.

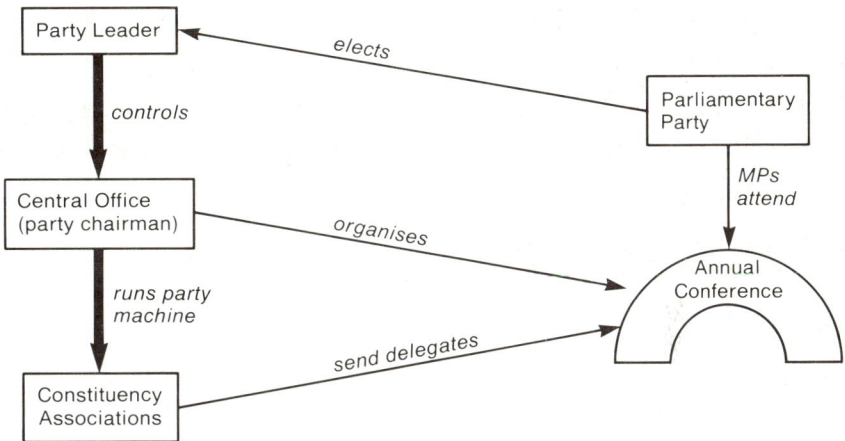

Figure 3.3 Structure of the Conservative Party.

Annual conferences of the Conservative Party tend to be rallies of the party faithful and real 'debates', indicating differences in the party, are rare. Conferences are designed to boost morale and allow party members to rub shoulders with the famous. Even if the annual conference passed a resolution disliked by the leadership, it carries no weight if the leader decides to ignore it.

However, the leader of the Conservative Party can still be influenced by the views of party members. The need to achieve, and keep, power means that the leader, and other important figures, have to take account of currents of opinions both inside and outside the party. Certainly Conservatives do not relish open disagreements within their own ranks, and there is always as strong feeling of loyalty towards the leader. But the absence of bitter public debate does not mean that it is avoided privately.

The decline in party membership since the mid-1950s has put an extra strain on the financing of the Conservative Party and forced it, increasingly, to rely on private business. A great deal of Conservative money is still raised through the efforts of constituency parties but private industry helps the Conservative Party in two ways. Firstly, it gives direct contributions to party funds, especially at election time when these are most needed; and secondly it supports organisations, such as Aims of Industry, which carry out their own campaigns through advertising, issuing pamphlets, and so on.

Left, right and centre

Before examining other political parties it will probably be helpful to explain two of the useful, if often over-used, words used in politics – 'Left' and 'Right'.

The origin of these words is simple enough. They come from the positioning of political parties in the semi-circular French national assembly, the equivalent of the British parliament. The more traditional, conservative parties sat on the right and the socialists and other parties who wanted change sat on the left. In Britain today the main political parties are usually thought of in the way explained in the inset below. However, these words may be used to describe variations within parties as well. 'Right-wing Conservative', 'left-wing Conservative', 'left-wing Labour', 'right-wing Labour' are some of the shorthand descriptions of politicians often used by the press. What do they mean? Having looked at the Conservative Party, let's begin with them. You can usually think of 'right-wing Conservatives' as people who are committed to a very rigid acceptance of party principles. They are likely to be fiercely in favour of free enterprise and competition, hostile to any form of state control of industry, and strong in their support of spending on defence and 'law and order'. A very typical right-wing view is that trade unions should be controlled by much tougher laws which must be enforced. And the right wing have never been very happy with our membership of the European Community because as they see it, Britain has lost part of her independence.

'Left-wing' Conservatives may well share some of these views but are unlikely to hold them so strongly. They see the state as having a genuine responsibility for reducing inequalities and believe that change, which is often necessary, is best brought about by agreement and compromise.

The use of 'left' and 'right' in the Conservative Party is another

Left	Centre	Right
Labour	Liberal and SDP Alliance	Conservatives

Parties are usually described as lying along a Left-Right line but there is a danger that this may exaggerate differences between them. The 'left-wing' Conservative may have a great deal in common with 'right-wing' members of the Labour Party. And the position of the Alliance does not emphasise its commitment to policies which could bring about considerable change in society. In some cases there is even agreement, although for different reasons, between members of the 'extremes' of the main parties about policies. One example of this is hostility to British membership of the EC which is found among left-wing Labour and right-wing Conservatives.

Figure 3.4 Description of political viewpoints.

illustration of how large parties are really coalitions which span a variety of views. The same is true of the Labour Party. But here 'left' and 'right' are reversed. 'Left-wing' in the Labour Party is associated with a firm commitment to Socialist principles and a desire to introduce a socialist society (see Figure 3.5). The 'right-wing' of the Labour Party regards necessary changes in society as only coming slowly and there is a firmer belief in the need to retain an economy which allows a large private industrial sector. 'Left-wingers', for example, would like to see a much greater programme of nationalisation, and would abolish both private education and private medicine. 'Right-wingers' fear that such a programme would lead to electoral disaster.

But a word of caution is needed. To begin with, these descriptions of 'Left' and 'Right' within parties are too exclusive. Political parties contain people with a range of opinions, very often a mixture of 'Left' and 'Right' views. Secondly it is important to distinguish between party *activists* and party *voters*; Figure 3.5 illustrates the difference.

Labour			*Conservative*	
Left	*Right*		*Left*	*Right*
Activists	Voters		Voters	Activists

Party activists take up different 'left' and 'right' positions in both parties compared with the typical person who only votes for the party in elections. This has become more apparent as partisanship has declined among voters. In the Labour Party, for example, the left is very strong among members of constituency parties but, according to opinion polls, many left-wing policies are unpopular with most Labour voters.

Figure 3.5 Voters and party activists.

The Labour Party

Unlike the Conservative Party which grafted a national organisation on to an existing parliamentary party structure, the Labour Party was created before it had any significant number of MPs. There was an 'upward' growth of its structure and many of the tensions within the Labour Party today stem directly from this process.

The people who founded the Labour Party were of two sorts: those who wanted a 'socialist society' and those who were more concerned with such defensive matters, such as trade union rights and improving the lot of working people, without necessarily wanting to change the whole political and economic system – a typical Left/Right divide. But socialism itself has had a considerable influence on Labour Party thinking, and it is necessary to look at and understand its principles more closely.

Socialism

The term **socialism** itself is very broad and, in many ways, unclear – especially when attempts are made to apply socialist principles to actual policies. The four main ingredients in socialist thought are based largely on criticisms of capitalism. **Capitalism** itself can be thought of as a way of organising an economy so that all forms of business life (industry, agriculture, banking, and so on) are run to make a profit, and control of business is in private hands.

First of all, socialism sees capitalism as a form of exploitation especially of the working class who own nothing but their skills and labour. Capitalism is based on self-interest and competition, whereas socialism emphasises the need for co-operation for the benefit of all. Secondly, it sees capitalism as responsible for producing huge inequalities of wealth and power. Greater equality can only come therefore through the means of production being taken out of the hands of the powerful few. And without economic equality, real equality cannot exist. Thirdly, capitalism is wasteful of scarce resources because making goods for profit does not mean that they are socially useful. For example, is it better to have bingo halls or improved housing? Lastly, capitalism denies people real freedom because only the wealthy few can afford to make real choices.

Shelton Bar Steelworks – checking the molten mixture. The Steel industry was one of a number of industries taken out of private hands and nationalised by the Labour government of 1945–1951. Nationalisation is seen by the Labour Party as necessary if governments are going to run the country for everyone's benefit.

These criticisms of capitalism point to the need for a completely new economic order – socialism. They do not, however, answer a vital question – how is socialism to be achieved? One way, of course, is through revolution – the violent overthrow of the system. This road to socialism has been rejected by the British Labour Party. Instead they have chosen the path of persuasion, the use of the ballot box, and an acceptance of the parliamentary system.

Democratic socialism is probably a fair description of the attitude of those on the Left of the Labour Party and many of the preferred policies of the Left reflect its influence; they include for instance a much larger programme of bringing private industry into state control; the abolition of the private sectors in education and medicine, which encourage inequality; the abolition of the House of Lords; and abandoning Britain's role as a nuclear power. This last point is a reflection of an important trend in democratic socialism which is a rejection of war and of the nationalistic fervour on which it is partly based.

Although many other Labour Party members are influenced by democratic socialist ideas the extent of this influence varies considerably. And the Centre and Right of the Labour Party is probably better described as being social democrat (not to be confused with the title of the new party formed in 1981). Their ideas would lay more stress on the need for gradual social reform. The state can be of great benefit in improving society and, through legislation, many of its worst features can be removed. There is a need for planning and some public ownership, but they accept that Britain is likely to remain a country with a considerable area of privately owned business. Wealth certainly needs to be redistributed, but through taxation and by strengthening the welfare state. Any move towards socialism can only be gradual.

Labour governments have leaned more to **social democracy** rather than democratic socialism in spite of frequent criticisms from the Labour Left. This seems to be partly because the kind of society which faced the early Socialist pioneers where the condition of many people was one of extreme poverty and squalor, does not really exist to anything like the same extent. There is poverty today and it is hard to deny the need for reform in areas such as housing and the treatment of the sick and the old. But Labour governments have in recent years avoided dramatic socialist change. There is however also a more practical reason, mentioned earlier. Labour right-wingers argue that many left-wing policies appear to be unpopular, even with Labour voters. They feel that in order to gain power the Labour Party must be prepared to move cautiously. The left wing of the party might argue that a real socialist set of policies has never been offered to the electorate.

The structure of the Labour Party

If you look at the organisation of the Labour Party (which is much more complicated that the Conservative Party) it is easy to see how it was constructed 'upwards'. The party was formed by a number of groups coming together – but of these the trade unions were particu-

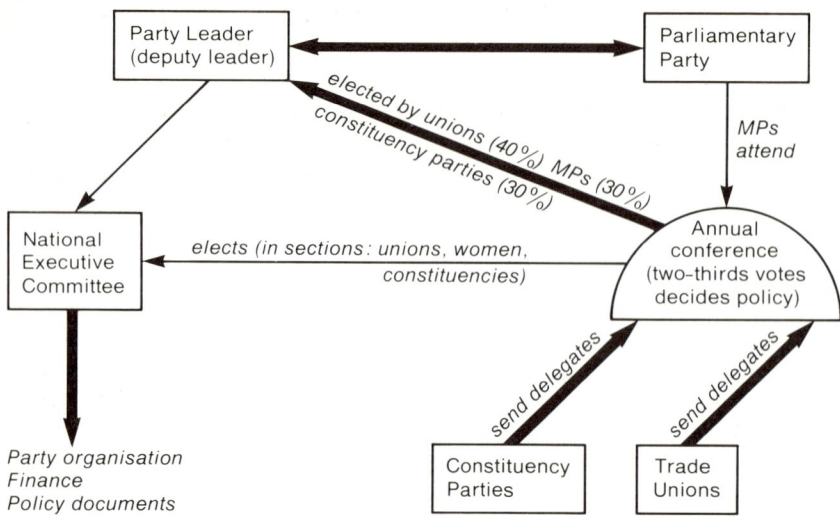

Figure 3.6 Structure of the Labour Party.

larly important. Indeed you may often hear Labour politicians and others talk about the 'Labour Movement' which emphasises the alliance between the unions and the party. The two work together at every level of the party structure and it has a considerable effect on the *idea* of Labour Party membership.

There are two main groups of Labour Party members. Firstly individuals can join in their own right by paying the subscription and, of course, agreeing to accept its rules. But trade unions can also affiliate themselves to the Labour Party. In this case the members of such a union who agree to pay a political levy, which the union collects and gives to the Labour Party, are *also* counted as members. At the moment union members who do not wish to contribute a political levy have to sign a document stating this – they have to 'contract out'. The result of this membership system is that the 'union members' of the Labour Party number over six million but individual membership is no more than 300,000.

The Labour Party annual conference

Delegates to the annual conference come from three main groups – individual members representing constituencies, trade union delegates and MPs. Voting however depends on the strength of membership of each group and this puts the unions in a dominant position. When votes are taken each constituency party is allocated 1,000 votes, although few constituencies have that many members, but each trade union can claim a voting strength of many thousands. MPs have no separate vote of their own except in elections for leader and deputy leader.

The effect of this is to put trade unions in the driving seat over conference decisions. But do conference resolutions really matter? There is considerable controversy over this within the Labour Party. If the conference passes a resolution on policy by a two-thirds majority then, according to the Labour Party constitution, it becomes party policy. But policies are put into operation ultimately by a Labour government and the conference has no power to force the parliamentary Labour Party (i.e. the Labour MPs elected to parliament) to adopt conference resolutions. It was stated earlier that Labour governments have been more inclined towards social democracy than socialism and this has created tensions at conferences. Constituency delegates are almost overwhelmingly drawn from the activist Left and, on certain issues, have received support from trade union leaders. In spite of this, Labour governments have been prepared to ignore conference decisions.

However, since 1981 a completely new dimension has been added to the importance of Labour Party conferences. In the past the leader and deputy leader of the Labour Party were both elected only by Labour MPs. The 1980 conference decided that they would be elected by, if necessary, a specially-called conference and that votes for both positions would be as follows: 40 per cent to trade unions, 30 per cent to constituency parties and 30 per cent to MPs.

All sections of the party therefore now have a say in choosing the leader. But it also means that if future leaders are challenged, or a new leader is needed, then they can be dismissed by a combination of constituency and union votes – even though Labour MPs themselves might support them or might detest the new choice.

Labour Party conference October 1983. Neil Kinnock becomes leader of the Labour Party and Roy Hattersley its deputy leader after a conference vote.

The National Executive Committee

One of the functions of the annual conference is to elect the National Executive Committee (NEC). The NEC is responsible for running the party nationally and controls party organisation. It produces policy documents, gives final approval to candidates chosen to stand in parliamentary elections and is responsible for party finance. Membership of the NEC is divided up into sections with each one electing people to serve for one year – they include the constituency parties, trade unions, Young Socialists, and a Women's Section. The Labour leader and deputy leader are automatically members.

The structure of the Labour Party may seem, from the outside, almost designed to publicise differences within the party. The Labour Party however has always argued that public disagreement is a strength rather than a weakness.

They believe that the emphasis on elections and the debate on the importance of the annual conference show that the party is continually concerned to be as open and democratic as possible. In the end, however, the Left/Right struggle is concerned with power within the party. That struggle is fought within the parliamentary party, the conference, the NEC, in constituency parties and trade unions.

The Labour Party and trade unions

As you saw earlier, the Labour Party and trade unions are frequently described as two branches of the 'Labour Movement'. Trade unions have a place at all levels in the party structure. Not only is this the case nationally, but it is just as true in constituencies.

Members of local branches of trade unions, as long as they are individual members of the party, can attend Labour Party constituency meetings, and the union branches themselves can nominate people to be considered as parliamentary candidates. Above all a trade union can 'sponsor' Labour candidates which means that, if they are adopted, a trade union will help to finance local constituency activity.

Trade unions also provide the Labour Party with the bulk of its finance – roughly 80 per cent – which is used to keep the national organisation going and, of course, to fight election campaigns.

The Liberal Party

The fortunes of the Liberal Party have changed dramatically in the twentieth century. In the late nineteenth and early part of the twentieth century it was a major political force, competing for power with the Conservative Party. Then, in the early 1920s it was replaced by the Labour Party. By the 1950s the Liberal vote in general elections had shrunk to well under a million during the high tide of the two-party system, but, since then, there has been a revival of support.

The recent history of the Liberal Party has been marked by four developments. Firstly, the party has scored some remarkable victories in by-elections especially when there has been a Conservative government. Clearly these have been largely due to dissatisfied Conservative voters but, in some cases, the Liberals have held on to these seats in later general elections. Secondly, the Liberals have placed an emphasis, at local level, on 'community politics' sometimes called rather disparagingly 'dustbin politics'. They have put a great effort into taking up local issues and have increased the number of Liberal councillors in local government. The third development came in 1976 when the Liberals entered a pact with the Labour government which had lost its overall majority in the House of Commons. They agreed to support the government in return for concessions on policies. How far the concessions, and consultations between the parties were real is a matter of dispute. But the pact lasted until 1978. For the first time in many years Liberals were at least associated with government.

Lastly, in 1981, the Liberals agreed to enter into an alliance with the newly formed Social Democratic Party and, in the 1983 election, the Alliance received the highest vote for a third party since the 1920s.

Modern liberalism

The custom of thinking of the Liberal Party as lying somewhere between the Right wing of the Labour Party and the Left wing of the

David Steel leader of the Liberal Party starting his national campaign for the 1979 elections. He was elected by some 20,000 party activists, the votes being weighted according to Liberal strength in constituencies.

Conservative Party can be deceptive. The Liberal Party is essentially a party of change and reform – but not through socialism. **Liberalism** has traditionally placed a considerable emphasis on the freedom and protection of the individual. The state is not seen as necessarily the best vehicle for achieving this. Liberals are suspicious of over-powerful and centralised government, and their policies reflect this suspicion. They want, for example, to give more power to localities and regions, and were in favour of devolution for Wales and Scotland. Their industrial policy is hostile to the union-versus-management battle and is based on the idea, as far as possible, of firms being owned jointly by workers and managers.

The Liberal Party was the first one to support Britain becoming a member of the European Community (EC). This was largely because they saw the EC as a way of breaking down national barriers and bringing the people of Europe closer together through identifying common interests and problems – and solving them together. But it also coincided with a more general Liberal emphasis on the need for greater international understanding and order. Liberals, for example, have been enthusiastic supporters of the United Nations.

The party is committed to the idea of electoral reform and argue that there must be a closer relationship between votes cast for a party in an election and seats won. The Liberal Party was the first to include people outside parliament in the process of selecting a leader.

The national executive is elected by the annual assembly of the Liberal Party but policy is decided by the leader who, nevertheless consults widely in the party.

The Social Democratic Party

The battles between the Left and Right of the Labour Party reached a climax in 1981 when four former Labour government ministers, the so-called 'Gang of Four', broke away from the Labour Party to form the Social Democratic Party. They came from the Right of the Labour Party and were soon joined by a number of other right-wing Labour MPs, one Conservative MP, a number of former Labour MPs, and other prominent members of the party. They also attracted support from many people who had never been involved in party politics.

In parliamentary terms they soon overtook the Liberal Party and, by 1983 had almost 30 MPs – so becoming the largest third party in parliament since the 1930s. However, these MPs had not actually been elected to parliament as members of the Social Democratic Party. When they did stand as members of the SDP in the general election in June 1983, only six were returned.

What do the Social Democrats stand for? On its formation in 1981 the party published a document outlining 'Twelve Tasks', which became the basis for its policies. The SDP supports the idea of a 'mixed economy' with a large private industrial sector as well as some state

The 'gang of four': Bill Rogers, Shirley Williams, Roy Jenkins and David Owen, who were the founders of the SDP.

control. But it puts a considerable stress on its opposition to what it calls the 'class politics' of the 'two old parties' with the violent changes of policies which this brings. It supports electoral reform, greater investment in industry, greater redistribution of wealth, decentralisation of power away from Whitehall, multi-racialism, and international co-operation which includes membership of NATO and the EC. Obviously in a number of key areas it shares policies with the Liberals although the decisions of both parties to form the Alliance for the 1983 general election was not seen as a merger by either party. For the moment they both want to keep their separate identities although there are members in both parties who would prefer a merger.

The work of political parties

Political parties are, obviously, a dominating influence on politics. But what is their real importance in the political system?

To begin with, parties make political choice much simpler. Although it can seem quite attractive for voters in elections to be given the opportunity to pick MPs, or local councillors, who are independent of any party, the idea being that we vote for the 'best person', the chances are that we would not have a clear idea of what that person really stands for politically. We wouldn't know, for example, how he or she would respond to new problems and it is unlikely that such a candidate would present us with policies covering the full range of political issues. Voting Conservative, Labour or Alliance makes our choice easier for two reasons. First we have some idea of what these labels mean and we can choose whether to identify with them. Secondly, parties offer us reasonably clear-cut alternatives in policies.

Choice may be made simpler but it also may become too restricted. We have seen that, in order to win power, political parties are a combination of interests which fight under the same label. But, for example, having two main parties can restrict choice too much: is it inevitable that people are divided into either Labour supporters or Conservative supporters? And, even if they vote for one or other party,

Ayatollah Khomeini who became leader of Iran after the fall of the Shah. Political leadership in Iran came from the dominant religious group.

do they agree completely with all the policies which the party wants to introduce? This problem is made more acute if the activists in a party, who decide the policy, are too much to the Left or Right of those who normally vote for the party. The right-wing policies of the Conservative Party and the left-wing policies of the Labour Party, for example, may both be too extreme for the majority of voters. The two-party system is under considerable strain and it might be that a wider, and more realistic choice of parties, could result: for example, a left-wing Labour Party, a centre/left Alliance, and a Conservative Party.

Political parties play a major part in mobilising political support and increasing participation in politics. They are anxious to draw into their structure, from local to national level, the largest possible numbers, to increase their support. They also act as a way of channelling people's views, and their demands, to politicians. They help to link people to the political system, and, by getting results, discourage action outside it. At election time political parties become involved in one of the most basic forms of political participation – getting people out to vote.

Recruitment into politics itself is a fundamental contribution of the parties to the political system: it is that recruitment which provides us with our political leaders. In countries without a well formed party system, political leaders may come from particularly strong interest groups – such as the military, traditional groups such as tribal chiefs, or even from the dominant religion.

The conflict between political parties is more than argument for argument's sake. Of course disagreement can be taken to petty extremes at times but political parties do reflect quite genuine differences in interests and beliefs – and play a part in enabling the political system to function in an orderly and peaceful fashion.

Discussion and essay questions

1. Why do people often argue that party politics is dirty. How would you answer these charges if you were a politician?

2. What are the differences between a political party and (a) CND (b) trade unions?

3. What is the evidence for and against the description of Britain as having a national two-party system?

4. What arguments would you put forward from (a) a Conservative and (b) a Labour point of view towards:
   the abolition of public schools?
   more government control over industries?

5. How useful are the terms 'Right, Left and Centre' in party politics?

6. What are the main differences between conservatism and socialism?

7. Compare and contrast the structure of the Conservative and Labour parties.

8. 'Political parties make choice easier.' 'Political parties limit choice too much'. Discuss these two descriptions of parties.

4 Voting and elections

Representation and elections

Most organised groups hold regular elections to decide who should hold various posts. Obviously elections can also be a chance to call to account those elected in the past. But why do we elect officers of a club, or members of parliament, to represent us? Why can't we all be involved in making decisions?

This may be possible sometimes, even at national level, and one device used is the **referendum**. In 1975, for example, a referendum was held about whether we should stay in the European Community and, in 1979, another was held in Scotland and Wales about devolution proposals. This can certainly be a useful way of finding out opinion on an issue, and the campaign itself helps to inform us about the arguments involved. But most issues cannot be easily reduced to a simple 'yes' or 'no'. In any case, the result of a referendum may carry great weight but parliament is not bound to accept the result.

In most organised groups, it is simply impossible to consult everyone before many decisions are made. Instead, we elect people to represent us, to make decisions on our behalf, knowing that future elections will provide the opportunity to judge how well they have done.

In national politics we elect MPs, but our vote depends heavily on our party preferences. At general elections we are usually far more concerned with the party label of candidates than whether, as individuals, they would make good representatives. The issue becomes which party can best represent us, our interests and beliefs, and above all which party we would prefer to see forming the next government.

Linked to this is the idea of **legitimacy**: the governments we elect claim the right to rule over us and we accept this claim because we elected them. The authority of government comes from the consent of the people. Naturally this right to govern is not given permanently and we expect to have the chance to express our views, and withdraw consent if necessary, at the next election.

The British electoral system

Constituencies

In general elections, voting takes place in 650 constituencies in order to elect MPs and to decide which party will form the government. The

c. 51   *Scotland Act 1978*

APPENDIX

FORM OF BALLOT PAPER

Parliament has decided to consult the electorate in Scotland on the
question whether the Scotland Act 1978 should be put into effect.

DO YOU WANT THE PROVISIONS OF THE SCOTLAND
ACT 1978 TO BE PUT INTO EFFECT?

Put a cross (X) in the appropriate box.

YES	
NO	

PRINTED IN ENGLAND BY BERNARD M. THIMONT
Controller of Her Majesty's Stationery Office and Queen's Printer of Acts of Parliament

*A ballot paper. In 1979 a referendum was held in Scotland and Wales over
government proposals for devolution. Can an issue as complicated as this be
reduced to a simple question?*

country is divided up so that, as far as possible, each constituency has
the same number of voters, but this equal balance is often difficult to
achieve. For example, a thinly populated rural constituency would have
to be huge in area if it was to have the same number of voters as an
urban constituency. Another difficulty in keeping constituencies the
same size is that their populations change over the years. For example,
many families have moved from the old central parts of towns to new
homes in the suburbs or even the countryside in the past thirty years.
It is the job of the Boundary Commission, which is independent of
government, to alter constituency boundaries accordingly. Between
1979 and 1983, the Commission made the largest number of changes
this century – virtually every constituency was affected.

How are party candidates chosen?

In all parliamentary constituencies the members of each political party
form a local constituency party (Conservatives prefer the term Association). These local parties have the power to select candidates and the
methods they use are similar to each other. If the party does not hold
the seat then a shortlist of four or five names is chosen by local officials,
after which a selection conference is held. There is no need for a
candidate to be born in, or live in, the constituency and many of those
ambitious to become MPs will apply all over the country.

In the past it has been rare for a sitting MP not to be chosen to stand again. However, the Labour Party has introduced a system of compulsory re-selection of MPs. One result of this was that some sitting MPs were not selected to fight their seats at the 1983 election. Some even fought as 'Independent Labour' candidates against their party's official choice.

Local constituency parties have considerable power in selecting candidates. Although a candidate has to be finally approved by national party headquarters, it is rare for the local party choice to be questioned. And, if the constituency is a 'safe seat' for their party, the selection meeting, which may consist of less than a hundred members, is effectively choosing the MP.

The timing of an election

This is the prime minister's decision, although under the 1911 Parliament Act, an election must be called within five years of the last one. Naturally, the prime minister will try and choose a time which gives maximum advantage to the government – for example when the economy is doing well and people have money in their pockets. An encouraging movement of opinion polls can be a factor as well. Sometimes there is no choice: on 28th March 1979, the Labour government lost a vote of confidence in the House of Commons by 311 votes to 310, the first time this had happened since 1924. Losing a vote on a trivial matter, or a 'free' vote where the political parties do not expect their members to vote in a particular way, is not nearly so serious. But when the vote is a vote of confidence in the government, and the government loses it, then it will be expected to call a general election. This is exactly what Mr Callaghan's government did in 1979.

Usually, however, the prime minister has the choice of when to hold an election. It is rare for governments to wait the full five years because, as the legal time for the election approaches, they lose the advantage of surprise and of fighting the election when it best suits them. In 1983, for example, Mrs Thatcher called an election when her government had a year to run. However, opinion polls showed that the government had regained a great deal of support and with a low inflation rate and signs of economic recovery, no doubt she felt that it was a suitable time 'to go to the country' – and she was right.

Ben Ford was Labour MP for Bradford North but failed to be chosen as Labour candidate for the 1983 election. He fought the seat as 'Independent Labour' and lost.

Preparing for the election

Marginal seats

Out of the 650 seats, about 500 are usually safe because one party has a majority which the others are not likely to overturn. The others are marginal seats where the MP has a smaller majority and where it is quite likely that he or she could lose to a candidate from another party. The national organisations of each party pay special attention to these marginal seats. For instance, they may arrange for their top speakers to visit them and they will try to find extra campaign workers to go to help the teams of local party members. In the 1979 election a net gain by the Conservatives of 55 seats gave them a comfortable majority of 43. This was a considerable victory, yet the key to the whole campaign lay in less than 100 marginal constituencies.

The build-up of the national campaign

The most important part of an election campaign, apart from special efforts in marginal seats, is at national level. Campaigns can be broken down into two time spans. First of all as a government moves into its fourth year of office, assuming that it has a comfortable majority, speculation about the election date is bound to increase and all parties begin their preparations. Secondly, there is the election campaign itself, which runs from the announcement by the prime minister, up to election day – normally between three and four weeks. The length of the 'pre-election' campaign can vary considerably as the elections of 1979 and 1983 illustrate. By mid-1978 the Labour government had lost its overall majority in the House of Commons and a pact with the Liberals, which had helped the government survive, was officially over. A defeat in the Commons over an issue of confidence seemed likely at any time. The government was not obliged to call an election until October 1979 but uncertainty about its survival meant that all parties had to be prepared for an election from the Summer of 1978.

The Conservative response began in March 1978 when it hired an

An advertisement used by the Conservative Party both on hoardings and in the press during the 1979 election campaign.

advertising agency, Saatchi and Saatchi, to work for them. In the past all parties had used people skilled in advertising to help in campaigns, but this was the first time a contract had been given to an agency. A committee of Conservative politicians and representatives from Saatchi and Saatchi was set up and it coordinated the campaign from April 1978. It used a mixture of press and poster advertisements, cinema commercials, and party political broadcasts. Following normal commercial practice 'target groups' were identified and these included skilled and semi-skilled workers, their wives, and first-time voters. The cinema was used to reach the 18–21-year-olds who now form the bulk of the cinema-going public, and press advertising was limited to the *Sun* and the *Daily Mirror*. At first the campaign concentrated on attacking the Labour Government's record but later the main emphasis shifted to presenting Conservative policies.

By contrast the pre-election campaign on 1983 was a very much shorter affair. Mrs Thatcher had a comfortable majority in the Commons and could have held on to power until May 1984. It was pointed out earlier that she had good reasons to call an election and there was considerable press and television speculation before she made her announcement but, compared with 1979, the national campaign was concentrated almost entirely on the three weeks up to polling day.

The election campaign

Once election day is announced a frenzy of activity begins with each party attempting to get maximum publicity for their policies and leaders. The parties appoint a campaign team of politicans and officials for this purpose. The presentation of the party case is regarded as particularly important and, in 1983, all three main parties used advertising agencies. Each party produces its **manifesto** which sets out the policies offered to the electorate, and decides which policies they are going to stress in their speeches and advertising. The party which wins the election will claim that its policies, as expressed in the manifesto were supported by voters so it has a **mandate** (legal authority) to carry them out.

Television

Campaigns have changed greatly in the last twenty-five years. Today television dominates the presentation of parties, their policies and, especially, their leaders. The great public meetings of the past have been replaced by politicians appealing for support through the television set in the corner of most living rooms and facing a national audience of millions. Virtually every activity in a national campaign is geared towards television exposure and because television is a medium which stresses personality and the idea of star performers the effect has been to turn elections into contests between the main party leaders, rather than being about a choice between parties and their policies.

Television and radio time in 1983 election

Television

Con: 5 broadcasts of 10 minutes
  (The Conservatives chose to have
  4 × 5 minutes and 1 × 10 minutes)
Lab: 5 broadcasts of 10 minutes
All: 4 broadcasts of 10 minutes
SNP: 2 broadcasts of 10 minutes (Scotland only)
PC: 1 broadcast of 10 minutes (Wales only)

Radio

Con: 4	broadcasts of 10	minutes
3	"	5	"
Lab: 4	"	10	"
3	"	5	"
All: 3	"	10	"
2	"	5	"
SNP: 2	"	10	"
PC: 1	"	10	"

Figure 4.1 Party election broadcasts.

For example, of the total amount of *news* broadcast time given to each party in the 1979 elections, Mr Callaghan was given 63 per cent of Labour time, Mrs. Thatcher 59 per cent of conservative time and Mr. Steel 73 per cent of Liberal time.

There are three ways in which television is used. Firstly, both the BBC and ITV put on special election programmes, and existing programmes such as Panorama, or World in Action concentrate on the election as well. Interviews, debates, analysis of different aspects of the campaign, are some of the techniques used. Secondly, news broadcasts are extended and increasingly parties attempt to provide 'newsworthy' items for inclusion. Major speeches by leaders for example are timed so that they can appear on the main evening news on both channels. In 1979 and 1983 a number of activities were deliberately engineered for television news and the press. These 'media events' only happened *because* television and the press were there and were set up just for the cameras. Thirdly, political parties are given time on television, and radio, to appeal directly to the public. These party political broadcasts are paid for by the parties themselves, who control the content. In 1983, however, the Conservatives, decided that party political broadcasts are not popular with viewers; so in four of their five broadcasts, they used only five minutes of the ten minutes available to them.

The press

Most national and local newspapers are totally committed to one or other party and usually it is the Conservatives. For example, in 1983, only one national daily paper, the *Daily Mirror*, supported Labour. Inevitably, newspapers are likely to select and present news stories to suit the party of their choice, and all editorial comments show political partiality as well. For example, in the 1983 election, a report from the National Institute of Economic Affairs brought the following responses. 'Gloom Report slams claims of recovery' (*Daily Mirror*), 'The Bumpy Road ahead to Recovery' (*Daily Express*), 'Britain is on the Up and Up' (*Daily Mail*). However, for both the Labour Party and the Alliance, television can partly offset the considerable press support received by the Conservative Party and, in any case, the influence of the press on voters is not at all clear. It may influence floating, (undecided) voters but as a 1983 poll showed, most readers are very clear about the political bias of their daily paper.

Opinion polls

Opinion polls taken during elections are probably the most accurate way of judging how the various campaigns are progressing and they are greeted with the same anxiety as a sick person's temperature. During the 1983 election six national polls were published regularly with others concentrating on regions and marginal seats, and private polls were taken for the parties themselves.

Opinion polls were particularly important in 1983 because, with three parties fighting the election and our 'first past the post' electoral system, the issue of **tactical voting** became more important. Anti-Conservatives, for example, might have voted either Labour or Alliance but this decision would be affected by which of the two parties had the best chance of defeating the Conservative candidate. Such tactical voting is not new and was common in previous elections, in seats where the Liberal candidate was seen as the main opposition to the Conservatives. In such cases the Labour vote was 'squeezed'. But in 1983 the potential for tactical voting was greater because the Alliance and Labour were very close in opinion polls and, for the first time for over fifty years, the election was a real three-party battle.

Such tactical voting has led some people to say that opinion polls should not be published during an election campaign, or at least not in its last few days. But it can be argued that it is only right that people should be able to make voting decisions on as much evidence as possible and that tactical voting is a perfectly respectable way of casting a vote – especially in an electoral system where all votes for a losing candidate are wasted.

The campaign in the constituencies

Victory in an election campaign, especially in marginal seats, often goes to the party with the best local organisation for getting its supporters to turn out and vote.

Every February a new Register of Electors is published for each constituency. This contains the name, address and electoral number of those entitled to vote in local and general elections. The first task of a well organised constituency party is to find out the voting intentions of everyone on that list. This is done through **canvassing** – going round every door and asking people how they are likely to vote. Canvassing is generally a method of finding out people's voting intentions rather than persuading them.

The results of the canvass are marked on cards as 'For', 'Against' or 'Don't Know'. In addition, people who need a postal vote are discovered. This means that if they are ill, have moved from another constituency or are likely to be away on work, a ballot paper is sent to them. In a marginal seat the party with the most efficient method of finding

Secretary of State for Defence, Mr Michael Heseltine, makes a point to a group of youngsters during the election.

its postal vote supporters may win for this reason alone. Canvassing also determines how many people will need transport to the polls; and it finds those willing to display posters, or join the party and help in a more positive way. It is rare to have a fully canvassed Register, although this is obviously the ideal to work towards. Canvassing continues up to election day itself.

Meanwhile the candidates get to know the area, discover its problems and meet as many people as possible. They try to get publicity in the local press and, above all, whip up enthusiasm amongst party workers. In other words, they carefully 'nurse' the seat. Existing MPs have an obvious advantage here, because appearances on radio and television and their activities in the Commons are reported in the local press.

The few weeks of the election campaign are especially long for constituency parties. They have to be sure that the right number of people sign the candidate's nomination paper and that it is handed in on time with the deposit (see Election finance). A local election address has to be written, printed and put in envelopes – each candidate is allowed to send one through the post free. They then have to work ceaselessly to meet people at doorsteps, factory gates, street corners and elsewhere. Public meetings are held, but they are usually badly attended unless a well-known national speaker is present. For party

DAVID DUNN
SDP/Liberal Alliance

How your vote can make a difference

On Thursday 3rd May your vote can make a difference. A difference to the future for you and your children. A difference to the future for Stafford and for Britain.

It's a chance to put Stafford on the political map. A chance to elect an MP who wants to bring the country together. An MP who will represent all of the people of Stafford, whoever they are. An MP who will be a local leader and a major asset to the House of Commons.

Britain can't afford two political parties which listen less and less to the people they claim to represent. With a Labour Party which shows no leadership and a Government which is no longer on the right track.

We all know Labour can't win Stafford.

We all know that a Conservative win won't make any difference, adding another member to the four hundred Conservative MPs already there.

If you want your vote to make a real difference.

If you want an MP with everyone's interests at heart.

Elect David Dunn and the SDP/Liberal Alliance on 3rd May.

DAVID DUNN

David Dunn is 37 and married with two children. He and his wife Patricia live in Stafford and have done for more than a decade. He is a lecturer in International Politics at North Staffordshire Polytechnic and a well-known expert writer on arms control.

Both David's boys, Mark and Paul attend Walton High School. David himself was educated in Manchester and worked in the aircraft industry before going on to study at London University and at universities in the United States.

David is also Chairman of South Staffordshire SDP and was the candidate here in Stafford at the last General Election when he came second to Sir Hugh Fraser with more than 13,000 votes.

Canvassing, 1983. Party publicity produced for David Dunn, the SDP/Liberal Alliance candidate in the Stafford by-election in 1984.

workers it is a time of great excitement, even if most people are un-moved and anxious for life and television to return to normal.

Election finance

Before an election there is no legal limit on how much a party can spend on putting its views across. That is why they sometimes organise big advertising campaigns in the months before they think an election is due. Clearly, this benefits the wealthier parties.

Once the election campaign starts, national advertising in news-papers or posters can begin in earnest. Spending on this is not limited but parties have to be sure that national advertisements do not mention candidates because there are very strict regulations about how much individuals may spend on trying to get elected. The laws on individual spending were first passed to stop candidates giving bribes to voters. Each candidate is allowed to spend so much per voter and has to hand in detailed accounts after the election.

Candidates have to pay £150 as a deposit which is lost if they do not get an eighth of the total vote. This was originally designed to discourage frivolous candidates but the deposit is now under review. In 1983, there were more 'fringe' candidates than ever before. For example, in Finchley, Mrs Thatcher's constituency, there were eleven candidates and the combined vote of eight of them totalled only 736 votes. In 1979 parties were entitled to party election broadcasts if they had more than 50 candidates so, for an investment of only £7,500 in deposits (which were all lost) the National Front, the Ecology Party and the Workers' Revolutionary Party, were all given television time. On the other hand a low deposit does mean that smaller parties can put up candidates and so bring their ideas to the notice of electors.

Election day

The key time in a constituency is obviously election day itself when the organisation of the party really matters. Ideally by this time canvassing

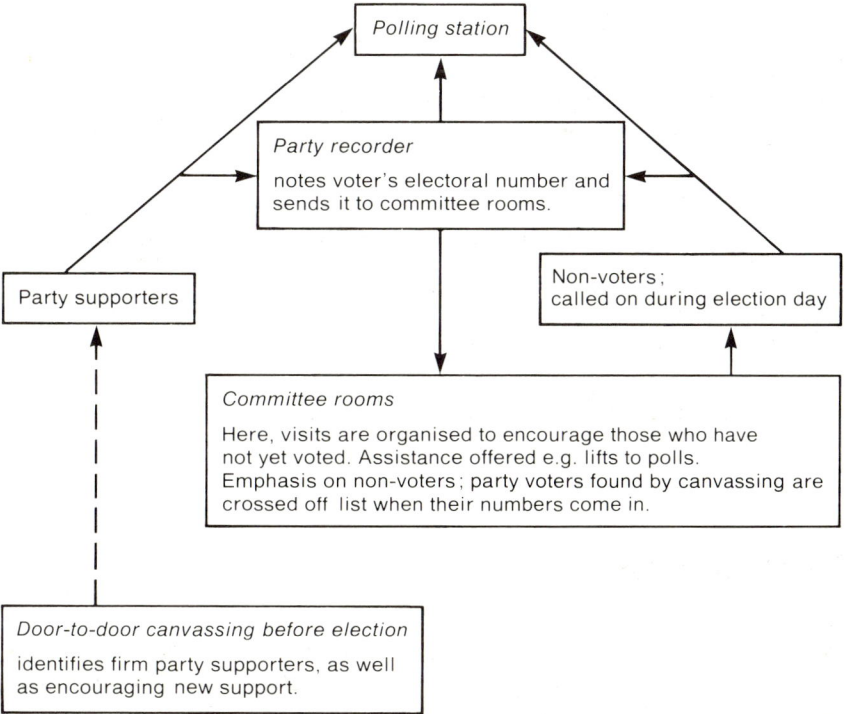

Figure 4.2 Getting out to vote.

is over, with the 'Don't Knows' revisited; and all known party supporters have been listed. Parties now concentrate on these. Figure 4.2 illustrates the usual method of 'getting out the vote' in each part of a constituency.

Results

Polling stations close at 10.00 p.m. The ballot boxes are sealed and sent to a central place, often a Town Hall, for the count. The first results are known in a few hours, although some rural constituencies do not start counting until the next morning. If a result is close – either in deciding the winner or in saving a deposit – there is a recount. In Peterborough the 1966 election produced eight recounts and a final majority of three for Sir Harmer Nicholls (Conservative).

If the overall result of the general election is that government has been defeated, the prime minister resigns and the leader of the new majority party is then invited by the Queen to form a new government.

The 1983 election: an analysis of the results

If we examine the 1983 election in terms of *seats* won by the parties then it was clearly a massive Conservative victory. They won 397 seats and gained an overall majority in the Commons of 144 – the largest majority of any party since 1945, and the first time in eighty years a Conservative prime minister had won two elections in a row. The Labour Party had the smallest number of MPs (209) since 1935 and, for them, the election was a disaster. The Liberal/Social Democrat Alliance completely failed in their aim of replacing Labour as the main opposition to the Conservatives and only won 23 seats (17 Liberal and 6 SDP).

This picture changes dramatically if we analyse the number of votes cast for each party. The Conservatives polled less votes in total, and gained a smaller percentage of the vote, compared to 1979, and the number of seats they won was out of all proportion to their support in the country. The performance of Labour is even worse if total votes are considered. They received the lowest percentage vote, 27.6 per cent, since 1918 – when they did not even fight a third of the seats. Fortunately for Labour they have a core of seats where their majority is so large that a political earthquake would be needed before they were lost. It was the success of the Alliance which drained away the support of the other parties – especially Labour. They had the highest percentage vote (25.4 per cent) for a third party since 1929.

Another feature of the election was turnout. Only 72.7 per cent of the electorate voted. This figure is always less than 100 per cent because the electoral register contains the names of people who have recently died and, with a June election, a number would have been on holiday. But this was still the lowest turnout since 1970. Figure 4.3 shows the vote for each party as a percentage of the total electorate.

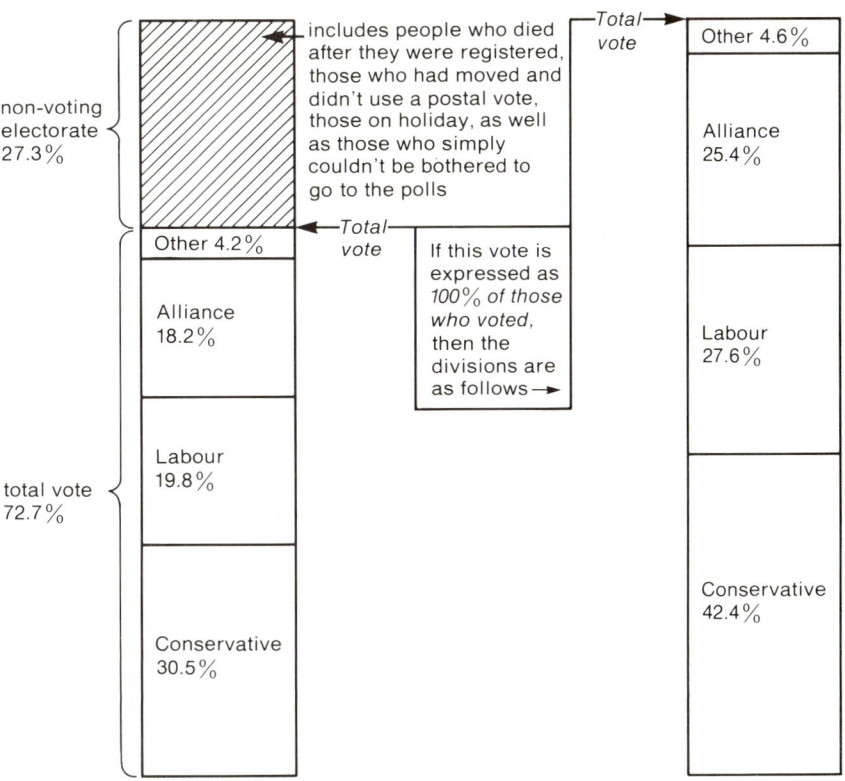

Figure 4.3 Two ways of looking at the 1983 election result.

The Conservatives, for example, received only 30.5 per cent.

Differences in the regional pattern of voting were apparent in 1979 and continued in 1983. In the south of England, including London, there was an average swing away from Labour to Conservative of 4.7 per cent whereas in Scotland this was 1.8 per cent and 1.5 per cent in the north-west. In Merseyside and Glasgow there were swings to Labour. Labour won only two seats in the south, outside London, while it held 41 of the 72 Scottish seats. In effect, Labour was driven back to its heartland in the north, Scotland, Wales and inner cities. The Alliance polled much more evenly than the other parties and tended to run second to the Conservatives in the south and second to Labour in the north. It came second in 313 seats compared with 180 for the Conservatives and 132 for Labour.

As in most elections since the 1950s there was a trend against voting mostly for the two main parties. Figures 5.1 and 5.2 in the next chapter shows a breakdown of voting based on such factors as social class, age, and sex. The importance of this kind of analysis is examined in the next chapter but it is clear that Labour lost a significant amount of support in some groups which are crucial for its success, such as skilled workers, and union members. The Alliance polled with evenness across all these groups. One explanation of its low number of seats is because its support is not sufficiently concentrated in any particular part of the country.

Is our electoral system fair?

The 'first past the post' system works best when the choice facing voters in each constituency is limited to two parties. It means that without any third candidate the winner will get more than 50 per cent of the votes cast in a constituency. And nationally there is a greater chance of a close relationship between votes cast for a party and seats won.

However, as the result on page 55 showed, the injection of a third candidate (and in Scotland and Wales there may be strong fourth candidates) with *reasonable support* frequently means that the winner will get less than 50 per cent of the vote. In the present system there is no mechanism at all for the votes of losing candidates to be reflected in parliament. One result of this is tactical voting where people vote to keep a party *out* rather than voting for the party they prefer. It they knew that their votes could count the probability is that they would vote for what they want, rather than against the party they dislike most.

The last few elections and especially the election of 1983, have seen a considerable imbalance between votes cast nationally for parties and seats won. The present system penalises the Alliance in particular (because its support is thinly spread around the country) and over-rewards the other two parties. The difference between votes cast and seats won has been one of the main reasons for the new interest in electoral reform. But there are other reasons as well. The decline in support for the Conservative and Labour parties has led to governments being elected – and in 1979 and 1983 with substantial majorities – on a relatively small percentage of the vote. Thus, another disadvantage of the electoral system is that a right-wing Conservative government or a left-wing Labour government can win office and pursue its policies – with the majority of people actually voting for other parties. It may be argued that one result of this is to weaken the legitimacy of government itself.

	Votes cast	MPs	Average vote per MP
Conservative	12,991,377	397	32,724
Labour	8,437,120	209	40,369
Alliance	7,775,048	23	338,046

Figure 4.4 Voting for three main party MPs in 1983.

In Chapter 2 it was pointed out that one virtue of the British political system has been its capacity to change over time in response to new forces which have emerged in society. Change can be slow and this may be justified as a way of distinguishing genuinely new forces from those which are much more temporary. For example, if the two-party system is restored in elections then demands for electoral reform will probably fade. However, if recent trends continue then pressure for change must increase.

Advantages of the present system

It would be wrong to assume that the present electoral system has no virtues. It is easy to understand, voters are only expected to put one cross on a ballot paper, and the winner is soon known. We vote in single member constituencies which are relatively small compared with other countries, and MPs can be easily identified with their constituencies and by their constituents.

The system may penalise smaller parties but it does enable us to have strong, one-party governments which can take clear decisions. Only twice since 1945 (1974 and 1976–79) has a government been forced to rely on other parties to stay in office. Virtually any change in the electoral system would mean that, assuming the smaller parties win more seats, we would have permanent **coalition** government consisting of different party combinations. This may reduce the chance of 'extremist' policies but it would also mean that parties would probably have to modify the policies they presented to the electorate in order to gain agreement with other parties to form a coalition. The effect of this would be to make smaller parties more powerful than their support would justify. However, the most important reason for continuing with the present system is probably the difficulty of choosing another. There are a large number of different electoral systems in use, (a few of which are outlined here), and it would be very hard to reach agreement on a new system for Britain.

Figure 4.5 Different electoral systems.

Alternative vote

How does it work?	1 Voter numbers candidates in order of preference (1, 2, 3, 4, etc).
	2 If a candidate receives more than 50 per cent of all first preferences then he is elected.
	3 If there is no clear winner on first count, the bottom candidate is eliminated and his second preferences are distributed among the other candidates.

Example:

Brown (Con)   22,110
Jones (Lab)   21,411
Evans (All)   8,320

Evans is eliminated and the second preferences of his supporters are divided between Brown and Jones. In this case Jones, who would be second in our present system, *could* win.

Where used: Australia.

Comments: Minority parties could still be 'squeezed', but candidates can stand without any fear of splitting the vote and letting in the party they dislike most.

Figure 4.5 Different electoral systems (cont.).

Double ballot

How does it work?

1 The seats in parliament are divided into two kinds: (a) normal constituencies; (b) those allocated by party voting strength in the country as a whole.
2 The voter has a double ballot paper. One is to vote for a constituency MP, the other to vote for a party.
3 The constituency MP is elected as in Britain, and this decides half the seats.
4 Then the total party votes are added up and the rest of the seats are allocated according to the percentage vote gained by each party. The parties will already have drawn up lists of people they would like to have in Parliament in order of preference.

Example:

If the 1979 United Kingdom election results are used, rounding off the percentage vote for each party, the 'list' could have produced the following result:

	Con	Lab	Lib
Vote	44	37	14
No. of MPs	141	119	56
Total 'list' seats:	316		

Where used: West Germany.

Comments: To qualify for MPs on the 'list' a party must obtain a minimum percentage of votes – 5 per cent in West Germany. This system produces larger constituencies than in Britain and would mean, on past voting patterns, permanent coalition or minority government. A modification to this would be to elect a proportion of MPs according to the 'list' system e.g. 25 per cent instead of 50 per cent.

Single transferable vote (STV)

How does it work?

1 Constituencies are made larger, with more than one MP. Assume a constituency with five members.
2 Each party puts up candidates for the seats – in this case five from each party.
3 Voters number candidates in order of preference and can either cast all five votes for candidates of one party or divide them, according to preference, between candidates of different parties.
4 A quota is calculated

$$\frac{\text{Total votes cast (total first preferences)}}{\text{No. of seats to be filled} + 1}$$

To work out how many votes are needed for each MP to be elected, e.g.

$$\frac{150,000}{5 + 1} + 1 = 25,001$$

To be elected a candidate in this seat needs 25,001.

Example:

5 First preferences are counted. Any candidate with more than the quota is elected. Then their 'surplus' votes are transferred i.e. the correct proportion of their supporters second choices are distributed to the other candidates. If no one reaches quota then second preferences of bottom candidate is distributed.
6 Process continues until five candidates have quota.

Where used: Ireland, Australian Senate.

Comments: Complicated and takes time. If it involves distributing second votes of bottom candidates then could distort preferences. But does mean people can express preferences across party.

Why have elections?

Criticism of our electoral system, and the search for alternatives, does not necessarily weaken the central importance for us of a method of choosing, and removing, governments peacefully. Elections must provide choice if they are to have any real meaning and the absence of choice can mean that frustration and hostility against government has no peaceful form of expression. In such cases violence may appear the only remedy.

Elections provide governments with legitimacy, a legal and moral authority for carrying out their policies. Even if many people show little interest in elections, apart from voting, they are a time when politicians attempt to defend their actions and explain their policies to the electorate. In this process people are encouraged to think about the kind of government they want. Both politicians and political parties are also forced to look at *themselves* and at whether they are really offering people what they want.

Figure 4.6 Election results in the UK 1979–83.

Election year	Conservative		Labour		Alliance (Liberals in 1979)		other seats	total seats
	% of votes	no. of seats	% of votes	no. of seats	% of votes	no. of seats		
1979	43.9	339	36.9	268	13.8	11	17	635
1983	42.4	397	27.6	209	25.4	23	21	650

Discussion and essay questions

1. In what different ways could it be claimed that the votes of some people are worth more than the votes of others?

2. What different problems, and advantages, are there in running an election campaign for (a) the government, (b) opposition parties?

3. Do you agree with the view that a party manifesto should be the basis for a mandate when that party is elected to office?

4. Does it matter if party politics and leaders are 'sold' to the public like commercial products?

5. How do political parties attempt to get the widest possible support in constituencies?

6. Which electoral system would you like Britain to have? Give reasons for your choice.

7. Do you think voting should be compulsory?

8. How would you organise a campaign for a party in a by-election?

9. Find out the election results in your constituency since 1945. Draw a graph to show the votes for each party and the percentage turnout. How often has the seat changed hands?

5 The basis of support for political parties

British party politics appears to be going through a period of change. Previous chapters have already illustrated that some of the old certainties of party politics are under strain. As the dominance of the Conservative and Labour parties has weakened, the electorate's changeable nature has intensified. By-elections have frequently produced sensational results where large majorities have been overturned; it was a series of such by-election truimphs which heralded the arrival of the Alliance between 1981 and 1983. But even in general elections such changeability, although less dramatic, has been apparent. In 1970 the swing to the Conservatives from Labour was the highest since 1945 – a record which was then broken by Mrs Thatcher in 1979.

A further change was mentioned in the previous chapter. Recent elections have produced wide regional, even local, differences in the way support swings between political parties. Until the 1970s, elections produced a fairly uniform pattern of voting geographically, and a swing from Conservative to Labour, for example, was likely to be roughly the same throughout the country. Now this is no longer so.

Why do people support one or other political party – and why should people change their allegiance? Both by-election and general election results point to one difficulty in answering such questions. Voting may be influenced by short-term factors such as the dislike of, or support for, a particular policy. For example, Conservative promises to cut taxes in 1979 were very attractive to skilled workers who normally voted Labour. By-elections, usually with little at stake in terms of bringing a government down, can be used to express discontent over various matters – even dislike of a particular candidate. Nevertheless the changeability found in by-elections is still much greater now than at the height of two-party competition in the period 1945–1964.

Any election is a kind of snapshot of the public mood however, there are still more long-term relationships between party support and certain groups in Britain. These relationships need to be explored.

Political socialisation

First, we need to understand what is meant by **socialisation**. From their earliest days children begin to build up an understanding of themselves – what they are like, how they are expected to behave, and their place in the world. A great deal of this understanding comes from the experi-

A sensational victory for the Social Democrats in the Crosby by-election, November 1981. Shirley Williams overturned a Conservative majority of 19,272 but lost the seat in the 1983 election by 3,401.

ence of being with family and friends, and is not taught directly. This process of socialisation continues throughout our lives, and shapes our values and our attitudes towards other individuals and groups. It is important in a political sense too.

Just think of someone you know well (like yourself) and how many of their (your) attitudes and opinions come from their family, their friends, their religion (if they have one), the place where their father or mother works, whether they belong to a youth club or a trade union. All these are agents of socialisation and so are some others: the school we go to, the part of the country we live in, the other members of our age group and the class we think we belong to. Of course, agents of socialisation don't have the same effect on all the people they are socialising. Some people react against what they are taught at home, school or church. Sometimes there are cross-currents; a machine-fitter's son who becomes a banker may be have been influenced by two very different sets of friends, work-mates, social clubs and so on. But it is still generally true that the agents of socialisation shape our values and attitudes towards other individuals and groups, and towards politics generally.

To begin with, we acquire attitudes towards authority and rules – in the family and in school for example – which may range from acceptance and conformity, to complete hostility. Our attitudes towards other people are important as well. The extent to which we are tolerant of people different from ourselves, whether because of colour or religion or sex, can have political consequences. It is not difficult in Northern Ireland, for example, for Catholic and Protestant children to have an intolerance towards each other when the family, their friends, their religions, even their school, emphasise differences – and when their chances of meeting someone socially from the other community are very limited. The same applies to racial intolerance. If we are brought up in families where blacks or whites are despised by our parents, and our friends have similar views, then the chances are that, at least when we are young, we will have acquired a great deal of racial prejudice.

Let us look at some of these agents, or influences in more detail and see how they affect our political views.

The family

The family is the first group where socialisation processes begin. Firstly it can help to create views about the importance of politics itself. Where parents are involved in politics, and regard political activity as normal, then it is likely to be accepted by their children. Secondly in party terms there is a strong relationship between the political views of children and those of parents, especially when both parents support the same party. If the parents views are divided between parties then which party a child supports is much less clear cut.

This kind of parental influence is particularly strong in teenagers, up to their earliest chance of voting. What happens after that depends on a variety of other factors which may either confirm the party preference or act as a counter-pressure against it.

Education

Taking the nation as a whole those who have experienced higher education – in colleges, universities or polytechnics – are, as a group, more likely to support the Conservative Party. Conversely, the Labour Party has more support among people whose education finished at school-leaving age. This may seem to conflict with the popular image of left-wing students, but it applies to *all* those who have gone into higher education and this stretches back over many years.

Does this mean that higher education has the effect of making people more Conservative? This question shows the danger of looking at each agent of socialisation in isolation. Those who have gone into higher education, especially until recently, have been drawn mainly from the wealthier sections of society. In other words they may well have been more inclined towards Conservatism in the first place. On top of this, higher education is often a way of going into jobs which are better paid, and it might be expected that this can be a Conservative influence too.

Religion

In the past, religion has been associated with support for one or other party. Non-conformists, for example, were predominantly Liberal and Anglicans tended to support the Conservative Party – the old Liberal jibe was that the Church of England was the Conservative Party at prayer. These influences, if they were influences, have declined. Uncertainty about the effect of religion alone is complicated by the point that non-conformists, for example, were drawn from people who also had economic reasons for supporting the Liberals. But religion has been, and is, an important part of Northern Ireland politics. Voting for many years has been divided on religious lines with the vast majority of Protestants and Catholics voting for different parties. But again religion in Northern Ireland is impossible to separate from the political arguments over partition. Protestants are overwhelmingly in favour of staying in the United Kingdom but the majority of Catholics would prefer to see a united Ireland. In recent years this association of politics and religion has meant the emergence of politicians drawn from the ministry, such as the Reverend Ian Paisley. In his case hostility to a united Ireland is bound up with extreme Protestant dislike of the Catholic Church.

Work

Different jobs bring people together from similar backgrounds, and they are likely to be affected by one another's views. Workers in the more traditional industries such as railways, steel, and especially mining, are generally strong supporters of the Labour Party. This is reflected in the huge Labour majorities in areas such as South Wales, and parts of the North of England and Scotland. Labour support is also greater in larger firms, including the more modern mass production companies, than in smaller ones. Again, workers in jobs where unions are powerful are stronger Labour supporters than those where unions are fairly weak. There are a number of possible explanations for this. Firstly, it could be that union activity encourages workers to support Labour. Secondly it could be that Labour supporters are more likely to join unions. Thirdly, there may be other influences, as we shall see below.

Class

The British have often been described as very class conscious and, as Figure 5.1 shows, there does appear to be some relationship between social class and support for different political parties. In Figure 5.1 class is defined mainly in terms of occupation, which shows how class and work can act as a joint influence.

   The Conservative Party are strongest in the AB and C1 groups with Labour ahead in the C2 and D groups. But it is equally clear that, although class is important, the parties are not divided rigidly on these lines. Indeed, if they were, it would be difficult for the Conservative

	AB	change	C1	change	C2	change	D	change
Con	62	−5	55	−3	39	−7	29	−3
Lab	12	−6	21	−	35	−12	44	−11
All	27	+12	24	+4	27	+16	28	+14

Figures show the percentage from each group voting for a political party. The Change column shows the gain (+) or loss (−) for each party since the 1979 election.

Key
AB   Professional & Managerial   C2   Skilled Workers
C1   Office and Clerical   D   Semi-skilled, Unskilled

(*The Guardian*, 13.6.83)

Figure 5.1 Class voting in the 1983 election.

party to win any elections because the C2 and D groups form the majority of the electorate.

There is a danger of reading too much into the results of one or two elections, especially as we are concerned with longer trends. But there has been a tendency since the early 1960s for the connection between class and voting to get weaker. The 1983 election continued this with 11 per cent or one in nine of the D group voters turning away from the Labour Party compared with 1979. The link between class and voting was further weakened in 1983 by the Alliance which took votes from both sides and received remarkably equal support from each social class. The connection may also be breaking down because the British people are less willing than they were twenty or thirty years ago to identify themselves with any one class.

That still leaves the question of why a large number of working-class people have always voted Conservative. This used to be explained as a 'deferential' vote in other words it expressed the feeling that the Conservative Party and its leaders are more used to governing and better at it. Today, the reason may simply be that more working-class people vote for whichever party will best suit their interests.

Age

Figure 5.2 shows a breakdown of voting in 1983 according to age. At first sight it seems to confirm the popular view that as people grow older they become more set in their ways and more resistent to change, therefore they are more likely to be Conservatives.

But other arguments link party support to the different background and experiences of each age group, which we call a cohort. People in the 65+ age group for example were brought up at a time when the Labour Party was fairly new. And, if family background is important in deciding party attitudes, there would not be as many with both parents strongly pro-Labour as in later generations. This theory would seem to be encouraging for Labour because they should become stronger in the 65+ age group in the future.

Voters by age group

	18–22	23–34	35–44	45–65	65+
Con	41 (−2)	45 (−)	47 (+1)	46 (−1)	48 (−3)
Lab	29 (−12)	32 (−8)	27 (−10)	27 (−13)	33 (−4)
All	30 (+13)	23 (+9)	26 (+10)	27 (+15)	19 (+7)

% of total vote in each group. Figures in brackets show change since 1979.

Voters by sex

	Men	Women
Con	46 (−1)	43 (−3)
Lab	30 (−9)	28 (−11)
All	24 (+11)	28 (+14)

Figure 5.2 Votes by age group and by sex in the 1983 election.

Another cohort theory is based on the experience of people when they first become aware of politics and of the differences in parties at the time. Those who became voters or interested in politics around 1945, for example, when Labour had a landslide victory, are likely to be a more pro-Labour cohort than the cohort who experienced politics for the first time in the late 1950s when there was a strong Conservative government and society was becoming much more affluent. This argument emphasises how important certain experiences are at key times in our lives.

Other influences on party support

Even if it is possible to establish a relationship between groups and party support this does not mean that such relationships can be easily explained. There are other patterns to bear in mind as well.

Women as a group have been more Conservative than men, and in all elections since the war the Conservative Party has had more women voters than Labour. One explanation may be that fewer women are likely to be affected by 'work influences', and that even working women are often employed in industries where unions are weak. However, this pattern may now be changing, and in 1983 more men voted Conservative than women (see Fig. 5.2).

There are also differences on a large scale. Scotland and the north of England have been heavily Labour for many years; the south-east solidly Conservative. This may be partly to do with the fact that the north is more industrialised, but that's not the whole story. The industrial Midlands, around Birmingham and Coventry, was mostly Conservative before 1945, then Labour, and has in recent elections shown a swing back to the Conservatives.

A particularly interesting factor in 1983 was the relationship between types of house ownership and voting patterns. Fifty-nine per cent of houses are owner-occupied and this percentage is increasing, whereas the number of council tenants has declined. The Conservative Party lead over Labour among house-owners in 1983 was 33 per cent whereas the Labour lead among council tenants was 21 per cent. Perhaps more significant was the breakdown of *working class* voters:

	Working-class house-owners	*Council tenants*
Conservative	47%	24%
Labour	26%	49%
Alliance	26%	24%

Short-term and long-term influences

In 1983 the 'Falklands factor' helped the Conservatives to win the election. Until the recovery of the Falklands in 1982, the Conservative government had fallen very low in the opinion polls but the 1983 election was fought on the anniversary of that military victory which had increased the Conservatives' popularity again. The Labour Party in 1983 was still suffering from disputes which had broken out within the party in 1980, and these clearly affected Labour results. In 1983 another factor was of enormous importance – the strength of the Alliance. It is not easy to measure the influence of all these factors. Surveys of opinion, or polls (on which much of the information in this chapter is based) can show important trends, but make no claim to be totally accurate.

Some events or circumstances only influence a single election – in other words they are short-term; others are the result of considerable social change and so have a long-term effect on an election and political life generally. There is no doubt that Britain has changed over the last forty years and some of these long-term changes *might* be an explanation of why, for example, Labour Party support has shown a steady decline since 1966. House ownership has expanded to include the majority of families – as has car ownership. Traditional industries such as coal, shipbuilding and railways are less important and newer industries, often not as strongly unionised, have developed. Fewer people feel the strong working-class identity which was associated with support for Labour. In other words, new interests have developed which people may not feel are defended by the Labour Party.

As the more traditional allegiances have declined so the particular policies of the parties appear to be more important. And, in 1983, it was Conservative policies on such issues as trade union reform, defence, taxation and nationalisation which were the most popular in opinion polls. Unemployment was seen as the *key* issue, but this didn't help Labour a great deal because of doubts about their claim to be able to cut it substantially. However, according to a Gallup poll in *The*

Guardian newspaper (14.6.83) 38 per cent of the electorate still believed that they were essentially Labour supporters though only 28 per cent *voted* Labour. The Alliance, on the other hand, lost votes because too few people thought that they had a chance of winning. Thirty-one per cent of those who thought of voting for them gave this as the main reason for not doing so.

All these influences on party support – both long-term and short-term – show a changing picture, even more so in recent years. In spite of the general level of continuity in British politics generally, the basis of individual party support is constantly shifting in accordance with social changes, political events, and the condition of the parties themselves. Although polls and surveys are valuable in showing some of this general picture, there are many areas of change which are difficult to evaluate – in particular the full consequences of the present three-way split in party allegiances.

Discussion and essay questions

1. What political attitudes do you think you have acquired from your family, friends, school?

2. 'If you are not a socialist before you are thirty then you have no heart. If you are a socialist after you are thirty then you have no head.' What is your view of this statement?

3. Do you know anyone who 'changed their voting habits of a lifetime'? What reasons did they give for their decision? Compare your findings with the rest of the class, and then with the data in Figures 5.1 and 5.2. Is there a pattern?

4. From the evidence in this chapter draw up 'profiles' of people likely to be strong supporters of (a) the Alliance (b) the Conservative Party (c) the Labour Party.

5. What problems face (a) the Labour Party (b) the Alliance (c) the Conservative Party in attempting to increase or maintain their support in the future? If you were helping to plan a campaign for one of these parties, what suggestions would you make?

Part Three: THE BRITISH EXECUTIVE

6   The prime minister and Cabinet

Forming a government

The prime minister is the leader of the majority party in the House of Commons. Only once since 1945 has an election given no party an overall majority – in February 1974. The then prime minister, Edward Heath, attempted to reach an agreement with the Liberals, but failed. He then resigned and the leader of the *largest* party, Harold Wilson, formed a minority Labour government.

   The first task of the prime minister after an election is to pick a government. The prime minister will take advice but has the final choice. In total there are about one hundred positions to fill with the twenty or so members of the Cabinet being the most important. Below them are different levels of junior ministers. All these posts carry a salary. Most of the positions are filled by MPs but some are members of the House of Lords. For example the new Conservative government of 1979 contained 86 MPs and 21 peers.

The Cabinet

The central body in government is the Cabinet which contains the most senior ministers and is chaired by the prime minister. In choosing a Cabinet prime ministers do not have a completely free hand. They have to consider which people are most respected in the party. These politicians are usually bound to get a post, although not always the one they most want.

   A prime minister will be concerned as well about the political balance of the Cabinet. Both the Conservative and Labour parties contain a range of political beliefs. Party unity could be weakened if a Cabinet did not contain some people from each of the main shades of opinion. This may involve including people whose views are not

The Conservative Cabinet in 1983, taken in the Pillared Room at No. 10 Downing Street, London.

always the same as the prime minister's but it can be better to have them in the Cabinet than building up support against the prime minister among back-bench MPs.

Cabinets, once chosen, do not remain the same through the life of a government. Every so often prime ministers will want to reshuffle the membership of the Cabinet and the government. Some ministers may prove ineffective while others may increase their reputations and there are always junior ministers hungry for promotion. Sometimes this is done to breathe new life into a government which is losing support in the country.

Every Cabinet contains some members who are not in charge of ministries or departments. They can be used to co-ordinate policy between departments, to chair Cabinet committees and take on special tasks. As Harold Wilson, lifetime supporter of Huddersfield Town Football Club, once said:

> I've come to believe that the strength of a Cabinet is in its non-departmental ministers. They are the half-backs of the government team. They don't often score goals or hit the headlines but no team can be a success without a good half-back line.

Most modern Cabinets have had a membership of just over twenty. The Thatcher Cabinet of 1983 was twenty-three. Twice, during war-time, prime ministers have preferred to have much smaller 'War Cabinets' which could concentrate on the war and make rapid de-cisions. These varied between five and nine members under Lloyd George (1916–1919) and Churchill (1940–1945).

In normal circumstances the Cabinet meets once or twice a week in the Cabinet Room of 10 Downing Street. As the executive arm of government its job is therefore to decide government policy and not to concern itself with minor details. To do this it relies heavily on certain groups which support its work.

Cabinet committees

As far as possible the issues which have to be decided in Cabinet have already been carefully examined, with information and recommen-dations sent to Cabinet members beforehand. This is the main task of Cabinet committees. The Labour government of James Callaghan (1976–1979), for example, included Cabinet committees concerned with: overseas policy and defence (chaired by the prime minister); the economy; home affairs; energy; legislation (to consider the govern-ment's legislative programme); Northern Ireland; urban aid. Modern Cabinets usually have about twenty-five committees, although the exact numbers and their work is never announced to the public. Apart from these committees there are a number of sub-committees and groups which bring departments and ministers together over more immediate problems facing the government. Membership of Cabinet committees is not just limited to Cabinet ministers. When necessary they can include junior ministers, members of the armed forces and civil servants. Most have representatives of the Treasury to speak on the financial consequences of anything that is decided. The chairmen and membership of the committees are decided by the prime minister. Some are chaired by the non-departmental ministers who have most time for such work but others, such as social services committees, are likely to be chaired by the departmental minister most concerned. Prime ministers will themselves take the chair at committees which deal with their special concerns.

Cabinet committees are hugely important both in investigating issues and providing a way of co-ordinating different parts of a government. Sir John Hunt, Secretary to the Cabinet (1973–1979), summed up their work in this way:

> The Cabinet Committee system grew up as the load on the Cabinet itself became too great. Through it matters of lesser importance can be decided without troubling the whole Cabinet. A decision by a Cabinet Committee, unless referred to the Cabinet, engages the collective responsibility of all ministers and has exactly the same authority as a decision by the Cabinet. (*Observer*, 14.11.76)

This description contains one nugget of information which is worth emphasising. Sometimes 'matters of lesser importance' can be decided without the Cabinet being consulted at all. But is it always true that only matters of little importance do not go to the Cabinet? For example, a Cabinet committee took the decision that Britain would build nuclear weapons after the Second World War. The full Cabinet were not consulted. Nor was the Cabinet consulted about the decision to spend £1,000 m. on modernising our Polaris submarine missiles in the 1970s. Even when important policies do go to the Cabinet for approval it may still find it difficult to challenge the recommendations of a Cabinet committee. The politicians and civil servants on the committee will have used their special knowledge and ministers from other departments may feel that they have not the information needed to disagree.

Cabinet office

The Cabinet office gives the administrative back-up to the Cabinet. It circulates papers and the agenda before meetings, records the minutes and passes on decisions to those affected. The office is the equivalent of a department for prime ministers. It helps them co-ordinate the work of government as well as keeping a watching brief on the activities of ministers and their departments.

Cabinet meetings

The prime minister is chairman of the Cabinet and has the power to decide on how it operates. Harold Wilson, for example, outlined his approach this way:

> I've followed very closely what I learned from Attlee when I was a member of his Cabinet; circulation of papers before a meeting; decisions not satisfactorily cleared at department level to be referred to the Prime Minister; extensive use of Cabinet committees so that we can economise on the use of the time of the full Cabinet; . . . insistence that all Cabinet reports must have a price tag, meaning that the financial implications must be previously agreed with the Treasury . . . And the key thing is that when the Cabinet takes a decision, that's it. There was one occasion when I noticed that a new minister had referred to something that had been decided in Cabinet as a 'proposal'. I sent him a short note saying that the Cabinet makes decision not proposals, and that was the end of the matter.

Mr Wilson's view illustrates a number of features about the Cabinet system. Prime ministers sum up after a discussion which gives them the chance to put a personal interpretation on what has been said. They try to decide what has been the main viewpoint or 'sense of the meeting' – Cabinets do not usually vote. This helps to get decisions without obvious divisions of opinion. The stress on decision-making means that a prime minister needs to be a skilled chairman. Clement Attlee, known as a man of few words, described his own attitude:

> The job of a Prime Minister is to get the general feeling, collect the voices. And then when everything reasonable has been said, to get

on with the job and say. 'Well I think the decision of the Cabinet is this, that, or the other. Any objections? Usually there aren't.

How important is the Cabinet?

Firstly, it is the body which co-ordinates the major activities of government. Many policies involve several government departments each one with particular knowledge to contribute and interests to defend. Although there are interdepartmental committees at all levels of government, *major* issues of co-ordination are settled by the Cabinet and its committee. The work of co-ordination is also necessary because many ministers have such large departments that they have little time to consider government policy as a whole. It is vital that they have information and an opportunity to discuss issues outside their department. Without this, a government can become fragmented, and may appear to be following different directions.

The Cabinet will also need to be satisfied that other groups are not in strong disagreement with government policies. For example, the government needs the support of MPs in its party. It is now customary for the Chief Whip to be at Cabinet meetings so he can pass on the feelings of the parliamentary party. Powerful organisations in the country such as the Confederation of British Industries or Trade Union Congress will also be considered. On some issues the views of foreign governments will be reported.

A second function of the Cabinet is to deal with disagreements between departments or ministers. For example, a government which wants to cut public spending is likely to find conflict between the Treasury, which wants to trim spending, and large departments such as Education and Science. These departments may accept the need for cuts but feel their work will suffer if they are given too little money. They may object if they believe that they have been asked to take too big a share of the cut-back. Much of this conflict can be sorted out in Cabinet committees, or through informal meetings between ministers. The prime minister may intervene as well if an agreement is difficult. But, if the matter is not decided, it must go to the full Cabinet.

Thirdly, the Cabinet is responsible for deciding the priorities of government. A new government will come to power claiming a mandate for the policies in its manifesto. It is one thing to claim a mandate and quite another to decide which policies shall go to the top of the list. A government simply cannot do everything it has promised at once – if at all.

The issue of priorities leads to a fourth function of the Cabinet – it decides the timetable of Bills that are sent to Parliament for debate. Unlike the system in some other countries, a British government controls the law-making body (the legislature). That is because the Cabinet is drawn from members of the majority party in parliament.

As long as it keeps the support of the party, it can see that its policies become law.

The last function of the Cabinet is to cope with the problems and crises which arise unexpectedly. Economic problems, industrial relations, actions by foreign governments are some examples. Since 1969 Northern Ireland has been a continual issue, with its crises and failed solutions. And, in 1982, the Falklands War came to dominate government activity.

Collective Cabinet responsibility

In British government there are many constitutional conventions, or ways of behaving which everyone accepts. One such convention is **collective Cabinet responsibility**. All members of a government, including the most junior, must accept and defend agreed policies – at least publicly. It is a means of maintaining the unity of a government. There may be bitter internal arguments about policies between members of a government but once agreement is reached in Cabinet then everyone is expected to accept the result.

If a member of the government is not prepared to accept such collective responsibility then the only option is to resign or to be sacked. That helps to preserve government unity at the time, but it does not necessarily follow that great harm is done to the individual in the long run. In the past such people as Anthony Eden (over negotiations with the pre-war Italian dictator, Mussolini), Harold Wilson and Aneurin Bevan (over Budget proposals), Peter Thorneycroft and Enoch Powell (over economic policy) have resigned from Cabinets and later achieved high office in their party. (Eden and Wilson became prime ministers.)

Resignations over policy disagreements are relatively rare, in spite of known battles in Cabinet where ministers have even lost over decisions affecting their own departments. Where disagreement involves more than one or two people, and has led to a major split in the Cabinet, collective responsibility can be hard to maintain. In 1975 the Labour government re-negotiated the terms of British entry into the EC. They decided to put the issue of whether Britain should stay in the EC to the electorate, by holding a referendum. But the Cabinet was hopelessly divided on its recommendation about voting. So they agreed to suspend the convention of collective responsibility. Most ministers campaigned for staying in, but others argued in public for British withdrawal.

The role of prime minister

How powerful is the prime minister?

In the past it was quite usual to describe the prime minister as 'first among equals', in other words just a little more important than other

Tony Benn, although a member of the Labour Cabinet, was one of a number of ministers who campaigned against Britain staying in the European Community in 1975.

Cabinet ministers. More recently it has been argued that Britain has moved towards a system of **prime ministerial government**, with prime ministers totally dominating Cabinets and getting their own way. What is the evidence for this?

The first step is to examine the basis of a prime minister's power. Prime ministers are responsible for appointing and dismissing Cabinet members. But we have already seen that prime ministers may not have a completely free hand because they need to include politicians who are powerful in their party.

The prime minister has the extremely important power of choosing members of the Cabinet committees. Each committee has only a few Cabinet ministers and prime ministers have the chance to pick those who agree with their own preferences. It can be difficult, as we have seen, for the full Cabinet to challenge a committee's firm proposals especially when the prime minister is known to support them. At times Cabinet committees take decisions and inform the Cabinet afterwards.

In both cases the prime minister's power to decide policies is greatly strengthened.

Some prime ministers have also used 'inner cabinets' where they meet a small group of senior and acceptable colleagues. On top of this, prime ministers will naturally discuss issues with individual ministers. Problems can often be sorted out, and agreement reached, before matters go to the Cabinet or one of its committees. With both the Wilson and Callaghan governments, for example, major economic decisions were taken by a small handful of ministers and officials, with the Cabinet merely informed. Later, Mrs Thatcher brought her own personal advisers on matters such as economics and foreign policies into Downing Street. This meant she could get advice which was independent from civil servants or even her ministers.

One political writer, Hugo Young, saw the position as follows:

> The Cabinet, a body of 22 people, rules little. It exists mostly to rubber stamp the decisions of small groups of its members, sometimes of one member – the Prime Minister. (*Sunday Times* 24.5.81)

The power of the prime minister is also increased by the planning and organisation of Cabinet meetings. The prime minister decides the agenda for the meeting. It is true that no prime minister would escape discussing items of outstanding importance, however awkward they might be. But they can delay discussion, or hold it before ministers have made up their mind. The prime minister sums up the discussion on each item and decides the Cabinet's view – which is not always the majority opinion. Often the prime minister will be influenced by the depth of feeling expressed and the views of certain key ministers. In a discussion on economic policy, for example, the Chancellor of the Exchequer's opinions will carry considerable weight.

Prime ministers have the right to ask for information from ministers, express their preferences, or just request action. There is a delicate balance between too little and too much interference by a prime minister; but if the prestige of a prime minister is placed firmly behind certain policies then it can be hard to resist. Frequently they take a special interest in certain departments or policies. Both Anthony Eden and Harold Wilson were virtually their own Foreign Secretaries and Harold Wilson took personal charge of negotiations with Ian Smith – the leader of Rhodesia when it rebelled against the British Crown.

This ability to take a personal interest in policies results from another resource available to the prime minister – time. The prime minister is not weighted down by heavy departmental duties and has time to concentrate on selected problems, and handle the unexpected crisis. In other words, the prime minister is able to be the final co-ordinator of government. This was Harold Wilson's view:

> The levers of power are all here in Number 10 in the Cabinet Room. The ability of the prime minister to use them depends upon being in touch with what is going on . . .

Prime ministers should be in a position to shape the total strategy of the government. If it lacks one, then they must accept much of the blame.

The notion of 'prime ministerial government' has also been strengthened by the way politics is presented, especially on television. Election campaigns are now dominated by television and the leaders of the parties get the most publicity. Television and press emphasis on personalities does not end with elections. The prime minister's speeches, visits around Britain and abroad, meetings with foreign leaders, question time in the House of Commons are all given wide coverage. This strengthens the impression that the prime minister is the government. It is generally impossible for other members of the Cabinet to achieve the same public attention.

The prime minister is also leader of a major political party. In most cases the 'loyalty factor' works strongly in their favour and the kind of publicity which surrounds them helps to reinforce it. The more a prime minister appears to be the government, the greater the pressure on other party members not to criticise or rock the boat. The loyalty of the party is increased when the prime minister is seen as the reason for success in elections or the likely cause of future victories.

The prime minister is always followed closely by the media. Here she is shown behind the wheel of a heavy duty tractor in Ogden, Yorkshire, during the 1983 general election.

The final resource available to the prime minister is the constitutional right to decide the date of the general election. This will be used, as far as possible, to give maximum benefit to the government. It has been claimed that this power is the ultimate weapon in forcing ministers to accept policies, or disciplining MPs who will not support the government. This is a doubtful argument, given that most MPs have safe seats; and it would be a foolish prime minister who called a election when the party was split. Yet the power is important, because policies can be co-ordinated and timed to give the greatest advantage in an election. For example: tax cuts could be delayed until the run-up to an election.

Up to this point it might seem that prime ministerial government is a reasonably accurate description of our system. No prime minister since 1940 has lost the job because of a Cabinet revolt or failure to be supported by the party in parliament – however unpopular the government, or even the prime minister, has become. This is hardly surprising considering the difficulties which would be faced by anyone planning such a change. There would need to be an obvious alternative candidate with support in the Cabinet, the parliamentary party and an ability to unite the whole party afterwards.

Prime ministers may be difficult or impossible to remove against their will, except at elections, but this does not mean that they are all-powerful. First of all, arriving at most decisions in government involves some compromise between a number of different interests. Departments in government, different wings of the party, powerful pressure groups in the nation, foreign governments are all major considerations when any decision is taken, even if the Cabinet is not consulted.

Every Cabinet contains powerful individuals, future prime ministers even, and a prime minister can find it difficult to force policies through if a determined majority, or even minority, opposes them. Sometimes disagreements do come into the open. Mrs Thatcher's economic policies led to bitter debates in Cabinet, the resignation and sacking of ministers, and considerable public hostility from certain Conservative MPs between 1980 and 1982. Prime ministers have sometimes lost over policies. Harold Wilson, for example, was forced to withdraw proposals on union reform in 1969.

So what do these often conflicting examples of prime ministerial decisions, and prime ministerial defeats, really tell us? To begin with the real basis of power of both the prime minister and the Cabinet depends on the fact that they *control the House of Commons*. Such is the strength of party loyalty and discipline that it is rare for an MP (especially on the government side) to vote against party decisions although, in recent years, the number of party revolts have increased. But they have not threatened to defeat the government on major issues. And if a policy is agreed in Cabinet, then it is virtually certain to pass through the House of Commons. But such loyalty must not be taken for granted. If the prime minister and government are going through unpopular times the 'loyalty factor' will still operate but demands for changes, at least in policy if not of the prime minister, are likely to be increasingly heard. The same applies in Cabinet. Certainly

The Falklands War in 1982. Did Mrs Thatcher's response to the Argentine invasion reflect a national – or a party mood?

it is true that removing prime ministers is extremely difficult but they are aware that the day of judgement for failure is likely to come after a lost election. For example, both Lord Home and Edward Heath lost the leadership of the Conservative party in opposition. In Heath's case the Conservative party rejected both the individual and his brand of Conservatism. Exactly the same kind of pressures built up in the Labour party after 1979. Important sections of the party rejected the policies and style of James Callaghan's leadership.

What makes a good prime minister?

From what we have seen it is not too difficult to describe the qualities which, ideally, a good prime minister should have. The political direction and co-operation of government needs a skilled administrator who must be able both to lead and delegate responsibility. As head of the ruling party in parliament, he or she must be able to perform well in House of Commons debates to keep up the morale of government MPs. As national party leader it is essential for the prime minister to be in touch with the mood of party workers and to be able to encourage them to give active support to the government. They must have mastered the vital skill of presenting themselves well on television. The prime minister is also the nation's political leader and should be able to rise above party interest and reflect national moods and concerns, especially at a time of crisis. Lastly, a prime minister needs energy and stamina together with the strength of mind to change the government team or its policies where they appear to be failing.

Discussion and essay questions

1. If you had just been elected prime minister what factors would you take into account in choosing your Cabinet?

2. 'The job of a prime minister is to conduct the orchestra and not play any of the instruments'. Explain and discuss.

3. What is meant by collective Cabinet responsibility?

4. 'The prime minister is first among equals'. 'Britain has a system of prime ministerial government'. Explain what these descriptions mean. Which one do you think is most accurate, and why?

5. If you were a government MP voting in an election to choose a new prime minister, what factors would you consider?

6. Conduct a survey of friends and relations to find out what particular strengths or weaknesses recent British prime ministers are remembered for.

7 Ministers and their departments

The increased size and scope of modern governments can be illustrated simply by looking at the names of the main departments of state. Some departments, and the titles of the ministers in charge, have been in existence for many years: the Treasury (headed by the Chancellor of the Exchequer) and the Foreign Office (led by the Foreign Secretary) for instance both go back to the days when the work of government was much more limited than now. Other departments have grown considerably, such as the Department of Education and Science, and some are relatively new creations which cover a huge range of responsibilities (see Fig. 7.1). Most ministers in charge of a department are known as secretaries of state and they have two main groups of people to help them in their work: junior ministers from the government party in parliament, and civil servants. In addition they may bring in advisers, usually experts from the academic world. In the Callaghan government, a secretary of state was allowed two outside advisers per department, but Mrs Thatcher reduced this to one in 1979. (See Fig. 7.2)

The path to office

It is rare for a person to be brought into government at the top level without having served a long apprenticeship in politics. This usually means some years as an MP in the House of Commons and successful experience as a junior minister in the lower levels of government. A prime minister will look for other qualities as well: a reputation for effective speaking in the Commons; the ability to argue out a case in detail; and a general popularity in the party (or with an important section of the party).

The work of a minister

The minister as a politician

Ministers are both important political figures and key administrators – although it is often difficult to separate the two. The main political task of ministers is to make sure that the policies, values and ideals of the governing party are known, and acted upon. All ministers share

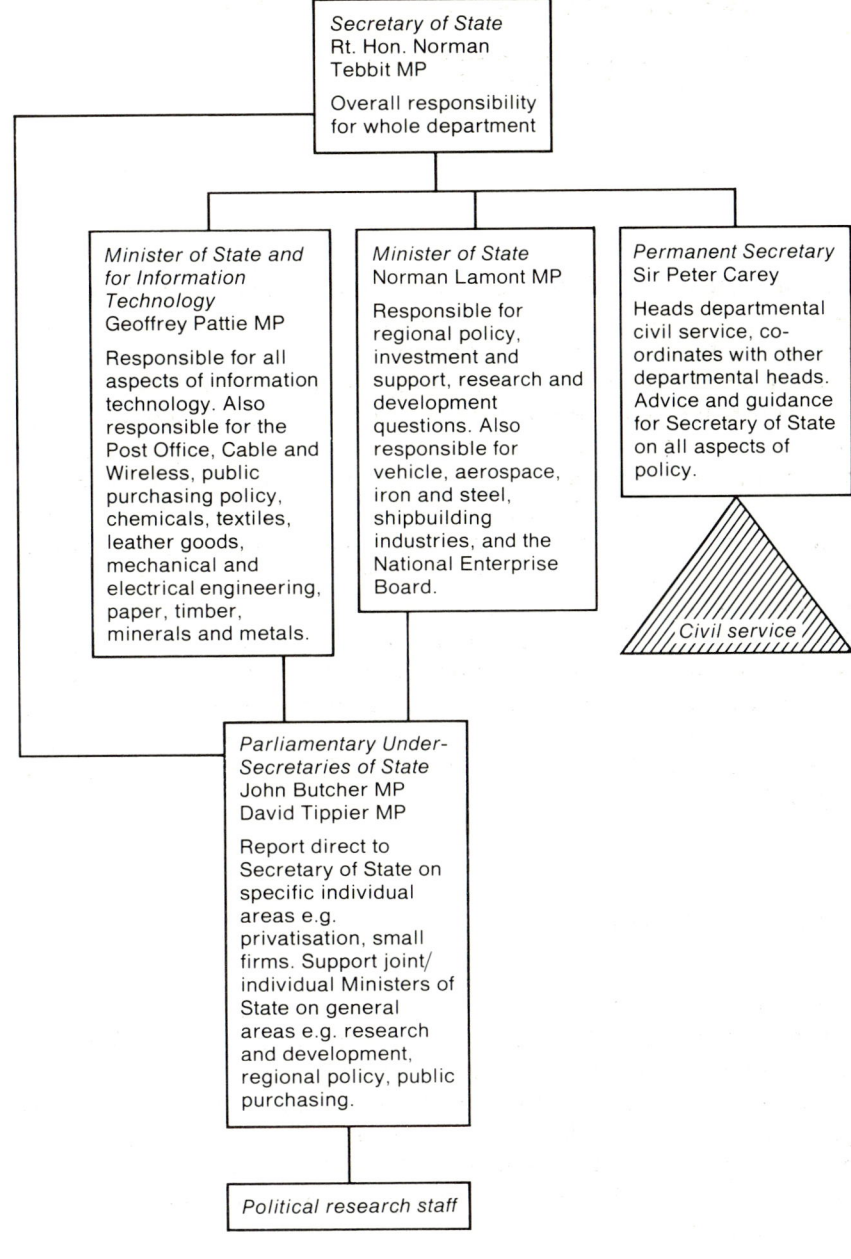

Figure 7.1 Department of Industry 1984.

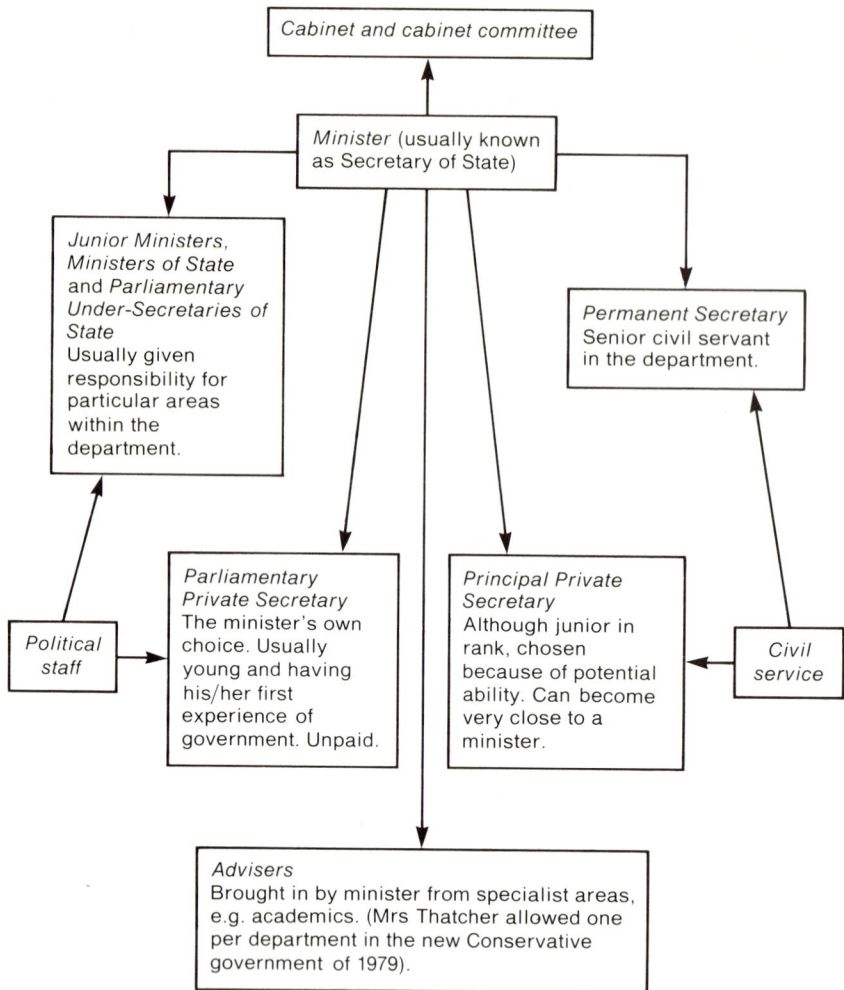

Figure 7.2 A minister and the department.

responsibility for all the policies of the government and have to defend them publicly. However, their most important political work is to develop policies for their own departments. In some cases the starting point is a firm promise in the party's last election manifesto. Other promises may have been more general so they need careful planning before they can be given a proper shape. The manifesto, for example, might have stressed 'greater educational opportunities for all'. That would raise many questions for the minister in charge of Education and Science: which area of education should be tackled first – nursery, primary, secondary, or higher and further? What kind of changes in education *could* produce 'greater educational opportunities'? And, inevitably, where is the money coming from and how much can be spent? However, the first question to consider is whether *that* promise is more important than other promises in the manifesto. In other words, what priority is it to be given? Essentially this decision belongs to the prime minister and Cabinet.

Neil Kinnock, born 1942, educated Lewis School, Pengam, South Wales and University College, Cardiff

1970	Elected to parliament
1974–1975	Parliamentary Private Secretary to Secretary of State for Employment
1978	Elected to Labour Party National Executive
1979–1983	Opposition spokesman for Education
1983	Elected leader of the Labour Party

David Owen, born 1938, educated Bradfield College, Cambridge and St Thomas's Hospital, London

1966	Elected to parliament
1968–1970	Under Secretary of State for Defence
1970–1972	Opposition spokesman on Defence
1974	Under Secretary of State for Health
1974–1976	Minister of State for Health
1976–1977	Minister of State, Foreign Office
1977–1979	Foreign Secretary
1979–1980	Opposition spokesman on Energy
1981	Founding member of Social Democratic Party
1983	Leader Social Democratic Party

David Steel, born 1938, educated Prince of Wales School, Nairobi, Kenya, George Watson's College, Edinburgh, and Edinburgh University

1965	Elected to parliament
1967	Sponsored the Abortion Act (a Private Members Bill)
1976	Elected leader of the Liberal Party

Margaret Thatcher, born 1925, educated Grantham High School and Oxford

1959	Elected to parliament
1961–1964	Parliamentary Secretary Ministry of Pensions and National Insurance
1967–1970	Member of Shadow Cabinet
1969–1970	Opposition spokeswoman for Education
1970–1974	Secretary of State for Education
1974–1975	Opposition spokeswoman for the Environment
1975	Leader of Conservative Party
1979	Prime Minister
1983	Re-elected as Prime Minister

Figure 7.3 Four career profiles.

Ministers have many ways of gaining maximum support for a particular policy or politics. They can send departmental circulars to groups who might be affected, or issue a 'green paper' which is a discussion document to put their arguments up to public debate. To build support they can use speeches in the Commons and outside,

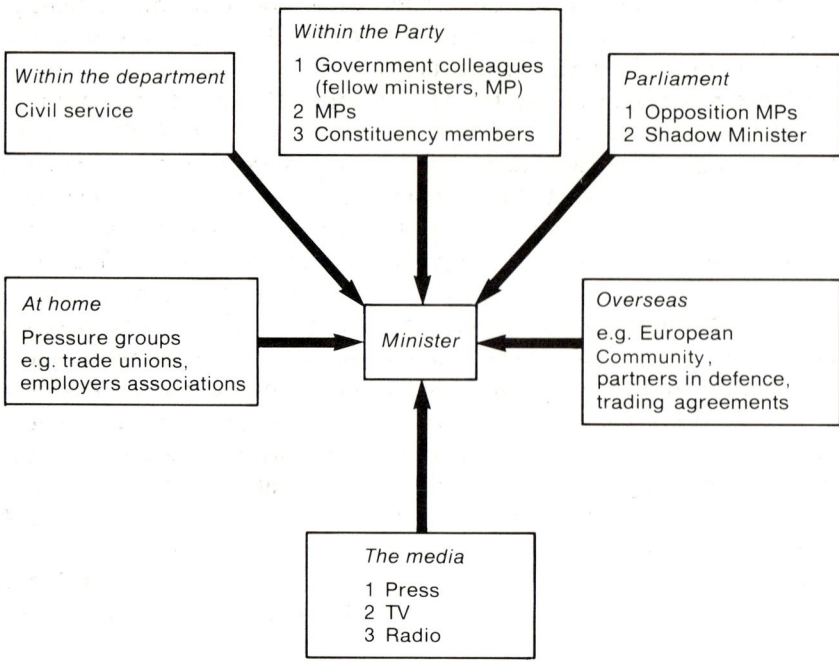

Figure 7.4 Influences on a minister.

television and radio interviews, talks with leaders of various pressure groups, visits around the country and meetings with party workers. For all these activities they can expect the backing of the civil service.

This side of their work ought to be where ministers have the greatest expertise. Normally they have a good deal of experience of speaking to MPs in debates and any successful politician has to be good at putting his ideas across to groups of every kind.

Few ministers have any specialist qualifications which match their department's work. A secretary of state for Education is rarely a former teacher or education official and chancellors of the exchequer are not usually economists. Richard Crossman, for example, was Minister of Housing in 1964 and admitted afterwards that he knew virtually nothing about housing issues at the start. The job of a minister is to give the right *political* direction to a department and not to be a detailed planner – that task belongs to the civil service. One former minister, Ernest Marples, once said: 'I have no brains myself. I don't need them. Other people have brains, I have judgement'.

The minister as administrator

As well as being in charge of policy making, ministers are responsible for the day-to-day operation of their departments. A department may be huge, broken into many different sections and with large numbers of civil servants. It is quite unusual for a minister to have previous experience of leading such a big organisation with so much spending power. So a minister has to rely heavily on the support of senior civil servants to ensure that the department runs smoothly and efficiently. This does *not* mean that ministers can neglect the constitutional convention of **ministerial responsibility**.

Ministerial responsibility means that ministers accept responsibility for all their own actions, *and those of civil servants in their department*. Even though a decision might be relatively unimportant, involving a very junior civil servant, the minister may have to explain what was done, and why, in parliament. Ministerial responsibility has a number of important results. Firstly, the public is given some protection against the abuse of power by civil servants, because complaints can go directly to ministers themselves. Secondly, the actions of civil servants are often likely to be cautious and based on what has been accepted in the past. The phrase 'red tape' is often used to describe civil service slowness in making decisions, and the fact that it always keeps detailed records of all stages in reaching them. This is hardly surprising, since decisions may be publicly investigated. Thirdly, it is usual for civil servants not to be named if something goes wrong. Ministerial responsibility protects civil servants from having to be directly involved in public and political arguments. Obviously, a serious error by a civil servant will not go unnoticed within the department and is likely to harm his or her career chances.

How far should responsibility be taken?

Ministerial responsibility has meant that ministers even resigned because of actions of their civil servants, unknown to themselves. But this has not happened since 1954. It now seems that, although ministers still have to take public responsibility, they do not accept that actions they know nothing about should cause them to lose office. The collapse of the Vehicle and General Insurance Company in 1971 was partly blamed on civil servants in the Department of Trade and Industry, yet the minister did not resign and a report on the affair blamed a civil servant by name. One estimate made during the 'V and G affair' was that only one per cent of all departmental decisions actually involve the minister directly. So it would be unreasonable to expect a minister to carry the blame in many such cases.

But there are cases where the ministers accept that the error was made in a judgement for which only they could have taken responsibility. A recent example came when Argentina invaded the Falkland Islands in 1982. Britain was not prepared for this so they could not prevent it. The Foreign Secretary and his junior ministers all resigned as a sign that they accepted responsibility for making a wrong judgement about Argentina's plans.

Ministers and civil servants

As we have seen, the size and complexity of government departments means that most of the issues never reach the individual minister for a decision, or even approval. At the same time, the minister has to carry considerable public responsibility for what goes on. How can these two features of ministerial government be balanced?

Obviously ministers must rely on the efficiency of their civil servants; and their working relationship with those at the senior level is particularly important. Traditionally, this relationship has been described in the following way. Civil servants are expected to offer ministers advice at all stages of policy development and to give them information on the likely results of any decision. This involves selecting the key issues which a minister has to decide, meeting with civil servants from other departments to help co-ordinate policies and often acting as the minister's representative in meetings with groups from outside Whitehall.

Ministers will be given various policy choices and it is quite normal, and reasonable, for civil servants to warn them about the dangers of each one. But the final decision rests with the minister and, once it is made, civil servants must agree to carry it out. Their own preferences should not colour the advice given to a minister nor the way a policy is administered by them. Civil servants must also accept the political leanings of the party in power.

But is this description of the relationship between ministers and civil servants realistic? Does it paint too simple a picture of civil servants playing only a supporting role in framing policies?

To begin with there are considerable problems facing any minister. We have already seen that they are likely to lack any experience of running large organisations. They also face real pressures from their workload. One survey of the working week of Cabinet ministers gave the following allocation of time:

Activity	Hours
Cabinet	4
Cabinet committees	4
Parliament	14
Party meetings	3
Visits	6
Interviews, deputations, press, MPs, Pressure groups representatives etc.	5
Formal receptions, lunches, meetings with ministers abroad	8
Constituency matters	2
Paper work, office meetings	15
	Total: 61

(*Source: B. Headey, New Society*)

George Brown, former Labour Foreign Secretary, described the pressures of work as follows:

Virtually no half hour is unfilled. I was seeing people in the department, receiving visiting statesmen and other groups . . ., attending cabinet committees, and so on. As Deputy Leader of the Party I was, of course, both in parliament and outside it. And quite often I would have to be in the House of Commons, either for questions, or to speak in a debate . . . And so, by the evening, I had already worked a very full day. But round about 6 p.m. the bowler-hatted chaps would start wending their way home, or to their clubs, depositing as they went the papers, the minutes, the telegrams which they thought I should deal with that night. The people in my own office, who of course themselves had already worked a full day, had now to start hours of hectic work, quite unknown in outside industry, in order to 'process' those papers so that I could receive them in relays from then on. I could be pretty sure of enough work to keep me at it until 2 a.m. at least!

With a day like this it is easy to see that developing policies, or even thinking about them, becomes difficult and can only be done at the end of a long working day.

A minister's chance of gaining specialist knowledge about his department's work is often weakened by frequent changes of office. For example, in the Labour government of 1964–1970 there were four secretaries of state for Education and Science, and four foreign secretaries. In the Labour government of 1974–1979 there were four secretaries of state for Education and virtually every other major department had at least one change of minister. Denis Healey was Secretary of State for Defence for six years (1964–1970) and Chancellor of the Exchequer for five years (1974–1979) but this kind of continuity is very rare. Between these two Labour governments we had a Conservative administration under Edward Heath when new ministers, and policies, were brought in. It is hardly surprising, then, that civil servants have far greater knowledge and experience of a department than the minister in charge and this can make it difficult for the minister to give firm leadership. Two former ministers gave surprisingly similar views about how new ministers ought to establish their position:

The first forty-eight hours decide whether a minister is going to run his office, or whether his office is going to run him. (Arthur Henderson, Labour Foreign Secretary 1929–31).

Ministers can be divided into those who run their departments and those who are run by their departments. I believe parliament finds out jolly quickly into which category ministers fall, and civil servants know within forty-eight hours of the minister putting his foot over the doorstep. (Iain Macleod, holder of various senior positions in Conservative governments of the late 1950s and early 1960s).

Indeed perhaps it can be too easy to be 'taken over' by civil servants. When Richard Crossman had just been appointed Labour Minister of Housing in 1964 he wrote this in his diary:

Thursday 22 October 1964 . . . Of course [civil servants] are profoundly deferential – 'Yes, Minister! No, Minister! If you wish it, Minister!'

It's also profoundly true that one has only to do absolutely nothing whatsoever in order to be floated on the stream . . . I turned to one of my private office [secretaries] and said, 'Now you must teach me how to handle all this correspondence.'

And he sat opposite me with his owlish eyes and said to me, 'Well Minister, you see there are three ways of handling it. A letter can either be answered by you personally, in your own handwriting; or we can draft a personal reply for you to sign, or, if the letter is not worth your answering personally, we can draft an official answer.'

'What's an official answer?' I asked. 'Well, it says the Minister has received your letter and then the Department replies. Anyway, we'll draft all three variants,' he said, 'and if you just tell us which you want . . .' 'How do I do that?' I asked. 'Well you put all your in-tray into your out-tray,' he said, 'and if you put it in without a mark on it then we deal with it and you need never see it again.'

I think I've recorded that literally, I've only to transfer everything that's in my in-tray to my out-tray without a single mark on it to ensure it will be dealt with – all my Private Office is concerned with is to see that the routine runs on (From *Diaries of a Cabinet Minister*, R. Crossman pp. 21–2.)

It's not difficult to see why senior civil servants are in a strong position. Firstly, they have considerable knowledge about the problems, the major and minor issues, the different interests inside and outside government which a department faces and the way it has coped with these in the past. Secondly, they are likely to have thought a good deal about what ought to be done in different areas and what is and isn't possible. This does not necessarily mean that they have a dangerous amount of power, because any major policy will still need the minister's final approval. But it can mean that ministers, who need time to understand their department's work, are in a weak position especially when they are first appointed.

It was pointed out earlier that an overwhelming number of decisions made by a department never reach the minister. But what about the one per cent that do? There is no doubt that civil servants have the chance to influence them in two ways. Firstly, they act as a filter through which advice reaches the minister. If there is an option, or a possible course of action, a civil servant can sway a minister's mind by presenting it either favourably or unfavourably. Secondly, civil servants may not give the minister a true picture of other options. In 1931 most of the Labour Cabinet resigned after they could not agree about how to avoid the pound being devalued by coming off the gold standard. The new government took Britain off the gold standard only weeks later and one of the ex-ministers complained: 'They didn't tell us we could do that!'

Civil servants are therefore in a position to limit both the information and the options reaching a minister, so that choice is restricted. Obviously civil servants do not always act in this way but it does show some of the problems in accepting the traditional view of their relationship with ministers.

What makes a good minister?

One person's 'good' minister may be another's 'weak' or 'poor' minister. For example, a minister who is good from a civil servant's point of view may be 'weak' as far as the party or government is concerned. If a 'good' minister is one who is determined to push for certain policies and give strong leadership in a department then it is clear he or she must have certain qualities. Firstly a minister needs to be decisive, especially over major issues. Secondly, a minister needs to win a fair share of the inter-departmental battles in Whitehall. This depends on such factors as determination, the advice, or briefings he gets from his civil servants, and the political standing of the minister. There is no doubt that civil servants appreciate a minister who can successfully fight for the department's viewpoint. Edward Heath explained in 1977:

> There is nothing that (civil servants) dislike more than to have a minister whom they feel is weak, who does not know his mind and who wants to leave it to them. That is not their mentality nor their approach. . . . What they like is to have a minister who knows the policy he wants to pursue, who will take advice on the consequences of it, and how it can be implemented, who will carry sufficient weight in Cabinet to see it through and will also have sufficient influence with the Chancellor of the Exchequer to get it financed. (Evidence to Expenditure Committee, February, 1977.)

The third quality a minister needs is the ability to do well in the House of Commons, especially at question time or when complicated legislation is being debated. They will face critics (usually, but not only, from the opposition parties) and rely heavily on civil servants for briefings, on arguments about policies and detailed legislation. In this, civil servants are rather like football managers who get great personal satisfaction, and reflected glory, from their 'players' putting on a talented, and successful performance. For the minister, the House of Commons can be a tense public arena where political reputation, and the prospects of higher office, may be at stake.

Fourthly, ministers need to have a clear idea about where decisions should be taken. The choice might be for them to make, or it might be sent down to a lower level in their department, or up to the Cabinet or one of its committees. Ministers who are not prepared to delegate decisions can soon become confused by detail. Some ministers prefer to concentrate on just a small number of key issues and push hard to get results there, leaving their junior ministers to cover the rest. This is especially the case when the minister is occupied with a major piece of legislation going through parliament.

In dealing with civil servants, ministers need the ability to ask the right questions and must be prepared to query the advice given. Ernest Bevin, Labour Foreign Secretary from 1945–1950, once said to his officials; 'You have given me ten good reasons why I should do what you suggest. You are very clever fellows. Go away and give me ten good reasons why I should do the opposite.'

Ministers may not be in a department long enough to become experts in its work but they have considerable political experience. And it is ministers who have to live with the political consequence of both success and failure. One former minister, perhaps under-estimating his contribution, simply said, 'Political heads of departments are necessary to tell the civil service what the public will not stand.'

Discussion and essay questions

1. What is meant by ministerial responsibility? What are the arguments for and against ministers resigning over actions by their civil servants which they knew nothing about?

2. Would you expect government attitudes towards the following issues to be decided (a) within a department (b) in a Cabinet committee, or (c) in full Cabinet?
    In each case give reasons for your choice.
    – The Home Secretary wants to release a man from prison because it is believed he was wrongly convicted.
    – The Treasury and the Department of Health and Social Security totally disagree on how much money should be spent by the DHSS next year.
    – The Secretary of State for Northern Ireland has put together plans for a new political structure in the province.
    – The Prime Minister has been invited to visit Moscow.
    – Government scientists in the Ministry of Defence claim that, for £2000 million they could perfect a death ray with an effective range of 500 miles.

3. If you were Secretary of State for Energy and you wanted more money spent on building nuclear power stations how would you try and get this policy accepted?

4. What problems are faced by ministers in being able to make sure that they really control their departments? How could they make this control more effective?

5. How might you describe a 'good' minister if you were (a) the prime minister (b) the minister's permanent secretary (c) a party worker in the country (d) a government MP.

8 The civil service

The last chapter examined the work of government largely through the eyes of ministers, and explored the relationship between them and their senior civil servants. However it is important to remember that these civil servants are the tip of an iceberg – which some people say is far too large. In 1979 there were 732,000 civil servants – for example, Social Services employed 101,000 and Employment 53,000.

About 75 per cent of all civil servants live and work outside London. Far from being in Whitehall and isolated from the general public, many are in daily contact through Job Centres, Social Security offices, Customs and Excise, Vehicle Licensing, and so on. It may be fashionable to think of civil servants as being 'faceless' bureaucrats who do not really 'produce' anything, but without them the welfare state, for example, simply could not exist.

Department structures

The ranking of civil servants can be seen in Figure 8.1. In each department the permanent secretary is the senior civil servant and is responsible to the minister for all that department's administrative work. Of

Figure 8.1 The structure of the civil service.

	Grade or post	No. employed	Salary (£ max.)	Entry and promotion
Open structure levels	Grade One (Perm. Sec.)	40	42,750	Under the administrative trainee scheme, graduate entrants can benefit from accelerated promotion, as shown below.
	Grade Two (Deputy Sec.)	136	34,250	
	Grade Three (Under Sec.)	505	27,450	
	Grade Four	177	26,450	
	Grade Five (Asst. Sec.)	2,032	23,159	
	Grade Six (Senior Principal)	3,346	20,794	
Administrative levels	Principal	4,171	16,656	
	Senior Executive Officer	7,274	13,144	
	Higher Executive Officer	22,186	10,729	
	Executive Officer	44,184	8,492	

graduate
entrant

There is a parallel system for 'specialist' civil servants, recruited as graduates, who act as advisers in various departments (e.g. economic advisers). They are able at least in theory to be promoted into the open structure levels.

course only a tiny proportion of all the decisions taken in a department will come directly to the permanent secretary.

The permanent secretary, as the department's official accounting officer, is also responsible for expenditure to the House of Commons and its committees. This means that he or she must ensure that any money spent by the department has been properly authorised. Below the permanent secretary, a department's work is divided into various areas of activity headed by deputy secretaries, under secretaries and other lower grades. This is illustrated by the structure of the Department of Transport. (See Fig. 8.2).

Entry and training

The most important group of entrants into the civil service are those graduates who usually join as administration trainees and are regarded as potential 'high flyers' who will reach the top levels. Entry is highly competitive. In 1980, for example, there were 2,281 external applications for just 100 vacancies and, in the end, 63 were appointed. Existing members of the civil service can apply as well and, in 1980, 31 administration trainees came from this 'in service' group. The selection process consists of a written examination and then a series of tests of ability and personality lasting two to three days.

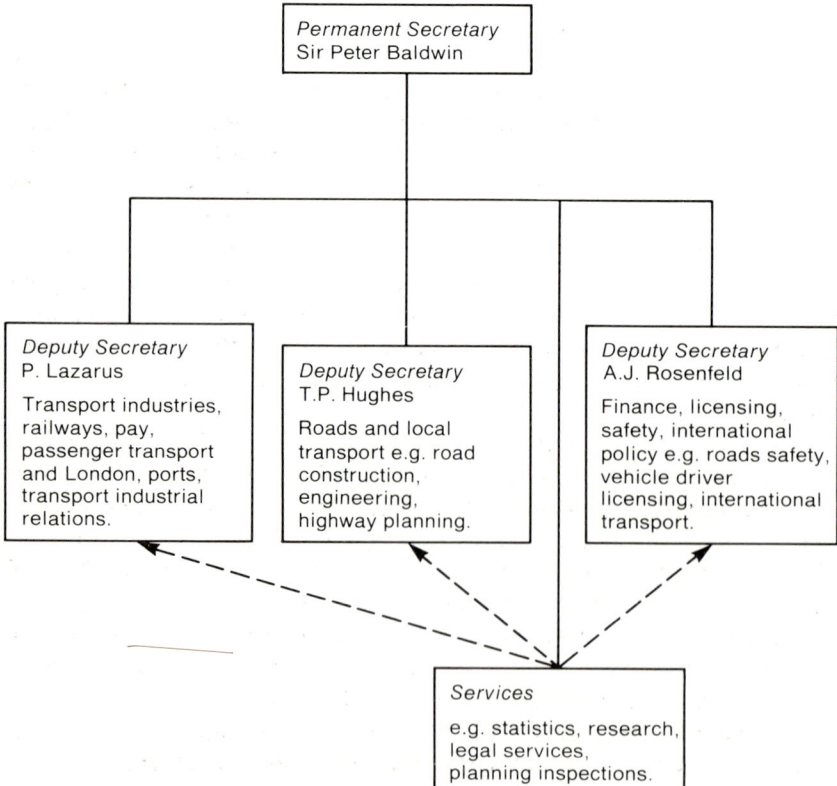

Figure 8.2 Department of Transport organisation chart (June 1980).

		External	In-service	Total
School	Total Entrants	233	120	353
	State Schools	109	86	195
	Direct Grant	55	11	66
	Private	63	18	81
	College of FE	4	3	7
	Other/Overseas	2	—	2
	Oxford & Cambridge	142	18	160
University	Other University or polytechnic	91	76	167
	Non graduate	—	—	—
	Arts	140	56	196
Degree subject	Social Sciences	68	25	93
	Science & Technology	23	13	36
	Other	—	—	—

Figure 8.3 Educational background of administration trainee entrants to the civil service (1978–80).

The background of successful applicants is seen in Figure 8.3, and illustrates certain criticisms which are made about the selection process. For example the pass rates of external candidates from state schools is 28 per cent whereas 41 per cent came from private or Direct Grant schools. There is also a heavy bias towards graduates from Oxford and Cambridge, although this is remedied, to some extent, by the background of 'in service' trainees who have already worked in the civil service. A further criticism is in the type of subjects taken in degrees. As the diagram shows, more entrants had taken Arts subjects (History, English, Classics) than Social Sciences (Economics, Politics, Sociology) which some argue are more relevant to the work of government. Even fewer entrants have a Science and Technology background.

The training of civil servants, including the potential 'high flyers' is very largely based on practical work within departments. As their career progresses, civil servants will usually be moved within departments, and to different departments, to widen their experience. However, many senior civil servants will still have spent the bulk of their time in one department, building up considerable knowledge and expertise in the process. When permanent secretary level is reached any change of departments is unlikely. Compared to the movement of ministers, the permanent secretary is well named!

A second element in training is the use of the Civil Service College in Sunningdale and its branches in London and Edinburgh. It trains some 8,000 civil servants a year in various management techniques. Subjects include economics, planning, organisation, personnel management, job appraisal, data processing and case studies in social policy. However, the college only carries out 9 per cent of total civil service training – the rest is still done within departments.

Other countries have a much more formal system. In France, for example, the trainee civil servant has to study full time for two years in one of two centres and the course is very intensive with a major emphasis on problem solving. The marks gained at the end of the two years decide which part of government is entered. Those with the highest marks are able to get into the prestige departments.

The work of the civil service

The senior civil servants in a department give their ministers considerable help and support. They write letters and speak for them, representing them in meetings with various groups, they prepare briefs, or statements of the way the department sees an issue, for the minister to use in public. A major part of this support is concerned with preparing legislation and helping the minister to pass it through parliament.

Much of this work, and especially legislation, involves a great deal of detailed planning and frequently means that a number of government departments have to be brought in at a very early stage. This is quite apart from consultations with the Treasury about finance. Such planning and coordination is provided by a complicated network of committees of civil servants both within and between departments. On top of this, most ministerial groups and committees will be 'shadowed' by committees of civil servants. This includes the Cabinet itself with the permanent secretaries of each department meeting once a week. The result is that by the time proposals reach a minister they will have been worked out in considerable detail. More important, they are likely to come to the minister *after agreement has been reached with other departments*, which can make it very difficult for a minister to challenge or alter any proposals.

There is also a danger that alternative proposals are dropped in the desire to get agreement before the minister is consulted. This is one reason why some ministers encourage as much debate as possible when they meet their officials and do not immediately accept the agreed solution.

A very typical civil service method is the use of internal memoranda and files. A senior civil servant needs to be skilled in writing memoranda which give a summary of issues and set out the decisions which need approval from a superior. If the memorandum is to go as far as the minister it will be placed in one of the 'red boxes' which he or she receives every day.

The most usual way of handling any issue which comes to a department in Whitehall is to open a file on it. The file includes all the documents on that issue and is passed to other civil servants or other departments affected, asking them to add their comments and suggestions. As the file becomes fatter it is passed up the system until it reaches a civil servant who feels that a decision can be made. It might continue travelling until it enters the minister's red box, especially if it has political implications.

Like the staff of any organisation, civil servants have less formal ways of oiling the machine: phonecalls, meetings over lunch, or simply meeting in someone's office. Such meetings have another advantage – that discussions and even agreements need not be written down.

Civil service reform

The civil service, as described in the last section, has its origins in the Northcote-Trevelyan Report of 1854. It arose from criticisms that civil service positions were given by patronage. The most usual form of patronage was for a politician or a senior civil servant to offer a post in a government department to a person they knew or who was recommended to them, perhaps by another politician. Each department dealt with its own patronage and civil servants could not move from one to another. The Northcote-Trevelyan Report led to reforms which completely altered all that. The civil service was unified so that recruitment was into the service and not a specific department. As a result, promotion could be achieved by changing departments. Even more important, patronage was abolished and replaced by a system of recruitment by examination and promotion by merit.

The Fulton Report

By the middle of the twentieth century there was a feeling that the civil service needed a thorough re-examination. This led to the Fulton Report of 1968, which began by stating, 'The Home Civil Service today is still fundamentally the product of the nineteenth century philosophy of the Northcote-Trevelyan Report. The tasks it faces are those of the second half of the twentieth century.'

The Report went on to say that the civil service was dominated by people who lacked proper background and training in areas vital to modern government. It criticised the emphasis on the idea of all-rounders or 'generalist' administrators:

> The ideal administrator is still too often seen as the gifted layman who, moving frequently from job to job within the Service, can take a practical view of any problem, irrespective of its subject matter . . .

Fulton added his observation of many generalist administrators:

> . . . [they] do not develop adequate knowledge in depth of any one aspect of the Department's work . . . often they are required to give advice on subjects they do not sufficiently understand.

To overcome such problems Fulton made a number of recommendations.

First he said that 'generalists' should have the chance to become specialist administrators in areas such as economics, finance, and in the main social problems of the day. Linked to this was a second recommendation that in future more graduate recruits should have degrees which were relevant for the work that civil servants were going to do. To support the development of specialist knowledge, Fulton suggested the formation of a Civil Service College which would run courses for civil servants as well as investigate problems related to the work of government.

Fulton also wanted change in the structure of the service. It suggested that a new Civil Service Department should be set up to be responsible for recruitment, pay and career development of civil servants. But the main purpose of the Department was to be a 'powerhouse' for changes which might need to be forced through against the hostility of civil servants. Fulton further criticised the civil service for not having enough contact with other sectors of society. It recommended, for example, that there should be more chances for people to transfer between industry (including nationalised industries) and the civil service in an attempt to give civil servants wider experience.

How effective was the Fulton Report? Certain of the recommendations were acted on quickly. The Civil Service Department and the Civil Service College were both established and, following Fulton, the grading structure was altered to make access to senior posts easier than before.

But the government rejected the idea of giving preference to graduates with 'relevant' degrees and argued instead that they should recruit the best brains, whatever their subjects. And they have a point. The content of subjects studied in a first degree can soon become dated and it can be argued that graduates should be chosen on the basis of their potential for becoming senior civil servants. However, the pattern of recruitment has changed a little since Fulton. This can be shown by looking as the background of new recruits for 1978–80 and comparing it with 1957–63 when only 3 per cent of administration trainees had degrees in science or technology and 85 per cent came from Oxford or Cambridge.

The English Report

In 1977 the first investigation by MPs of the civil service since 1873 was published. The MPs were a sub-committee of the House of Commons Expenditure Committee of the day, and their chairman was the Labour MP, Michael English. Part of their Report dealt with the same questions as Fulton about recruitment, training and pay of civil servants. Two recommendations in this part took an opposite point of view. Firstly the 'English committee' wanted the work of the Civil Service Department cut back, with such matters as efficiency, internal auditing, applying cash limits, to be taken over to the Treasury. Secondly, they wanted the Civil Service College to be wound up and suggested that courses run by universities and polytechnics could be used much more.

However, the English Report took a similar view to Fulton on the choice of civil servants and the need for them to have experience of the wider issues. It criticised the system of selecting 'high flyers' right from entry. The Report argued that recruitment should be widened to include non-graduates and promising individuals from, for example, local government and the health service. A higher management training course essential for top promotions should be available to civil servants only after they had already shown ability. This course would include academic study, 'on the job' training (which might include working for an opposition MP, in local government, in industry, or in the regions) and tough 'case study work' to stretch them. Civil servants could have had five to fifteen years experience before they took such a course. The Report saw it as a way of giving future senior civil servants a much great understanding of political, economic and social issues and a way of breaking down the isolation of the civil service. Like Fulton, the Report urged the need to transfer civil servants temporarily to other jobs – and it showed how little had been achieved since Fulton in this area.

By the 1980s little was left of the changes begun after Fulton. In 1981 the Civil Service Department was abolished and most of its work, such as deciding on the manpower needed or the pay of civil servants, was given to the Treasury. In part this was because it made little sense to separate these questions from the Treasury which was responsible for the government policy of limiting public spending. But more important, the Department had failed to become a 'powerhouse' for reform. Fulton had suggested that senior appointments in it should be made from outside organisation. This was not done and those in charge of the Department were described by *The Guardian* as 'civil servants steeped in those very traditions which Fulton wanted to replace and well placed to frustrate the Fulton reforms. Moreover, the first Permanent Secretary at the CSD, Lord Armstrong, admitted candidly after he retired that he had managed to deflect many of the proposed changes.' (Editorial 13.11.81.) Nor has the Civil Service College become as important as Fulton intended, and the vast bulk of training is still carried on within departments.

Power to the civil servants?

The most controversial part of the English Report dealt with a topic which the Fulton Report had left alone. This was the question of just how powerful the civil service is and whether it is really under the control of elected politicians.

The main body of the Report listed a number of grievances about civil servants. The MPs on the committee had heard about how difficult it was for ministers to change the 'firmly held policy views' of the civil servants in their department. There were complaints that civil servants tried to wear down the political will of ministers and 'delay and obstruct them' sometimes by even briefing other ministers on ways to stop policies going through.

Some members of the committee took an even more outspoken line. All the Labour MPs on the committee except Michael English himself agreed with an alternative first chapter to the Report. It was written by Brian Sedgemore MP, who had once been a civil servant. He spoke of the need to restore political power against bureaucratic power which was 'part of the struggle for democracy itself'. He went on:

> ...most of the problems of the civil service stem from the fact that top civil servants misconceive their role in our society. The role they have invented for themselves is that of governing the country. . . . They seek to govern . . . according to their own narrow, well defined interests, tastes, education and background . . . They can and do relegate ministers to the second division through a variety of devices. These include delay, which is a potent one when Governments are in a minority situation or coming to the end of their political life; foreclosing options through official committees which parallel both Cabinet sub-committees and a host of other ministerial committees; interpreting minutes and policy decisions in ways not wholly intended; slanting statistics; taking advantage of Cabinet splits and politically divided ministerial teams. In doing all these things they act in what they conceive to be the public good. Some would say they perceive that good in the interest of their own class.

These ideas received support from other Labour MPs especially those on the left of the Labour Party. Tony Benn argued, in 1981, that the civil service would always try to 'steer incoming governments back to the policies of the outgoing government minus the mistakes the Civil Service thought the outgoing government made'. (*The Listener*, 18.6.81)

Michael Meacher MP, a former Labour Under Secretary of Trade wrote in 1979 about some of the devices he believed were used by civil servants to manipulate their ministers. They 'filtered out' vital information so it never reached the minister, leaving the decision to the permanent secretary. He stated that one official, after a meeting with a minister, said, 'That went well – I didn't tell him anything he wanted to know.'

Meacher also described how civil servants worked with each other in meetings of inter-departmental committees, to obstruct the policies of some ministers. One way this was done, he claimed, was simply by saying that any decision must be delayed until a committee had produced a report. He summed his views up with the claim that civil servants are acting 'against ministers rather than in support of the political manifesto of the governing party'.

There is no doubt that much of this criticism comes from the left-wing of the Labour Party, which regards civil servants as essentially cautious and unreceptive to new ideas. But criticism of the civil service has not come only from the Labour Party. One minister in the new Conservative government headed by Mrs Thatcher in 1979 said this to a *Daily Telegraph* reporter:

Unless we break out of the civil service straightjacket now, we'll never get another chance to rule. It is beginning to look to many of us that civil servants are a breed who really believe they run the country, and that all they've got to do is knock new ministers into shape.

Ministers were also said to doubt whether they would 'be prepared to carry out their proposals impartially and not try to submit alternative and unacceptable proposals'.

Yes, minister?

These accusations are by no means accepted by all politicians. Peter Shore argued the following when he was Labour Secretary of State for Trade in 1976:

I came here with a strong view that demanded we leave the Common Market. It was contrary to that held by the Department. But they adjusted, and assumed a policy that must have been very disagreeable to many of them. Proposals were put to me that were intended, inevitably, to reflect the outlook of previous Governments, but I can't think of an occasion where the Department failed to respond when I felt a new approach was needed. I expect people in responsible positions to have views, and to argue strongly for them. At the end of the day they accept the political decision. (*Observer*, 29.2.76)

Two former prime ministers gave evidence to the English Committee on this issue:

I would say quite clearly . . . that the civil servants were under ministerial control. I have absolutely no doubt about it. In my ministerial life this has always been the case. (Edward Heath.)

I have always taken the view . . . that if a minister cannot control his civil servants, he ought to go . . . I do not think any minister should, or can, shelter behind civil servants and say, 'My civil servants won't let me do it'. (Harold Wilson.)

The criticisms naturally have been vigorously denied by senior civil servants themselves. For example, Sir Brian Hayes, Permanent Secretary to the Minister of Agriculture: 'the civil servant has no power of his own – he is there to help the minister and to be the minister's agent'. (*The Listener* 18.6.81.) Similarly, Sir Patrick Nairne, Permanent Secretary to the Department of Health and Social Security: 'I have never known a situation where civil servants were working together to defeat ministers' political objectives.' (*The Listener* 18.6.81.) Lord Rothschild found in his experience that where there was delay it was 'because issues were complex, [and] . . . the divergent interests to be reconciled legitimate and well argued'. (*The Times* 7.11.77.)

A balance of power

The English Report made some recommendations affecting the relationship between ministers and civil servants. They argued that 'a minister should be free to adopt any organisation he thinks fit for the efficient discharge of business'. It may be surprising, but ministers are *not* free to do this. For example, it is extremely hard for a minister to change the permanent secretary or other senior officials in a department. Michael Meacher MP pointed out (*The Guardian* 14.6.79) that when Barbara Castle was Minister of Transport she failed to remove her permanent secretary when all the other permanent secretaries threatened to resign if she persisted in trying.

The English Report suggested that permanent secretaries should be *required* to change or reshuffle civil servants if a minister wished, although permanent secretaries themselves should only be removed with the consent of the prime minister. Secondly, it was proposed that ministers should be able to bring MPs and/or outside advisers into their departments and that there should not be a narrow restriction on the numbers. Thirdly, the Report suggested that ministers could take up the system used in many Western European countries, of having their own cabinet. This would mean that Ministers could have far more MPs in their departments, backed up by staff drawn from outside the civil service. Not surprisingly the idea of 'ministerial cabinets' does not receive much support from senior civil servants who argue that it would weaken the link between ministers and civil servants in their departments.

These suggestions of the English Report have not yet been acted on – Mrs Thatcher even reduced to one the number of outside advisers whom a minister can bring into his or her department. Even if the English Report's ideas were taken up, it is likely that the outcome of any departmental disagreement would depend on the personal strengths of civil servants and politicians themselves. As one writer has argued, 'The balance of ability may well, in the end, determine the balance of power.' He added that it was quite proper for civil servants to point out the snags and problems facing ministers. Certainly arguments between civil servants and ministers are essential – if only to reduce mistakes. And it is unrealistic to expect that very experienced civil servants will not have their own views about what ought to be done. But this is a long way from claiming that there is a conspiracy to block the wishes of elected politicians.

Discussion and essay questions

1. What have been the main suggestions for reforming the civil service since 1968? How much has been achieved?

2. The Fulton Report suggested that civil servants did not have enough contact with the community at large. How far would you agree with this? What suggestions can you make for increasing such contacts?

3. If you were a minister how would you try to ensure that you were in control rather than your top civil servants?

4. What kind of tactics have been used by civil servants, according to some writers, to weaken the power of ministers? How could ministers counter them?

5. How might civil servants defend themselves against the charge that they are trying to run the country?

6. Imagine that you are Permanent Secretary at the Ministry of Transport. The minister is quite keen on licensing bicycles (£5 a year) but you are against it. Draft a memo to him which will gently, but firmly, convince him that it would not be a good idea.

7. What is meant by the political impartiality of civil servants? Why do people like Tony Benn and Brian Sedgmoor argue that it is not a correct description?

Part Four: PARLIAMENT

9 Parliament – the House of Commons

The British parliament is divided into two chambers – the House of Commons and the House of Lords. The Lords still has important powers but it is the Commons which is the central body of parliament.

The place of the House of Commons in British politics

First of all, the Commons is the main **legislature**, the place where laws are passed. In practice that means that the legislative powers are in the hands of the government because it controls the majority party in the Commons. It follows that the second important job of the Commons is to *maintain a government*. It does not pick a government. It simply ensures that a government is able to rule effectively – which is achieved by party organisation in the Commons. A third important aspect of the Commons' work is to question and criticise the actions of government. Although the government is normally able to 'control' the Commons, this does not mean that it can do just as it pleases. There are some parliaments or political assemblies in the world which are little more than 'rubber stamps' for official policy, because all (or practically all) their members are devoted supporters of the government. In Britain the existence of an official opposition ensures regular public criticism. Government MPs too will often express disagreement, at least privately, if they feel that their party's leaders are following the wrong policies. This ability to act as a public 'watchdog' on government depends to a large extent on ministerial responsibility. As we saw in Chapter 7, ministers are expected to account in parliament for the work of their departments and take responsibility for complaints against them or their civil servants.

These three main aspects of the Commons' work help to make it the most important forum in British politics. It is still the main arena where political parties fight their major battles and where any issue of public concern can be raised. Consequently it is important in extending the political education of the people. Debates, questions, and the passage of Bills all add to public awareness of politics – especially through reports in the media.

A member of parliament

New MPs arriving at the Commons must feel a sense of triumph. The highest positions in British politics are normally obtained after a long apprenticeship in the Commons, so they have their feet on the bottom rung of the ladder of political promotion. For the future there is the vision of ministerial office or even of 10 Downing Street itself. For many MPs it may be a job for life because 'landslide elections' where a large number of seats change hands, have been rare. But for MPs who have won a marginal seat, the performance and popularity of their party and its leaders will be vital if they are to survive the next election.

MPs receive £16,904 a year (1985), with free travel within the United Kingdom on parliamentary business, and an allowance of up to £12,546

Neil Kinnock was first elected to Parliament in 1970. Like many MPs he has to spend a considerable amount of time travelling. As leader of the Labour Party he now spends even more time in trains.

House of Commons after 1983 election

(a) Educational background	Alliance	Conservative	Labour
Oxford and Cambridge	6	187	30
Other universities	9	93	83
Total universities	15	280	113
Military colleges	0	12	0
Technical colleges and Colleges of Technology	2	20	34
Public schools (e.g. Eton, Harrow, Winchester)	9	244	19
Grammar schools	14	129	97
Elementary and other secondary schools	0	10	64

(b) Occupations			
Barristers and solicitors	5	80	18
Journalists and publishers	3	40	11
Teachers and lecturers	4	21	45
Doctors	1	3	2
Farmers and landowners	1	38	2
Company directors	2	130	5
Accountants	1	14	2
Insurance underwriters, brokers and bankers	0	43	0
Managers and executives	1	52	18
Other businessmen	1	16	4
Engineers	1	9	18
Clerical and technical workers	0	0	8
Trade union officials	0	0	24
Mine workers	0	0	13
Railway workers	0	0	4
Other manual workers	0	0	6
Party officials	0	8	4
Local and central government	2	12	16
Women MPs	0	13	16

(c) Age groupings			
Over 60	2	47	52
50–59	6	118	76
40–49	7	138	62
30–39	6	83	29
Under 30	2	8	0

Figure 9.1 What kinds of people are elected MPs?

(1985) for research and secretarial assistance. They get free stationery together with free calls and postage from Westminster. If they lose their seat in an election there is a maximum severance grant of the full annual salary although the amount will vary according to age and time spent as an MP. They are also allowed overnight subsistence up to £6,696 a year (1985) for the time they spend in London. Many MPs have to run two houses, especially because most local parties are keen to have an MP living in their area.

The salary and allowance may seem generous but they are well below the rates paid to MPs in most other countries. Most MPs in Britain have to share office accommodation, and do not have the suite of rooms which would be made available in many foreign assemblies. When the Commons is sitting, they may work up to fourteen hours a day. Five months holiday is some consolation, but part of this, and many weekends, are taken up with work in constituencies. With these kinds of demands on their time, most MPs are forced to give up their own jobs, and have little or no opportunity to take up any outside work to supplement their incomes or insure against future unemployment in the event of losing an election.

The Chamber of the House

The old House of Commons was destroyed in an air raid in 1941. When it was rebuilt after the war it was deliberately planned to be almost an exact replica of the previous one. This was not just based on tradition or sentimentality. It was strongly felt that the size and shape of the old Chamber suited the working methods of the Commons.

The Chamber is surprisingly small. There is not enough room to seat all MPs on the benches at any one time. This is rarely a problem, however; a 'full house' is unusual – because sitting in the Chamber listening to debates is only one part of an MPs life. The great advantage of having a small Chamber is that it allows a relaxed, almost conversational, style of speaking. On important occasions, when there is a good attendance, it produces a sense of packed excitement.

In many foreign parliaments, speakers have to go to a rostrum in front of the assembly. In the Commons they merely stand up in their places once they have been called by the Speaker. When MPs vote, they walk into one of the two lobbies ('Aye' or 'No') and are counted as they emerge through a type of gate.

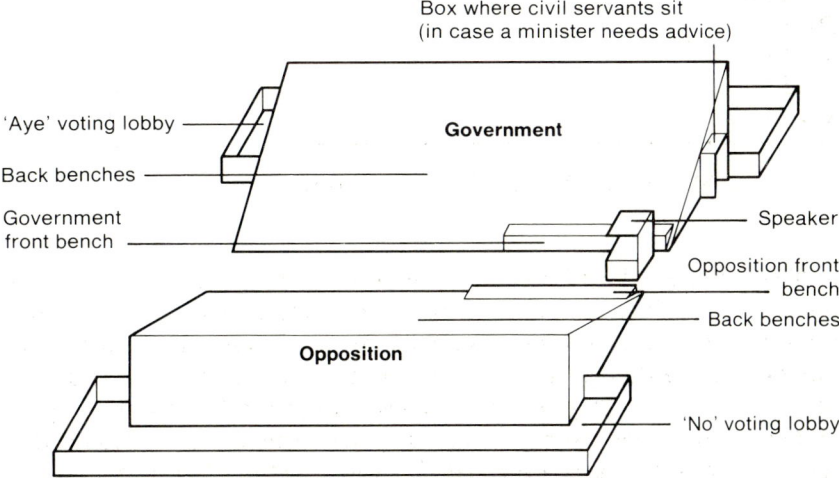

Figure 9.2 The House of Commons: general layout.

Interior of the House of Commons, showing the Speaker's Chair, seating for the Clerk of the House and assistants, the table on which is the Dispatch Box and place for the Mace. The galleries are used by the press, distinguished strangers, and by members of the public.

The main government and opposition leaders sit on the front benches facing each other. The phrase 'back-bench MPs' refers to members who do not hold any official post and sit on the benches at the back. The rectangular shape of the Commons gives a strong impression of the government and opposition being engaged in conflict. More important, it emphasises the idea of the opposition being an alternative government. The members of the Shadow Cabinet speak from their own front bench, and there is an obvious alternative prime minister in the leader of the opposition who is leader of the second largest party.

The chairman in the Commons is the *Speaker*, who is chosen from among the MPs themselves, usually by agreement between the main parties. On becoming Speaker he remains an MP but he must be politically impartial, for he has complete control of procedure in the House. All speeches are published daily in *Hansard*, a record of the proceedings of the Commons.

Outside the main chamber of the Commons are other rooms, or lobbies, where for example MPs can meet members of the general public. The practice of confronting MPs about grievances or attempting to persuade MPs to support particular policies is, as a result, known as **lobbying**.

The Chamber of the Commons appears to be the public cockpit of British politics where political parties and their leaders confront each other. The media frequently supports this view in their reporting of dramatic activities such as the main debates. But much of the work of the Commons is far less spectacular, for example, when details of a proposed new law are considered. It is also important to remember that MPs spend a great deal of time in activities outside the Chamber especially in the various committees of the Commons.

Political parties in the Commons

Political parties are central to the working of the Commons. Whether maintaining the government or attacking it, it is the party system which makes these activities effective.

Supporting the party is a particularly important responsibility for government MPs. Although the prime minister and Cabinet members are the most powerful people in British politics, this is only because they can command a majority in the Commons. If they lose this majority in a vote over a major issue, then they may be forced to resign – as happened to Labour in 1979. Equally, the opposition will want to show that it is united enough to form an effective alternative government.

Party organisation

Each political party has certain MPs called *Whips*, who control day to day organisation in the Commons. The name comes from a hunting expression (whipping in) but although it sounds fierce and disciplinary, it does not mean that MPs are bullied into supporting their parties. The vast majority of them would do so freely, whips or no whips. Their belief in their party and its policies, coupled with a reluctance to cause disunity, will usually be enough.

The main task of the whips is to send out details of forthcoming business to their MPs and to ensure that the party votes at its maximum strength on important debates. If MPs cannot be in the Commons to record their vote, perhaps because they are in their constituencies, then their party whips will try to get them 'paired' with MPs on the other side. This means the rival whips agree that neither MP will vote; thus keeping the relative strengths of the parties equal.

A more general responsibility of the whips is to keep their party leaders in touch with the views of back-benchers. As a former Cabinet minister, Lord Hill, put it: 'A [government] Chief Whip's job is to listen and learn, to gather up the scraps of gossip, to assess other people's opinions. He is the Prime Minister's ears and eyes in the smoking room and in the lobby.'

Although political parties are united on most issues, they do nevertheless contain groups with differing opinions. Every now and again some back-benchers will be unhappy or even critical with official party policy – it is the job of the whips to try to prevent a split. Friendly persuasion is likely to be more effective than threats or bullying, and the most severe threat of all – expulsion from the parliamentary party – is avoided if at all possible.

If a revolt by government MPs against the party leadership cannot be prevented, its seriousness will depend on the size of both the rebel group and the government's majority in the House. When a government has a tiny majority, as did Labour from 1974 to 1979, even a handful of rebel MPs can threaten it with disaster. But they may well be reluctant to go that far. Indeed when a government has a large majority the supporters are more likely to be rebellious simply because the government is safe. This was the experience of the Conservative government after 1983.

Party meetings

These are held regularly and, because they private, MPs express their views frankly. Meetings of government MPs are often addressed by ministers, who can face sharp criticism on controversial issues. But it does not follow that these meetings decide policy. That is largely the job of party leaders; although they must obviously take account of what is generally acceptable to MPs.

In the end, unity is maintained simply because no party can do without it. To win power, or keep it, is the main aim of parties and their leaders. Public arguments and splits within them can ruin their chances of winning the next general election.

The opposition

A basic task of the opposition is to examine government decisions critically and provide a check on any misuse of power. It is true that some party battles in the Commons, in which the opposition objects to practially everything the government does, can seem petty and trivial. But it is the responsibility of the opposition to ensure that as many objections as possible are put forward and discussed before the government goes ahead with its policy.

Criticism for its own sake, however, it not enough. The leader of the opposition and the Shadow Cabinet are the alternative government. They are expected to be constructive and put forward positive policies of their own. The electorate cannot be expected to trust them with office in the future unless they give the impression of being able to run the country.

In the day-to-day business of the House, opposition arguments may appear to have little or no effect. The voting of MPs is rarely in any doubt; and at the end of every major debate the government will almost certainly win. Does this make debates a sham – rather like watching a football match when the result has been decided beforehand? Not really, because the main purpose of party battles in the Commons is to force the government to explain and defend its actions. This is an old Commons tradition, dating back to the days when the government was the monarch. Today it is largely the task of the opposition rather than the Commons as a whole, although a government's own MPs may be critical of government as well.

Many people would like to see MPs vote less frequently along party lines. At present this only happens when there is a *free vote* – usually on such issues as divorce, abortion, capital punishment or licensing laws, where party loyalty might stifle the MP's own belief or conscience. Should free votes be extended to more politically controversial areas? If they were, then government as we know it might become unworkable. The present near-certainty of voting in the Commons does at least make governments secure enough to carry out a full political programme.

Pressures on the MP

Party leaders and policies

In all parties there are groups of people, including MPs, who will have widely different views about what the party ought to be doing. Such disagreements may not always spill out into the open and MPs are able to express their doubts 'behind the scenes'. But sometimes there is virtual open warfare as was the case in 1981. Many Conservative MPs, including former ministers and even a Conservative ex-prime minister (Edward Heath), publicly opposed the policies of the Conservative government under Mrs Thatcher. At the same time the Labour Party became a battleground between the Left and the Right wings with much of the conflict centred on whether Tony Benn or Dennis Healey should become deputy leader of the party. In both cases the battle inside the parties was based on a mixture of personality and policy clashes, and each faction claimed that *it* represented the 'real party'. In other words some MPs were facing the problem that their loyalty to the party clashed with their belief that party leaders and official policy did not reflect party principles.

Constituency parties

It would be a very foolish MP who did not attempt to establish a good relationship with the constituency party. The constituency party will have chosen the MP as their candidate. It is the local activists in the party who keep the organisation running; this can be a vital factor in holding a marginal seat. If an MP loses the support of the constituency

Mrs T calls Tory critics crackers

by ADAM RAPHAEL and WILLIAM KEEGAN

Conservative critics of Mrs Thatcher's policies brought an angry response in 1984.

Calls by Tory ex-ministers for change of tack over economy

By Colin Brown.

party they then may choose someone else as their official party candidate next time. This has become particularly true in the Labour Party because the party's constitution lays down that MPs must offer themselves to be re-selected for each general election. Before the 1983 election some sitting Labour MPs were not chosen to fight their seat again.

The national interest

We would normally expect MPs to believe that their own party policies are in the national interest, but there may be occasions when they conflict. This occurred in the debates over devolution for Scotland and Wales (1978–1979) when a number of MPs on both sides voted against their party leadership. Of course one person's idea of national interest can be another person's idea of national betrayal. But MPs have justified voting against their own party on the grounds that national interest was not being served by certain policies. In 1940 so many Conservative MPs either abstained or voted against their own Prime Minister, Neville Chamberlain, in a debate about the conduct of the war, that he was forced to resign. Winston Churchill took his place.

Moral and religious beliefs

Conflict may occur between the deeply held moral or religious beliefs of MPs and party loyalties. Party leaders try to minimise such conflicts

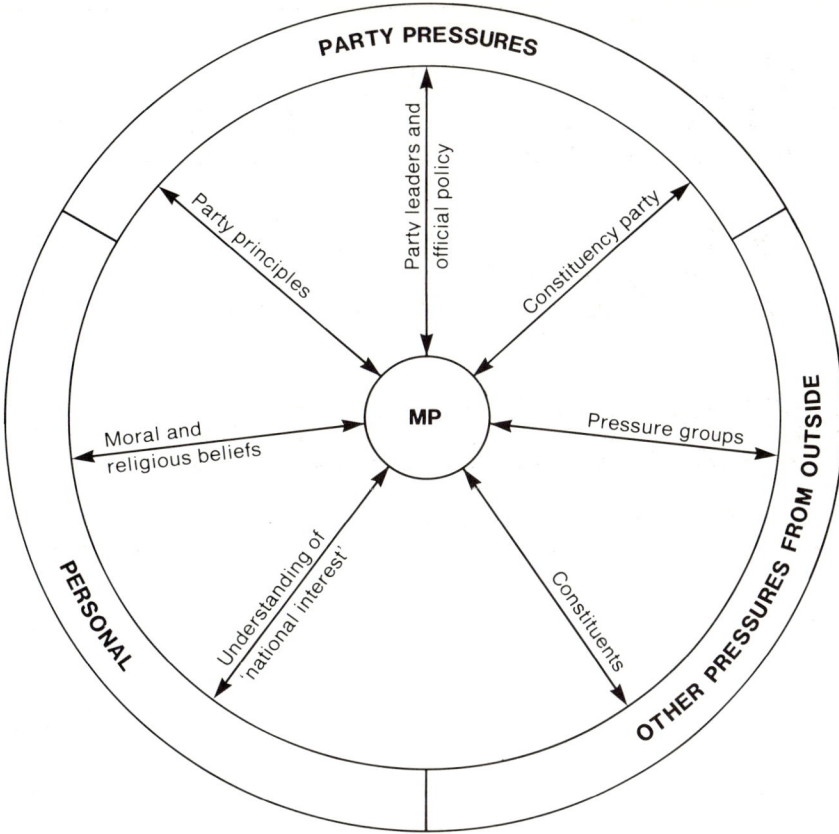

Figure 9.3 The loyalties of an MP: party loyalties may be challenged by other deeply-held principles, causing an MP to break with the party, and perhaps with politics altogether.

by allowing free votes in the Commons when obvious matters of conscience are debated. In the 1960s, for example, such issues as divorce reform and legalising abortion could not easily have been made party isues. New laws were passed but after debates on Private Members Bills, not Bills proposed by the governments.

Constituency interests

There may be times when party policy conflicts with the clear interests of an MP's constituency as a whole, or an important group of constituents. Defence cuts may close naval dockyards or the government may decide to close factories. MPs are always aware of the need to press the government to develop their constituencies, perhaps by new projects or financial help to industry. It may be rare for MPs to vote against their own party on such matters in the Commons, but they are expected to pursue constituency interests as vigorously as possible. This may mean speaking out against their own party's policies if their constituency is badly affected. This is not as easy as it sounds. There may be conflicting views about what *is* in the interests of a contituency. For example, some might want a new motorway running through but

Issues raised in one weekly 'surgery' in a Midlands constituency

	Issue	Action taken by MP
Housing	Two requests for places in old people's bungalows	
	Young couple living with parents in overcrowded house want council flat	Letters sent to local council's housing manager. Some put in touch with a local councillor
	Middle aged couple in damp council house want transfer	
	Crippled woman with small child wants ground floor flat	
Pensions and superannuation	Two want an increase in pensions for the disabled	Letters to Health Service Superannuation Division
	Two men worried about redundancy scheme for miners	Letter to Department of Health and Social Security
	Widow of a man who died after a pit accident believes she is not receiving enough Social Security	Letter to Department of Health and Social Security
	War widow angry because two-thirds of her pension goes back in tax – the result, she claims, of working to support her sons	Letter to the Chancellor of the Exchequer
Other problems	Complaint about interference on a television set caused by a local amateur radio operator	Letter to local GPO Manager
	Presentation of a petition to put a footpath through part of a local village. Letters sent seven years ago to the county council not answered	Petition accepted and sent to the county council with the MP's support
	Mother claims that her daughter, sent to a home for maladjusted children, is not allowed to see her. The girl is now pregnant	Letter sent to the children's home
	During the same 'surgery' two people called to thank the MP for his efforts in the past – one had got back a lost sewing machine, and the other had been granted a transfer of council houses. In this particular constituency the MP always writes the necessary letters while the people concerned are present. And he has a member of the local council with him, to help sort out local issues, especially housing.	It has to be admitted that not all MPs are as conscientious as they should be in their constituency work, and some do not actively encourage their constituents to see them. But the vast majority of MPs consider the protection of the rights of constituents to be a central part of their work.

Figure 9.4 An MP's 'surgery' record.

others would oppose it. Some groups may want policies which the MP totally rejects.

When it comes to individual constituents, most MPs spend a great deal of time helping to sort out their problems. They hold regular 'surgeries' where constituents can bring their problems; often an MP's action can produce rapid results. Where government departments are involved, MPs can raise matters directly with the minister by writing a letter or even speak about cases on the floor of the Commons itself.

In their constituency work a major responsibility of MPs is to protect people's rights under the law. Many laws are very complicated, and individuals often have the greatest difficulty in picking their way through the maze of welfare benefits, social security payments, housing legislation and so on. MPs are well equipped to give advice in these areas.

The Parliamentary Commissioner for Administration

In 1967 a new post was established by parliament – the Parliamentary Commissioner for Administration, or ombudsman. The task of the ombudsman is to investigate cases where there appears to have been maladministration in a government department. The term 'maladministration' is difficult to define but it certainly covers cases where civil servants have been neglectful or incompetent and, especially, where their decisions seem to be arbitrary. To a great extent, the ombudsman has discretion in deciding what is covered by 'maladministration'. He has the power to obtain the papers relevant to a case and, after investigating it, can produce a report and make recommendations.

Members of the public can only contact the ombudsman through their MPs – which can be seen as a weakness in this grievance system. On the other hand MPs are in a position to say whether any case is likely to be covered by the ombudsman's terms of reference, and if so, can help in framing the arguments. A more important weakness is that the ombudsman has no power to enforce his recommendations. In the end it is up to the minister concerned to accept or reject any findings. At least the existence of the government ombudsman is an incentive for civil servants to be careful in their dealings with the public. No department likes any adverse publicity which can come from a critical report. Usually over half the cases referred to the ombudsman are rejected as being outside his terms of reference, but each year there are cases where maladministration is established.

The system was expanded in 1973 when the ombudsman became Health Commissioner, responsible for investigating complaints of hardship or injustice in the National Health Service. In this case the public can send in complaints directly, although they may not question medical judgements of Health Service staff. In 1974 four Local Government Commissioners were appointed – three for England and one for Wales. Their task is to investigate complaints against the actions of local government.

The Commons – government control?

It is rare for the government to be defeated in either the Commons chamber or in committee. This is hardly suprising because virtually all governments in recent times have had a majority. Such factors as the natural loyalty of MPs, party organisation, and the belief that party splits could be harmful, all help to maintain the government's position. Prime ministers can also reward their own MPs by promotion, and a reputation for being 'awkward' is not likely to win many friends among party managers in the Commons.

The platform for government control may be the solid support of their MPs but governments also have considerable advantages in the day-to-day business of the Commons. They can plan when to bring legislation forwards. They have all the resources of the civil service behind them so that government proposals will be thoroughly worked out in advance. Compared to this the resources of MPs are meagre – one secretary, a cramped office, and no research staff of their own.

But that is only a part of the picture. Firstly, opposition parties wait in ambush. They may not defeat the government but can, and do, expose policy weaknesses and government failure. No government likes adverse publicity and embarrassment. Secondly, the smooth running of the Commons depends on a degree of co-operation between the parties, for example in timetabling or pairing. If the opposition parties decided to be completely obstructive a government could run into difficulties. Thirdly, the Commons has introduced a new committee system. This is examined in the next chapter but it has meant that MPs are now better informed about issues and better able to challenge the government.

Governments may be confident about winning votes in the Commons but they must also remain sensitive to the views of their own MPs. As we have seen, MPs face a number of often conflicting pressures, and their support must never be taken for granted. It may be that the ultimate rebellion, voting against their party, is rare but there are different ways of expressing discontent as Figure 9.5 shows. However, in the last few years, even voting against your own government has become a little more common.

Between 1945 and 1970 there was not one example of a government being defeated in the Commons itself because of the actions of its own back-benchers. There were a number of cases of government MPs abstaining or even voting against their government. But in no case was the government majority really at risk. Probably the most serious threat to a government came in 1969 when the Labour government, which had a large majority, attempted to reform industrial relations. They published a White Paper, 'In Place of Strife', which outlined the

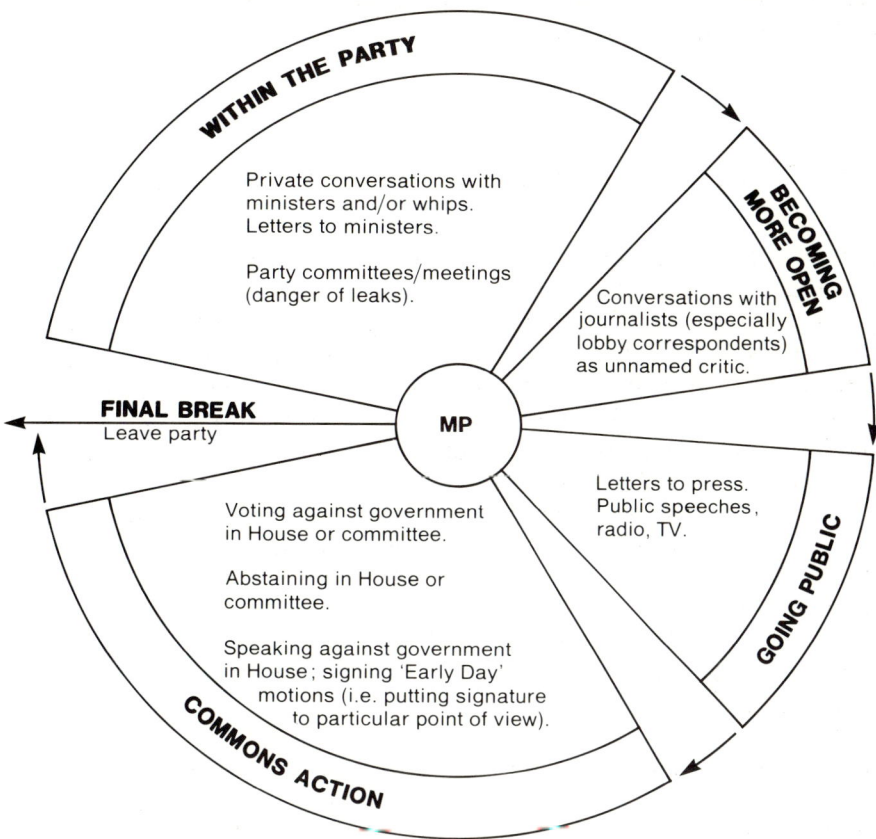

Figure 9.5 The government back-bencher – ways of expressing discontent.

proposals and, in the debate which followed, fifty-five Labour MPs voted against and a number abstained. There was considerable trade union pressure against the proposals but the most significant opposition came from a group of 'middle of the road' Labour MPs. In June 1969 the plans were dropped, mainly because the government accepted that they would have great difficulty passing them through the Commons. In the same Parliament the reform of the House of Lords was also withdrawn but, in this case, because of an 'alliance' of backbench MPs of both parties.

In 1970 the Conservatives took office with a majority of thirty. Between 1970 and 1974 it was defeated five times on the floor of the House because of a mixture of Conservative abstentions and votes against. And, in those years, two thirds of all Conservative MPs voted against the government at least once. If the committee stage of Bills is included then the government lost sixteen times in 1972/73 alone. Although none of these defeats were regarded as votes of confidence which could mean an election, nevertheless it was the actions of Conservative MPs which made them possible.

At first glance it may not be surprising that the Labour government of 1974 to 1979 was defeated many times. In October 1974 it won the election with a majority of three. Between October 1974 and

December 1975 it lost twenty-six times in the Commons and in committee. (Between October 1964 and March 1966, when it had an equally small majority, it lost only four times.) By February 1977 the majority had disappeared through by-election defeats, and the government was able to carry on only by making a pact with the Liberals. In the next two years until the May 1979 general election it still lost on another twenty-five issues. But some of the important defeats were engineered by its *own* MPs. For example, Jeff Rooker and Audrey Wise, two Labour MPs, forced the government to accept the 'Rooker-Wise' amendment to the Finance Bill. Against the Treasury's wishes, the House of Commons voted for the amendment that certain income tax allowances should be inflation-proofed.

In 1979 the Conservatives returned to power with a comfortable majority of forty-three. Mrs Thatcher found it necessary to change certain policies because of pressure from groups including her own MPs. Proposed cuts in the BBC's external services, for example, were halved and even the Finance Bill in 1981 was modified because of Conservative MPs reluctance to accept a major increase in the tax on oil. And government proposals on MPs' pay were changed because of the likelihood of a Commons defeat. The same pattern was seen after the 1983 election — stimulated now by a large majority which protected the government from defeat. Public criticism by Conservative MPs and abstaining or voting against the government was seen on issues such as economic policy, local government changes, transport, grants and fees in higher education and so on.

Yet it would be foolish to believe that the balance has swung the other way. The vast bulk of government legislation, for example, is still passed with little real difficulty and voting against your own leadership once or twice in a session which contains hundreds of different voting opportunities hardly makes MPs all that rebellious. Naturally, as a general election approaches, all MPs think more carefully about breaking ranks and threatening unity.

Discussion and essay questions

1. Would you say that the House of Commons is just a 'talking shop'?

2. 'MPs should be full time so that they do not have jobs outside the House of Commons?' Give the arguments for and against this view.

3. MPs are sometimes accused of slavishly following the 'party line'. How would you defend this loyalty towards the party?

4. What problems would there be in the House of Commons if there were many more MPs who were independent of political party?

5. Imagine you are an MP. On which of these issues would you want to follow your own views rather than following the party line?
   Abortion   Nuclear disarmament   Capital punishment
   Wage control   Abolishing private schools.

6. In what different ways could it be said that the House of Commons fails to represent a cross-section of the people? Does this matter?

10 The Commons at work

Each parliament works on an annual timetable called *sessions* which begin with the Speech from the Throne in late October or early November. The Queen's Speech outlines the policies which the government intend putting to parliament in that session and is written and approved by the prime minister and Cabinet. A considerable part of the Queen's Speech is taken up with government proposals for new laws and these must pass all their stages in that session. If not, then the process has to start again from the beginning in the next session of parliament. Figure 10.1 shows a breakdown of Commons business in the first session of Mrs Thatcher's Conservative government, 1979–83. This was an unusually long session – because it ran from the Queen's speech in May 1979 (just after the general election) to October 1980. Sessions usually last only about 180 days.

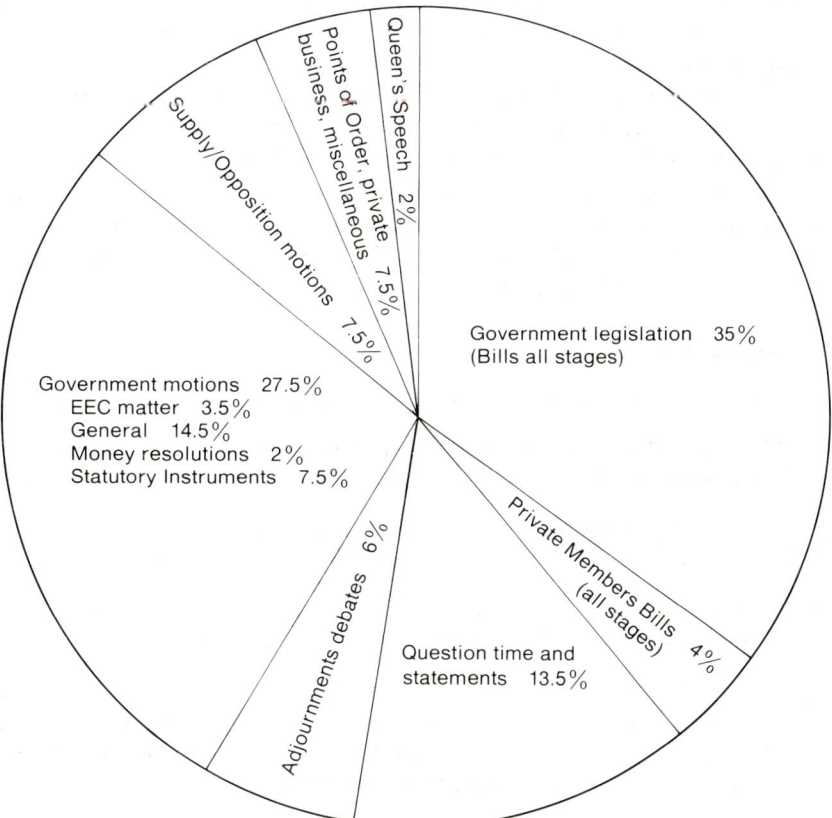

Figure 10.1 The Commons chamber – time spent on various kinds of business.

The debate on the Queen's Speech gives the government and opposition parties the change to meet head on over the general direction of government policies. The debate tends to be concerned with wider issues of policy rather than detail, and for Mrs Thatcher in 1979 it was the moment when the priorities of the new government could be explained and defended.

Legislation

When legislation is passing through parliament it is called a Bill. It becomes an Act of Parliament when it has been agreed by the Commons and Lords and signed by the monarch. It is then the law of the land.

There are two types of Bills: Public and Private. **Public Bills** are concerned with matters affecting the whole nation. The majority of them are sponsored by the government and take up most of the time spent by the Commons on legislation. A few Public Bills are also known as Private Members Bills. That is because they are presented by backbenchers from any party. A ballot is held to choose the lucky MPs, and about twenty Fridays in each session are set aside for the Bills.

Private Bills usually deal with the powers of local authorities. They may be of great interest to certain regions of the country, but rarely have any national importance. Much of the detailed work on these Bills is done by the House of Lords.

Even when a government has a clear idea about what it wants to see in a new law, there is still a great deal of work to be done before a Bill is presented to the Commons. Consultations with individuals and groups most directly concerned are a neccessary first stage. A 'Green Paper', or discussion paper, may be issued by the Government. It will contain the general ideas behind the legislation, together with a great deal of background information. A 'White Paper' may then be produced setting out more concrete proposals, with supporting arguments. Well before a Bill is finalised, the government will have a fairly clear idea of opinions and reactions towards it. At some stage a Public Bill goes before a Cabinet committee and then, for final approval, to the Cabinet itself. During this time it is drafted into a clear and definite form, with the help of government legal departments.

Procedure in parliament

Bills can be presented first either in the Commons or in the Lords, after which they go through the same procedure. Bills can be a lengthy and complicated business but in an emergency, the proceeding can be speeded up considerably if there is no serious opposition. The Zimbabwe Bill in 1979 which granted independence to the former colony of Southern Rhodesia, took only 14 days to pass between the

First Reading	The title of the Bill is read out, and printed copies made available so that MPs can study the proposals.	No debate.
Second Reading	Debate on general principles. Usually takes place in the Commons, but can be in committee.	Bill is either rejected, or (as is almost certain if sponsored by the government) accepted.
Committee stage	Bill is examined in detail and amendments can be made. This is the vital stage for the minister or junior ministers in charge of the Bill.	There are eight regular or 'standing' committees. Between 25 and 40 MPs will be involved at this stage (in proportion to party strength in the Commons) and they often have a specialist interest in the subject. Some important Bills are considered by a committee of the whole House, in the main Commons chamber.
Report stage	The amended Bill is 'reported' to the Commons. It can go directly to the Third Reading.	
Third Reading	A debate, similar to the Second Reading. But it need not be held.	
Review in the Lords	The Bill then goes to the Lords (or to the Commons if it started in the Lords) and through similar stages.	If there is a conflict between the two Houses, then the Bill must take the form decided on by the Commons – although the Lords can delay it for up to a year.
Royal Assent	Now automatic – a *convention*.	In theory the monarch can refuse to sign the Bill, but this has not happened since 1707. If the monarch refused, it would bring the Crown directly into politics and threaten its independence – and survival.

It can be tempting for the opposition, when faced with a Bill they heartlily dislike, to try and delay proceedings. This seems worth doing as a Bill has to be passed in one session and cannot be left to the next. The government has various ways of dealing with delay. Debates can be brought to an end if an MP moves successfully, and the Speaker agrees, 'that the question now be put'. This is called the 'closure'. In committee a government can limit discussion by setting a time limit for considering clauses (*guillotine*) or allowing the chairman to select only certain clauses for discussion (*kangaroo*).

Figure 10.2 Stages of a bill passing through parliament.

first reading and royal assent, with the second reading, committee stage, report and third reading all taking place in one day!

The slowest stage is usually when a Bill goes to committee. For every Bill which reaches the committee stage a new committee is set up to consider it. The great advantage of this is that MPs with a special interest or expertise can be included. Committee procedure is less formal than in the Commons Chamber, for example, an MP can speak more than once as an issue is discussed.

This stage of the Bill is the first time that changes, or amendments, can be made and this gives backbench MPs a chance to influence legislation – if only in its detailed application. Generally the best chance of changing legislation in committee is either when clauses have not been drafted clearly or when the legislation is not seen as politically controversial. The Bill is not likely to have its main aims drastically altered because the government party has a majority on the committee just as it does in the House of Commons.

The committee stage can frequently last months with a couple of mornings a week given up to its work. This contrasts sharply with the second and third readings which last only a few hours as the general principles of the Bill are debated.

Private Members Bill

Those MPs who win a chance in the ballot to present a **Private Members Bill** will soon be swamped by suggestions about the kind of Bill they should take on. Outside organisations send them completely drawn up Bills ready for their use and other MPs will be eager for them to adopt Bills they wanted to present themselves. However, the majority of Private Members Bills are unlikely to pass the long process of becoming law unless they are one of two kinds: firstly, the fairly non-controversial Bill which few MPs oppose, and secondly Bills which are supported by the government. In such cases, the private member may have help in drafting the Bill and extra time in the Commons if this is necessary. Governments may prefer Private Members Bills to be used as a way of passing legislation, for example in sensitive areas where moral judgements may be involved and any controversy about the Bills will not then fall on their shoulders. Private Members Bills have been used to abolish capital punishment, change divorce laws and lift restrictions on abortion.

Discussion and debate

Question time

Four days a week, ministers have to answer questions put to them orally by MPs. The prime minister appears on Tuesdays and Thursdays and government departments are represented, usually by ministerial heads on a rota basis. Ministers can only be questioned about activities

	Questions answered in writing	Questions answered orally
Monday	118	31
Tuesday	132	33
Wednesday	116	34
Thursday	74	38
Friday	54	—

A selection of oral questions asked in the House (week beginning 16.7.84)

Question raised by	Directed to	Question	Answered by
Sir David Price (Con) EASTLEIGH	Secretary of State for the Home Department (Home Secretary)	'What information he has as to changes in the level of drug addition in Hampshire over recent years and, in particular whether there has been an increase in the use of heroin.'	David Mellor Parliamentary Under-Secretary for Home Dept.
Mr B. J. Heddle (Con) MIDSTAFFS	Secretary of State for Education and Science	'what steps he is taking to monitor trunacy levels.'	Peter Brooke Parliamentary Under-Secretary for Education and Science
Mr Ian Grist (Con) CARDIFF CENT.	Secretary of State for Wales	'what is his latest assessment of the effects of the miners' strike on the economy of South Wales.'	Nicholas Edwards Secretary of State for Wales
Mr D. Nellist (Lab) COVENTRY S.E.	Prime Minister	*'if she would list her official engagements for Thursday, 19th July.'	Margaret Thatcher Prime Minister

*It is often difficult to address a question directly to the PM because, if it concerns specific government policies, it is likely to be regarded as the responsibility of the minister concerned. This kind of question is clearly addressed to the PM, and once answered, the questioner has a chance to raise virtually any issue. (David Nellist went on to ask about the coal strike.)

Figure 10.3 Question time in the Commons – a breakdown.

over which they have a direct responsibility. However as we saw in Chapter 7 ministerial responsibility means that the whole range of a department's work can be raised. About 3,000 questions are answered this way each year. Questions may be asked for a variety of reasons: to embarass the government, to obtain information, to press for action on an issue, and so on. Sometimes innocent-looking questions are followed by supplementary (additional) questions which catch the minister unprepared and question time can easily turn into a small, and noisy debate. However, if MPs are searching for information they usually prefer to put a written question to a minister. There can be more than 30,000 of these each year. Departments take oral and written questions very seriously indeed. In answering oral questions, ministers are as well briefed as possible, even rehearsed, and great care is taken to cover any likely supplementary questions. Question time does give MPs a chance to keep a watchful eye on government, and forces ministers and civil servants to take care, but it has become a party political ritual as well. For example, prime minister's question time on Tuesdays and Thursdays has become very predictable in recent years, and seems to be mainly an opportunity for scoring elementary debating points.

Adjournment debates

These are held at the end of every day and last for half an hour. An MP, selected by ballot, introduces the subject for debate and a junior minister, responsible for that particular area of government, replies. MP's reasons for picking topics can be as varied as those for asking questions at question time, and local constituency matters are often chosen.

Main debates

Until the 1982–83 session the opposition were given 29 'supply days' when they could choose the topic for debate. Supply days were originally intended as a means of discussing government spending estimates but they became debates on any aspect of policy. The opposition chose topics as a way of launching the strongest possible attack on an aspect of government policy. However, the Commons agreed in July 1982 to abolish the term 'supply days' and replace it with 'opposition days' and also to reduce them to 19 days. Certain topics which had been dealt with in supply days (for example, the Armed Forces and the EC) were then taken in government time. However, three days were to be allocated for discussing estimates which, in the past, had too frequently been allowed to pass with little or no debate.

On the government side, the equivalent of supply days are debates on government motions (known as 'general motions'). Naturally the government chooses areas where they want to emphasise their achievements. These government or opposition motions are the main way in which the Commons takes part in 'great debates', apart from major new Bills. They are widely reported and the range of topics considered is vast.

European Community matters

The impact of the EC on British politics is examined more fully in

Chapter 22 but membership of the EC has had an important effect on the work of parliament. One of the most traditional descriptions of parliament was that it was 'supreme'. We have already seen that parliament cannot make decisions which limit the power of any future parliaments and there is no body in Britain which can declare that the decisions of parliament are 'unconstitutional'. This is why it is customary to talk of 'the supremacy of parliament'.

However, when Britain joined the EC in 1972, it agreed to accept both the laws that controlled the EC then, and any new laws which were made afterwards. Community laws now automatically become our laws. But, in another sense, the supremacy of parliament still holds. A future British parliament could decide that Britain should leave the EC – although unravelling all the ties that bind us to the EC would not be easy.

EC matters now come, increasingly to the Commons. Examples include motions on general aspects of belonging to the Community and consideration of specific EC laws. The Commons has a number of committees which concern themselves with EC matters. There is a standing committee on European Community documents which receives EC proposals and consultative documents sent by ministers. The select committee on European legislation can refer any proposals for Community laws back to the Commons for further consideration. The Government has accepted that, when this happens, it will withhold agreement with other EC countries until the Commons has discussed the matter.

Statutory instruments

Every year parliament passes roughly one hundred Acts of Parliament. But, at the same time, as many as 2,000 rules and regulations are made, not by parliament, but by ministers with the authority of parliament. Such rules and regulations are known as **delegated legislation.** There are considerable advantages in such system. Modern legislation, for example in such areas as social welfare, cannot cover every possible case and parliament simply does not have the time nor expertise for a close examination of each new regulation. Delegated legislation also allows ministers to deal with changing circumstances when an Act is being applied without having to come back to parliament for further legislation. It enables ministers to experiment with regulations, for example road safety, and there may be times when they need to act very quickly to cope with, or head off, some disaster.

Delegated legislation effectively makes ministers law-makers in their own right even though the power is granted by parliament. Many people have said this puts too much power into the hands of ministers, especially because it can be difficult to forecast how far future ministers will be able to stretch the use of delegated legislation. This is especially so when an Act gives ministers the very wide power to act as they 'think fit'.

House	Monday 29.6.81 2.30 pm	Wednesday 1.7.81 2.30 pm	Thursday 2.7.81 2.30 pm
Private bills	Whitehaven Harbour Bill (Lords amendment agreed to) Northumbrian Water Authority Bill (Third Reading)		Northumbrian Water Authority Bill (Royal Assent)
Question time	Secretary of State for Trade. Minister for Overseas Development	Secretary of State for Transport. Minister for Civil Service	Chancellor of Exchequer. Prime Minister
Ministerial statements etc	Minister for Civil Service on Civil Service Pay	Prime Minister on European Council meeting (followed by short debate)	Leader of House on following week's business, followed by questions and comments from MPs.
Main debates etc.	1. Yorkshire and Humberside Region (supply debate) 2. *EEC* proposals re: proprietary medicine (decision deferred) 3. New Statutory Instruments approval (motion agreed)	1. National Health Service Act — amendment debate 2. Opposition motion condemning government policy re: Motor Industry (supply debate) 3. Orders setting up London Docklands Dev. Corp. approved	1. Government resolution to continue powers given by Northern Ireland Act 1974, Northern Ireland (Emergency Provisions) Act 1978 — agreed in series of votes.
Adjournment debate	W. Shelton MP on gypsy encampment in constituency. Reply: Under Secretary of State for Environment.	4. N. Baker MP on loss of agricultural land. Reply: Secretary of State for Environment.	A. Morris MP on cuts in office of Population Censuses and Surveys. Reply: Under Secretary of State for Health and Social Security.
House rose	11.03 pm	12.25 am	12.33 am

Figure 10.4 The Commons at work – three typical days.

Most delegated legislation comes into force through **statutory instruments**. These are rules, orders, and regulations made by ministers under an Act of Parliament. (The term also includes the power of local authorities to pass by-laws.) Parliament has a number of ways of trying to control the use of statutory instruments. Obviously the first control must be in the wording of the powers any act gives to ministers. Secondly, each Act requiring delegation of powers must state how such a delegation will take place. There are different ways of doing this. The most far-reaching delegated powers must have the approval of the

Commons and the government must grant time for this to happen. However, most of them are only *presented* to the Commons. Unless someone objects and MPs then annul or cancel the minister's regulation it will come into force after forty days. Thirdly, the Select Committee on Statutory Instruments (the Scrutiny Committee) has the power to bring any statutory instrument to the notice of the Commons. The chairman is a member of the opposition and can ask a department to justify any new regulation.

The committee system in the Commons

The Commons has two main types of committees – **standing committees** and **select committees**. Standing committees mostly deal with the committee stage of legislation, but two others are the Scottish and Welsh Grand Committees which consist of all the MPs from the two countries. They consider matters which are concerned exclusively with Scotland and Wales.

Select committees, unlike standing committees, have a membership which usually lasts for the lifetime of a parliament. There are four types. Firstly, some have the responsibility of controlling the running of the Commons, ranging from domestic issues such as catering to the

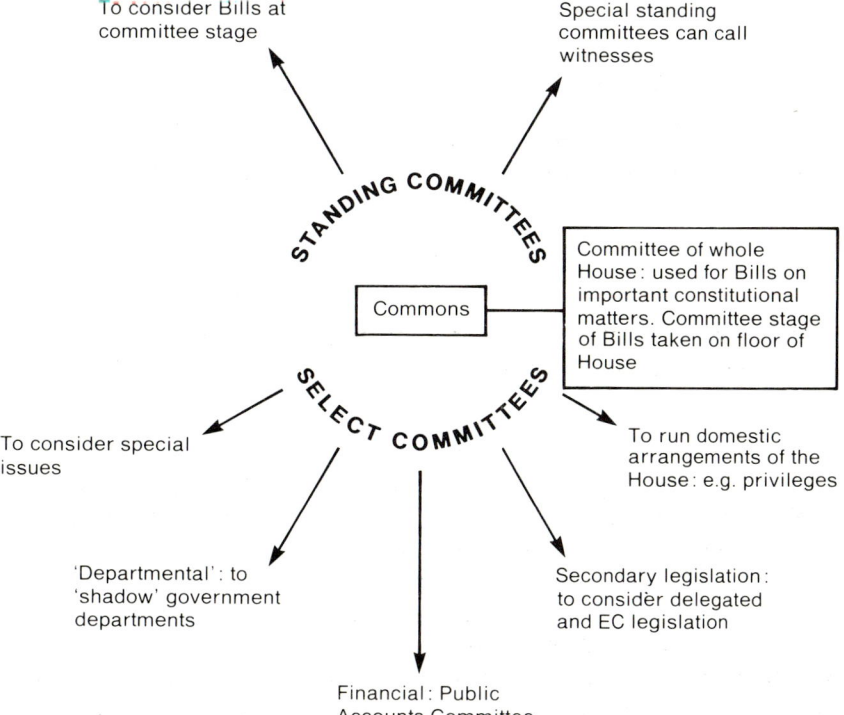

Figure 10.5 House of Commons Committee system.

work of the Privilege Committee in protecting the rights of MPs and the Commons itself. Secondly, there is a group of select committees concerned with 'secondary legislations' such as delegated legislation or EC matters. Thirdly, select committees are set up from time to time to consider specific issues. In 1980, for example, one was established to consider improvements in supply procedure, which is the way the Commons votes money for the government. Lastly, there are select committees which exist to examine the work of government and administrations – the departmental committees and the Public Accounts Committee.

'Departmental' select committees

In 1979 the Commons agreed to establish a completely new system of departmental select committees. Fourteen of these new committees

Name of committee	Principal government departments concerned	Maximum number of Members	Quorum
Agriculture	Ministry of Agriculture, Fisheries and Food	9	3
Defence	Ministry of Defence	11	3
Education, Science and Arts	Department of Education and Science	9	3
Employment	Department of Employment	9	3
Energy	Department of Energy	11	3
Environment	Department of the Environment	11	3
Foreign Affairs	Foreign and Commonwealth Office	11	3
Home Affairs	Home Office	11	3
Industry and Trade	Department of Industry, Department of Trade	11	3
Scottish Affairs	Scottish Office	13	5
Social Services	Department of Health and Social Security	9	3
Transport	Department of Transport	11	3
Treasury and Civil Service	Treasury, Civil Service Department, Board of Inland Revenue, Board of Customs and Excise	11	3
Welsh Affairs	Welsh Office	11	3

Figure 10.16 Structure of 'departmental' select committees set up in 1979.

were set up based on the major government departments. Why was this done? Norman St. John Stevas, then leader of the House, explained:

> The objective of the new committee structure will be to strengthen the accountability of ministers to the House for the discharge of their responsibilities. Each committee will be able to examine the whole range of activity for which its minister or ministers have . . . responsibility . . . It will provide opportunity for closer examination of departmental policy . . . It will also be an important contribution to greater openness in government. (*House of Commons Debates*, Vol 969 c. 49, 25.6.79)

The committees were appointed to examine the expenditure, administration and policy of each department, as well as bodies which come under various ministers, such as nationalised industries. As there is no committee corresponding to the Northern Irish Office, each one examines Northern Ireland matters relevant to the department it covers.

Members of the government and regular opposition front bench speakers are not included and, once appointed, MPs normally serve for the life of a parliament. The government has a majority on each committee, but some chairmen come from the opposition. Each committee can appoint people from outside parliament to act as specialist advisers.

Both the committees and any sub-committee they set up can send for 'persons, papers, and records' to assist their work. From the beginning, the government pledged, in the words of Norman St. John Stevas, 'that every minister from the most senior Cabinet minister to the most junior under secretary will do all in his or her power to co-operate with the new system'. However, the government rejected the

---

	Select committee on employment
Chairman	J. Golding (Lab)
Members	J. Aitken (Con) A. Bowden (Con) M. Calvin (Con) J. Craigen (Lab) J. Gorst (Con) O. McDonald (Lab) R. Powell (Lab) K. Wickenden (Con)
Specialist advisers	M. Hanson R. Lewis B. Harvey
Published reports	The Manpower Services Commission Corporate Plan The Legal Immunities of Trade Unions
Inquiries include	(a) Training, mobility and unemployment (b) The work of the Department of Employment group (c) The EEC fifth directive – The structure of societies anonymous

---

Figure 10.7 Departmental select committee on employment, 1983.

Select committee on home affairs

Chairman	Sir Graham Page (Con)
Members	A. Dubs (Lab) G. Gardiner (Con) J. Hunt (Con) R. Kilroy-Silk (Lab) Mrs J. Knight (Con) A. Lyon (Lab) Dr E. Marshall (Lab) J. Richardson (Lab) W. Waldegrave (Con) J. Wheeler (Con)
Specialist advisers	Dr. S. McConville D. Williams
Published reports	Proposed New Immigration Rules Race Relations and the 'Sus' Law Deaths in Police Custody The Law Relating to Public Order

Figure 10.8 *Department select committee on home affairs, 1983.*

Home affairs sub-committee on race relations and immigration.

Chairman	J. Wheeler
Members	G. Gardiner J. Hunt A. Lyon J. Richardson
Specialist adviser	D. Smith
Current inquiry	Racial disadvantage

Figure 10.9 *Home affairs sub-committee on race relations and immigration, 1983.*

Department select committee on treasury and civil service.

Chairman	Rt. Hon. Edward du Cann (Con)
Members	A. Beaumont-Dark (Con) Dr. J. Bray (Lab) J. Bruce-Gardyne (Con) T. Eggar (Con) M. English (Lab) T. Higgins (Con) M. Meacher (Lab) R. Shepherd (Con) R. Wainwright (Lib) K. Woolmer (Lab)
Specialist advisers	Dr A. Budd Dr P. Neild T. Ward Prof. W. Buiter Prof. D. Hendry Prof. M. Miller Prof. H. Rose
Report include	Provisions for Civil Service Pay Increases in 1980–81 Estimates The Budget and the Governments Expenditure Plans (1980/81–1983/84) Monetary Control The Future of the Civil Service Department The Government's Economic Policy

Figure 10.10 *Departmental select committee on treasury and civil service, 1983.*

idea that committees should have the power to order ministers to attend. They can report to the House 'their opinion and observations on any matters referred to them' together with special reports on any matters they think fit. But the government would not agree that time should automatically be set aside for debates on such reports.

How important are the new select committees?

The new system has only been working for a relatively short time. However, it has already produced a number of improvements in the way the Commons operates – especially in its role of scrutinising government activity. Firstly, it gives MPs a chance to become more familiar with the work of each government department and the technical detail behind its policies. Secondly, the government is forced to think more carefully about how it justifies its policies in detail. The committees have frequently cross-examined both ministers and civil servants – with MPs from all parties, including the government, joining in the close questioning. This means the committees can expose weaknesses in the way policies are put together, or highlight the absence of a policy. Thirdly, a committee can probe more deeply and carefully than a Commons debate. Fourthly, the committees have produced many reports, some of which have been given wide publicity in the press and on radio or television. In this way MPs have been able to widen both their own, and the public's, understanding of a number of issues.

Lastly, the committees have not been afraid to examine issues which are politically controversial. It might be assumed that this would result in reports based simply on the party political composition of the committee, but this has not necessarily been true. For example, in a report by the Treasury Committee on Monetary Policy, Conservative MPs put their names to strong criticism of their own government.

The major doubt about the effectiveness of the new committees must be how far governments will take action on their reports. A report which criticises the government could simply be ignored, but even if this is not the case, there is no guarantee that reports will be debated. If a committee is divided, especially politically, the government has even stronger reasons for down-grading any criticisms of its activities.

On the other hand the new committee structure can be seen as essential if MPs are ever going to be able to examine the actions of government in any kind of detail.

The Commons and government finance

The increased size and scope of government in the twentieth century is clearly shown by the totals for public income and expenditure in Figure 15.3. These show how much is spent by central government on different programmes, either directly, or as grants (rate support grants) to local authorities which are responsible for putting certain spending programmes in matters such as education and housing.

Governments raise money for their expenditure in a number of ways: taxation, by the public paying for certain services, or selling assets such as government shares in BP. The rest is borrowed. The amount of borrowing needed to cover the gap between government income and expenditure is known as the **Public Sector Borrowing Requirement** (PSBR). It is only the government which is entitled to initiate expenditure, and MPs are not allowed to propose any changes in legislation which would increase the amount of money spent. But government proposals for expenditure and taxation must be finally approved by the Commons.

The procedure for Commons approval

Government finance is handled through a number of funds or accounts. The most important of these is the Consolidated Fund which is the government's account with the Bank of England. The revenue from taxes and other money received by the government is paid into this account and most of the money spent by the government comes out of it. There is also a National Loan Fund (NLF) which deals with all government borrowing, including paying interest to those who have lent it money, for example, by buying government stock. The National Insurance Fund (NIF) handles the income and expenditure needed for the national insurance schemes.

Parliament has two ways of giving permission for the government to use these funds. Firstly, there is the annual 'supply' procedure which gives authority for most expenditure from the Consolidated Fund. Secondly, there is more permanent legislation which covers the Government using the NLF, NIF, and the rest of the Consolidated Fund (which includes payments to the EC and judges' salaries).

Annual supply procedure

About 90 per cent of government expenditure from the Consolidated Fund is given through annual Acts of Parliament. These are known as 'Consolidated Fund Acts' (which give permission for overall sums to be spent from the Consolidated Fund), and 'Appropriation Acts' (which give details of how particular services are to be financed). Both relate just to one financial year and they cannot be carried forward to the next year. This means that the annual agreement of parliament is necessary for a wide area of government spending.

Commons control over government finance

Raising money through taxation is dominated by the great set-piece event of the Budget. The details of the Budget are kept secret until they are announced by the Chancellor of the Exchanger. Obviously a great deal of money could be made if people knew in advance what taxes were being changed. Neither the Commons as a whole, nor any of its committees, are, in any sense, consulted before any tax changes are announced and the Budget proposals themselves are incorporated in the Finance Bill which passes in the House with little difficulty.

The Commons does have a bigger part to play in considering government expenditure. In this, the committee system is useful. Departmental committees examine expenditure proposals, as they affect each department. They are concerned with finding out whether policies implied in the expenditure estimates could be carried out more efficiently. Both ministers and civil servants are questioned for their views and arguments.

The overall economic policy of the government, including expenditure plans, can be investigated by the Treasury and Civil Service Committee which often asks detailed, and tough, questions about what the government is doing. But government expenditure involves spending vast sums of money on a wide range of programmes and committees do not have the time to investigate every aspect.

On top of this the government has the final advantage of being able to command a majority in the Commons if its plans for expenditure are threatened. In the last resort, even the sternest criticisms of its economic policy by the Treasury Committee can simply be ignored, so long as the government can count on enough support in the Commons.

In the Commons itself the supply days, mentioned earlier, were never used in recent times to investigate expenditure plans. In effect Commons approval for expenditure simply went through 'on the nod'. One MP, stated quite simply 'The truth and reality is parliament hardly controls public expenditure at all.' It can't be claimed that there has been any real improvement on this, even with the three days now set aside for discussing expenditure.

Value for money?

Although there are weaknesses in the way the commons can investigate government *proposals* for public expenditure, there is greater control over how the money is finally spent.

Central government expenditure is audited by the Controller and Auditor General (C and AG) and a staff of about 600 in the Exchequer and Audit Department. The Department is independent from the government. For voted expenditure, accounts are prepared and have to be submitted by government departments to the C and AG within six months of the end of the year they refer to. In each government department the permanent secretary is also the accounting officer and is responsible for the efficient spending of money. The C and AG makes sure that permission was given for any expenditure.

The C and AG presents reports to the Commons and these are considered by the Public Accounts Committee (PAC). The C and AG and the PAC work closely together. They are not just concerned with 'checking the books' but also with whether value for money has been obtained. The C and AG emphasises those cases which ought to be examined carefully by the PAC.

The PAC is the senior select committee in the Commons. It was set up in 1861, and its chairman is traditionally a member of the opposition, usually with experience of being a Treasury minister. The main witnesses at hearings are the accounting officers of departments and the C and AG. PAC reports are presented to the Commons together with any reply from the government.

The PAC has often highlighted inefficiencies in the way money has been spent. From them we know, for example, that the cost of building the Inland Revenue centre at Bootle trebled because construction was not properly planned, that the administration costs of the Manpower Services Commission went up seventeen times when its budget rose four times. Exposing such cases of inefficiency is one part of the PAC's work, but it goes further, and makes recommendations on avoiding mistakes in the future.

Discussion and essay questions

1. If you were an MP and had the chance to introduce a Private Members Bill, what new Law would you like to see passed? How would you try and get maximum support for your Bill? What problems do you think you would face?

2. What are the main ways for an opposition to criticise the actions of government? How effective do you think they are?

3. What is meant by the 'supremacy of parliament'? How has this changed in recent years? What are the arguments for and against the present position?

4. What is meant by 'delegated legislation'? How does the House of Commons attempt to control its use?

5. Raising and spending money by the government needs the approval of the Commons. Does this mean that the Commons controls government finance?

6. Why were new select committees set up to shadow government departments? What advantages are there for MPs in this new structure? If governments do not have to accept their reports are they bound to be ineffective?

11 Parliament – the House of Lords

The House of Lords is the second chamber of the British Parliament. Over 1,100 peers are entitled to take part in its proceedings, but the average daily attendance is just under 300. At one time it was as important as the Commons but the increasingly stark contrast between an elected Commons and a Lords dominated by hereditary peers, and overwhelmingly Conservative, led to both a loss of power and reform.

Under the 1949 Parliament Act legislation, passed by the Commons, can be delayed by a year, although this does not apply to Bills affecting government finance. In 1958, life peerages were first created which broke the hereditary principle and also allowed women to become members for the first time. Peers were given attendance allowances and travelling expenses but, unlike MPs, no salary. The 1963 Peerage Renunciation Act made it possible to give up hereditary titles for life although they can be resumed by successors. This was particularly important for politicians who wanted to pursue a career in the Commons. Indeed it was the refusal of Anthony Wedgwood Benn to accept the title of Viscount Stansgate when his father died in 1960 which sparked off a campaign to change the law.

The present composition of the Lords is seen in Figure 11.1. It includes the small, but important, group of Law Lords. The Lords is the final court of appeal for the whole of the United Kingdom in civil cases and for England, Wales and Northern Ireland in criminal cases.

The work of the House of Lords

The Lords is part of the legislature, with all Bills passing through it. It has its own political party structure, but the atmosphere of the place is less highly charged than the Commons. Its hours are shorter – it meets for about 36 weeks in the year and normally sittings begin at 2.30 p.m. and end at around 7 p.m. Debates lack the high drama of the Commons – largely because the key political figures in each party are found in the other House and if the government is defeated in the Lords it does not have to consider resigning. Each party has its own leader in the Lords and there is a 'whipping' system to maximise party support. But the Lords also has a considerable number of 'crossbench' peers who do not belong to any party and this helps to make debates less politically predictable.

The Lord Chancellor presides over the Lords but, unlike the Speaker, has clear party political responsibilities. He is a member of

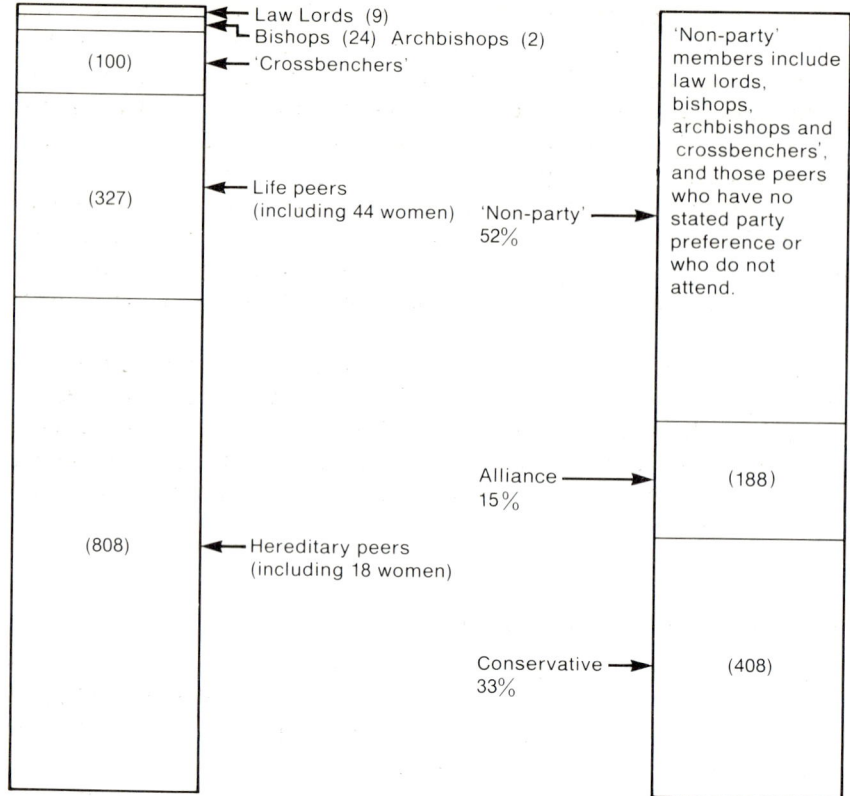

Law Lords (9)
Bishops (24) Archbishops (2)
(100)   'Crossbenchers'

(327)   Life peers
(including 44 women)   'Non-party'
52%

'Non-party' members include law lords, bishops, archbishops and crossbenchers', and those peers who have no stated party preference or who do not attend.

Alliance   (188)
15%

(808)   Hereditary peers
(including 18 women)

Conservative   (408)
33%

Figure 11.1 Membership of the House of Lords.

the Cabinet, can take part in debates from the benches and expresses support for his party and its policies in the country.

The Lords and legislation

Even when Bills have passed through all their stages in the Commons, the Lords does not merely act as a rubber stamp. Even the most careful work by the Commons and its committees can still mean that amendments may be needed to strengthen a Bill or make it clearer. The more complicated the legislation the more likely such changes become and the Lords is a convenient place to do this. Secondly, Bills passing the Commons may have been speeded up by the 'kangaroo' or the 'guillotine' (see Figure 10.2). In other words, clauses in some Bills may not have even been discussed. Again the Lords can be used to remedy this, and possibly point out weaknesses. In both cases the amendments made in the Lords are often accepted by the Commons.

The House of Commons is a very busy place and the Lords can relieve the burden by being the chamber where certain Bills are first introduced. Sometimes they will be Public Bills but the largest group are Private Bills which, for example, affect the powers of local authorities. In these cases the Lords does the bulk of detailed examination so that passing the Commons can be more of a formality and less time-consuming.

The power of the Lords to delay legislation passed by the Commons is more controversial. A one year delay can make a great deal of difference. The Lords still has a built-in Conservative majority and, if the power of delay is used, it is almost certainly against a Labour government. If that government is in its last year of office then the Lords can effectively stop legislation being passed until the next election. This happened in 1949 when the Labour government Bill to nationalise steel was thrown out. The Lords uses this power sparingly because any over-use against an elected government would obviously increase pressure for either a major reform of the Lords or its total abolition.

Those who defend this delaying power argue that a government can be guilty of very hasty decisions on legislation which may need to be delayed in the 'public interest'. But should the Lords or the elected government define the public interest? Clearly an elected government has the strong claim that its idea of public interest has been approved by the voters.

The Lords and the 'great debates'

Like the Commons, the Lords spends part of its time debating issues of current importance. There is a wide range of experience and knowledge among peers, especially as many life peers have reached the top of their professions. So it is not surprising that Lords debates can be very informative. Debates on foreign policy, for example, may include speakers with previous experience in government, the armed forces, the diplomatic service as well as people from university. The same is true of most other areas which are debated. Do these debates really make much difference to public opinion? Certainly some of them are widely reported and they are a way of exerting pressure on government and raising public issues.

The Lords and the EC

Both the Commons and the Lords have set up committees to examine proposals for European legislation and report back to each House. In the Lords the European Communities Committee has a salaried chairman and there are seven specialist sub-committees to look at proposals in different fields and submit reports to the main committee. Each sub-committee is helped by part-time specialist advisers with expert knowledge in their particular field. It hears evidence from civil servants and organisations affected by the European laws.

On average, fifty-one Community proposals are deposited each month although they are sorted out into about a third which need further examination, and the rest which do not. The Lords Committee co-operates closely with the Commons Select Committee on European Legislation to avoid overlap. The sub-committees of both the Commons and Lords main European Committees often hold joint meetings, although they produce separate reports.

The reform of the House of Lords

In spite of its useful work, the very existence of the Lords in the British system of government can be difficult to justify. It hardly seems in keeping with a modern democracy that people should be part of the legislature simply because they were born with the right parents. Without being elected they have the power to delay legislation put forward by the Commons. The political balance of the Lords as a whole is tilted firmly on the side of the Conservatives, whichever party is in government.

On top of this is has been argued that the values represented by the Lords, such as inherited privilege, tradition, and the existence of titles themselves, help to reinforce a class system we could do without.

Abolition or reform?

Plans for major reforms in the membership and power of the Lords have been put forward for over a hundred years but agreement has never been reached on a number of basic issues. The first of these is whether we need a 'second chamber' at all. There is no doubt that the Lords does perform some useful functions as a second chamber. It gives government a chance to re-think and revise legislation after it has left the Commons. It eases pressure on the Commons by taking on most of the detailed work for Bills, especially Private Bills, which are not politically controversial. Membership of the EC, with the need to check carefully on proposals affecting Britain, has given the Lords an extra and important task. On the other hand, some claim that we could do without a second chamber. Some countries, such as Sweden, manage perfectly well with a single chamber.

Even if a second chamber is desirable, there is another more difficult issue: how should its members be chosen? If members of a new House of Lords (perhaps with a new name such as Senate) were directly elected then two results might follow. Firstly, one party might have a majority in the Commons and form a government, with another having a majority in the Lords. This could happen if the Lords were elected on a regional basis or by using a different voting system from the Commons. Secondly, the Lords would be in a much stronger position to claim that they represent the views of the people. The power of the Commons could be weakened with increased tension between the two houses. A solution to this difficulty might be to give a guaranteed majority in the Lords to whichever party formed the government. This is opposed by those who fear that the Lords would merely become a 'rubber stamp' for Common legislation.

Most proposals for reforming the Lords have argued against having any hereditary element. But what about the life peers who bring valuable expertise into the work of the Lords? Should they have a place in a new structure?

The final issue concerns the power of a reformed Lords. Some proposals have suggested that delaying powers should be increased, others that they should be reduced. The answer is bound to be related to the composition of the Lords. If it were elected it would have a stronger claim to longer delaying powers because it would represent the views of voters. Some MPs dislike this idea as a threat to the power of the government, especially over controversial legislation.

With such important questions and so many different proposals for reform, it is hardly surprising that little has been done and it is essential that reform of the Lords is agreed between the major parties. Otherwise a new second chamber might become a political football, with its membership and power being continually altered as governments change.

Discussion and essay questions

1. What are the advantages in having life peers in the House of Lords? What kinds of people would you like to see appointed as life peers?

2. Discuss ways in which a second chamber could be elected, listing the advantages and disadvantages of each method.

3. How has the power, work and membership of the Lords changed since 1945?

4. What arguments would you put forward in favour of (a) keeping the House of Lords as it is, (b) abolishing it?

5. Why do you think we still have a House of Lords in the 1980s?

Part Five: POLITICAL COMMUNICATION

12 Pressure groups

The growth of government in the last 100 years, and the extra range of responsibilities it has taken on, led to the emergence of two groups – political parties and pressure groups. What is the difference between them? Political parties seek public office by fighting elections and appealing to a wide range of different interests. In order to win political power they must develop policies which cover the whole range of government responsibilities and appeal to a wide range of different interests. Pressure groups have more limited aims. They are concerned with a much narrower range of issues, or even one issue, and try to *influence* decision makers, especially governments.

How do national pressure groups operate?

Figure 12.2 summarises the main activities of pressure groups. The first target must be the government itself because it is at the centre of political power. Here pressure groups try to achieve three major objectives. Firstly they need information about government attitudes towards those areas of policy which affect them. Secondly they would like the goodwill of decision makers including ministers and civil servants. This goodwill can be important in deciding how far the government will consult with a pressure group in the future. Thirdly they hope to influence government thinking and so help to shape government policy.

The relationship is two-way because governments also benefit from contact with pressure groups. First, governments get practical information about how well policies are working. Pressure groups collect their own statistics and information from members. Secondly, pressure groups may be consulted before policies are decided. Farming policy benefits from a close working relationship between the Ministry of Agriculture and the National Farmers Union (NFU), although of

Protective or defensive groups	
Examples Trade unions, CBI (Confederation of British Industry), National Farmers Union, British Medical Association AA, RAC.	Protect a particular interest. Defining the interests of their members can mean that these groups support policies which are apparently outside their more obvious areas of concern. Unions, for example may support *causes* such as CND
Promotional or cause groups	
Examples CND National Council for Civil Liberties, Anti-Apartheid Movements, Viewers and Listeners Assoc., Welsh Language Society.	Promote a cause or a set of beliefs.
National groups	
Examples See all the above organisations.	Protect or promote a cause or an interest of national concern.
Local groups	
Examples Residents associations, Civic associations, Local environmental groups, Protection societies	Most of the pressure groups above will have local branches. But many pressure groups exist only at a local or regional level. They can be protective (e.g. opposing the building of an airport/nuclear reactor) or promotional (e.g. local festival society)
Single issue groups	
Examples 'Troops Out' movement of Northern Ireland, 'Save the Whale' campaign.	At both national and local level there is a distinction between permanent groups, and temporary groups such as these, which are often disbanded when their cause is won or lost.

Note: There is more than one way of categorising any pressure group, as the example here shows: CND/cause/national and local/single issue.

Figure 12.1 Types of pressure groups.

Whitehall	
Representatives on 'official' committees; contact with civil servants and ministers — through meetings, letters, phonecalls, lunches etc.	Used by groups accepted as important and useful to government. Most valuable time for pressure groups is *before* the government makes a decision.
Westminister	
Delegations to see ministers or 'lobby' MPs; attempts to gain the support of particular MPs.	Used by groups which may have little direct contact with government (and also by important groups if they are not successful with Whitehall). Many groups will already have MPs as members or supporters (e.g. CND).
Political parties in opposition	
	Pressure groups hope that the main opposition party will commit itself to pressure group aims. Only used when there is likely to be existing sympathy in party and can reduce support in other parties.
Public campaigns	
Includes press advertising, demonstrations, marches, sit-ins, petitions, strikes.	Used by groups which would otherwise have difficulty in attracting the attention of the government (and also by more powerful groups to reinforce other methods).

Figure 12.2 Methods used by national pressure groups.

Lobbying government. In 1984 the Chancellor of the Exchequer put VAT on takeaway food. These protesters are outside the Chancellor's house in Downing Street but their efforts had no effect.

course the government does not have to accept the views expressed by NFU leaders.

Consultation can take different forms. For example, government departments have a range of advisory committees which bring together ministers, civil servants and pressure group leaders so that views can be exchanged. Thirdly, pressure groups can help in carrying out policies. This is true, for example, in agriculture. Lastly, a government hopes for support from pressure groups. An example of this was the agreement reached between the Labour government and the trade unions in the mid-1970s, known as 'the social contract'. In return for certain concessions over policy by the government, union leaders agreed to wage restraint.

Clearly some pressure groups have access to government, and are actively welcomed into Whitehall, whereas others do not. Trade unions and employers meet regularly with government ministers in bodies such as the National Economic Development Council to discuss economic policy. But the CND (Campaign for Nuclear Disarmament) does not have regular meetings with the Ministry of Defence!

In addition to the formal (and open) types of contact between pressure groups and government there are a number of informal contacts. As a senior manager of a large company once put it, 'Whitehall is only two tube stations away; we have a permanent secretary to lunch from time to time.'

Another 'target' for pressure groups is parliament. It may not make policy but having MPs on your side can be a help in putting pressure on government as well as increasing publicity. Richard Crossman described the relationship of MPs and pressure groups in the following way:

> A considerable number of MPs on both sides of the Commons act as paid political agents of outside bodies . . . lobbying ministers on their behalf, and sometimes, when they rise to speak, reading aloud almost verbatim [word for word] the brief they have received from the body which retains their services.

There is nothing necessarily sinister in this. Parliament, as a national forum, ought to be a place where such arguments are heard. Yet MPs are not expected to be 'controlled' by outside interests. The House of Commons is always hostile towards any attempt to threaten MPs who do not support the 'line' of any outside group they may be associated with. An example of this would be a Labour MP who is sponsored by a trade union but who does not agree with union policy on an issue. But with 650 MPs the chances are that the widest possible range of pressure groups will be able to find 'friends' in parliament.

Another method used by pressure groups is to gain support within the main opposition party. The ideal position is, of course, to get the party to commit itself to specific policies which it will carry out if it wins power. Naturally the political parties often find themselves closer to some pressure groups than others. CND, for example, has more support in the Labour Party than the Conservative Party. The reverse is true of the Institute of Directors.

Pressure groups carry out public campaigns and use a variety of tactics, such as demonstrations, marches and petitions, to increase support and give their arguments the widest possible publicity. But it does not follow that the most effective pressure groups are the noisiest and most visible. Some groups, such as unions have traditionally held marches but also have access to Whitehall. But many other groups, lacking such access, have only the public campaign to show the strength of their feelings. Of course in time they hope to gain more powerful friends.

What makes a pressure group successful?

Why is it that some pressure groups are more powerful than others? A pressure group, if it is to be influential, must have access to decision makers whether at local or national level. This depends, to a great extent, on the importance of the pressure group to the decision makers themselves. As we have seen some pressure groups have a close relationship with government and *both* sides benefit. Such groups can put their case directly. The resources of a group can also be important.

A CND demonstration in 1981. CND puts great stress on public demonstrations with several marches against Cruise missiles in 1983.

A pressure group is likely to be more effective if it can afford a large staff, facilities for research, provide briefings, advertise in the press, hold seminars, conferences and public meetings. But in the end, the real power can only be to persuade and governments face many different pressure groups, all of which can't get their own way.

Do pressure groups make the political system more democratic?

Pressure groups provide a wide range of opportunities for people to participate in politics. A group of people who get together to press for a zebra crossing in a road may not regard themselves as being political, but they are. They are expressing a demand that certain decisions should be made about how a local authority spends its money and they are trying to influence decision makers. In doing this, pressure groups increase the number of 'access points' into the political system. They are a way of expressing, or transmitting, people's political demands. Without them, governments would find it more difficult to know which demands existed and people could feel frustrated and divorced from the political system as a result. It follows that pressure groups help to develop support for the system by helping to turn demands into action.

Pressure groups also act as a check on the activities of government. In most areas of government policy there are pressure groups which provide criticisms and alternative policies. The Child Poverty Action Group, for example, continually measures government policy against the needs of poor families and gives detailed evidence where it affects them badly or does not do enough. In this work, pressure groups are part of the continual process of educating people about political issues. The Child Poverty Action Group itself was formed in the late 1950s, largely because there was widespread ignorance, within government as well as generally, about the extent of poverty in Britain and the number of families who were living below the poverty line. In other words they helped to *identify* an important social and political issue.

But pressure groups don't necessarily make the different sections of society more equal. Groups with contacts, wealth or power may get a better hearing than others equally deserving. Engineers and miners, for example, are well organised and may be prepared to use their considerable industrial power. Nurses are weaker, partly because they may be reluctant to strike. Some groups such as the unemployed are hardly organised at all.

A further problem is that the views of a pressure group may reflect the opinions of its leaders rather than its members it claims to represent. An opinion poll in 1980 (*The Sunday Times* 31.8.80) showed, for example, that the majority of trade unionists believed that the police should have the power to stop mass picketing, that the closed shop (where everyone in a work place must belong to a trade union) is a threat to individual liberty and even that the unions should not be so closely linked to the Labour Party. They also believed that strikes should only be called after a secret ballot. These members' views ran completely against those of virtually all union leaders and were not the official policies of unions. They illustrated some important differences between union activists who attend meetings and help to formulate policy, and ordinary members.

Leaders of pressure groups can protect themselves from criticism by their members in a number of ways. They control the running of their organisation, they can put out appeals for unity or loyalty and label opponents as 'trouble makers'. Although pressure groups may be essential to democracy, they may not always be very democratically organised.

Trade unions as a pressure group

Trade unions are among the most powerful of the protective pressure groups in Britain. But what is the basis of their power?

Firstly, since 1945, productivity, inflation, wage levels, employment, and so on have been key problems for all governments. These are of central importance to trade unions as well so that governments and unions are both vitally concerned with the attitudes and policies of each other on such issues. There are over 100 government advisory committees where trade unionists, civil servants and government ministers can meet.

Secondly, the union movement has a large membership of over 13 million and represents more than 55 per cent of the workforce – a

Number of members	Number of unions	Total membership (000's)	% of total number of unions	% of total membership of all unions
250,000	11	7,555	2.6	62.0
100,000	14	2,175	3.3	17.9
50,000	14	978	3.3	8.0
25,000	17	617	4.1	5.1
15,000	18	354	4.3	2.9
10,000	4	54	1.0	0.4
5,000	25	167	5.9	1.4
2,500	37	132	8.8	1.1
1,000	54	86	12.8	0.7
500	45	32	10.7	0.3
100	113	28	26.8	0.2
less than 100	69	4	16.4	0.0
Total	421	12,182		

It is common enough to talk of trade unions, or the trade union movement, but this can hide the wide differences which exist between unions themselves. The majority of trade unionists belong to one of the top eleven with memberships of over 250,000. The Transport and General Workers Unions (T and GWU) is the largest at 1.88 million members (1980). Other unions are much smaller. Members of the T and GWU are found in many different types of work ranging from lorry drivers to car workers. Other unions are industrial and found in only one type of activity, for example the National Union of Mineworkers (NUM). In mining there is a closed shop so that the NUM has 100 per cent of its potential membership, but this is not true of other types of work – for example agriculture. The National Union of Agricultural and Allied Workers (NUAAW) had only 50 per cent of its potential membership (1980) because workers on the land do not have to belong to a union. Unlike mining where workers are geographically concentrated and have a long history of union loyalty, agricultural workers may work alone or in only small groups – and are widely scattered throughout the country. This weakened the NUAAW's ability to call for industrial action. One way of strengthening the position of such workers is to join a more powerful union. In 1982 the NUAAW as a whole did this and merged with the T and GWU. In recent years unions have expanded considerably among white collar workers, for example the National Association of Local Government Officers (NALGO), and they now form 31 per cent of the total of all trade unionists – skilled workers account for 41 per cent and semi-skilled and unskilled 28 per cent

Figure 12.3 The structure of trade unions membership (end 1981).

higher percentage than any union movement in Western Europe or North America. Many types of work are totally organised and union leaders are highly skilled at negotiating with management on behalf of their members. Such skills are useful for trade unions in presenting their arguments to a wider public, and to government itself. Backing this up are, in many cases, the considerable financial resources of unions which, as a last resort, are available to support industrial action.

Thirdly, there may be a gulf on some issues between leaders and members but loyalty to the union is still a powerful force.

Fourthly, unions have a place, at all levels, in the structure of the Labour Party. Whenever Labour are in power, with union members and sympathisers holding office, trade unions have a close relationship with government.

Fifthly, unions have, and are prepared to use, their industrial power. The strike can now be a more far-reaching weapon than in the past

Demonstration during the miners strike in 1984. In this example it was the Trade Union Congress which was being lobbied for support against pit closures.

because of the way industry has become more integrated and techno-
logically based. Strikers in the electricity and gas industries, lorry
drivers (especially oil) can have a rapid impact on the economy. Strikes
in one industry, or even in part of an industry, can soon affect others.
Car firms, for example, may only carry a couple of days' supplies of
components so that a strike affecting one key car component could
quickly bring the whole car firm to a halt.

However, the unions' strength needs to be balanced by other factors.
To begin with it would be wrong to assume that they apply to all trade
unions. Some trades are hardly unionised at all and others such as the
retail trade, have a much smaller percentage of union members than
'closed shop' industries such as mining. Equally there is no doubt that
calls for industrial action over wages, for example, have met a less
enthusiastic response in recent years because of unemployment.
Another result of unemployment has been a fall in union membership
and a consequent loss of funds. And, although there was general
hostility in the early 1970s among unionists to attempts to control a
union's activity by law, the same determination was not shown ten
years later. On top of this the changing pattern of industrial development has meant that the older industries, such as railways, mining,
steel, where unions had a tradition of strength and militancy, are
declining. In newer industries, for example electronics, union activity
tends to be weaker. Lastly, the Conservative government since 1979
have tried more than previous governments to keep unions at arms
length. There is nothing like the close relationship which unions
normally enjoy with Labour governments – nor even the kind of
working partnership which they have had with previous Conservative
governments.

Case study of pressure group activity: the Vale of Belvoir

The Vale of Belvoir (pronounced 'Beeva') is in the north east of
Leicestershire. It is an important farming area and is also a popular
place for day trippers – especially in the summer. In August 1973, the
National Coal Board (NCB) announced that they were sinking bore
holes in the Vale to look for coal. In July 1976 the results of this survey
were published. The Vale had one of the largest coal reserves in
Europe, over 500 million tons which was equal, in energy terms, to the
largest oil field in the North Sea. The next year, 1977, the NCB
recommended developing three mines and in 1978 submitted planning
applications.

It is common enough to talk of an 'energy crisis' but Britain is
fortunate in having large coal reserves and North Sea oil. However,
many coal mines are reaching the end of their life and new coalfields
will be needed to replace them and help to find new work for miners.
North Sea oil will begin to run out towards the end of the century. It

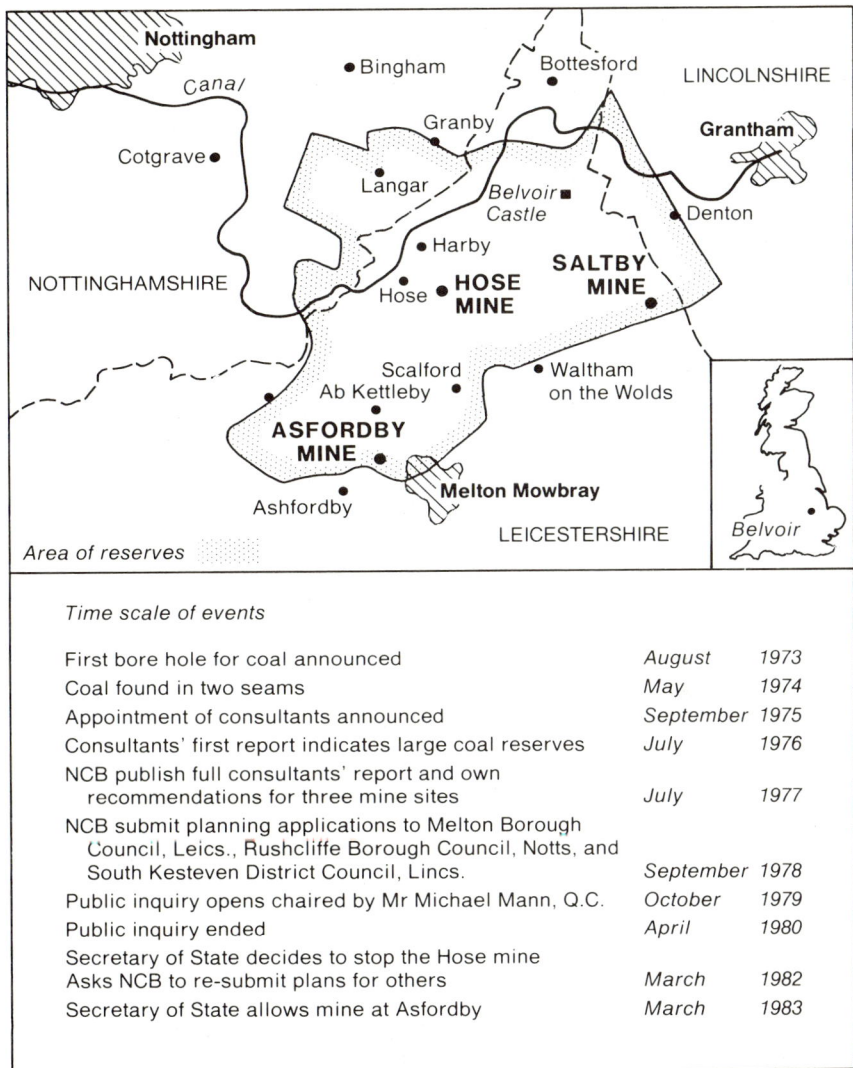

Figure 12.4 The Vale of Belvoir.

can be argued that the 'national interest' must mean that areas like the Vale should be opened up to coal mining. But coal mining is not easy to hide. New mine buildings, slag heaps, a greater volume of traffic on the roads, an influx of 2,500 miners and their families, possible damage to drainage pipes on agricultural land, are some of the likely consequences of mining in the Vale. Modern mines are not as damaging to the environment as those built in the past and the NCB has become very skilled at landscaping – especially when mining is finished. But if the mines were opened, the Vale could be a mining area for as long as seventy years. Even though most people might accept that mining in the Vale was in the national interest it is quite a different matter for those who live in the area affected. What was their response?

At first the people in the Vale were simply angry and there were rather disorganised protests. They then formed groups to give these protests some shape. The Vale of Belvoir Protection Society was established and drew up a petition against mining which attracted 30,000 signatures. Thirty parish councils also came together to co-ordinate opposition. Local MPs, raised the matter in parliament, with ministers and with the NCB. A fighting fund was started with a target of £100,000. However, even among people in the Vale, there was not total opposition to mining. Members of the Agricultural Workers Union saw the job opportunities which mining would bring either as a chance to be employed by the NCB or as a way of forcing up wages on the land. Shopkeepers and other traders could see the advantages of a large increase in customers. Naturally both the NCB and the National Union of Mineworkers (NUM) were in favour of the project.

Matters reached a head in October 1979 when a public inquiry opened to consider whether mining should take place. However, the inquiry went beyond the issue of mining in the Vale and became involved with the whole question of Britain's energy needs. Those against mining argued that coal from the Vale was not needed at the time. They were prepared to accept that, if it could be shown that Britain needed the coal, mining should be allowed. The inquiry closed in April 1980. Like all public inquiries of this sort the minister responsible has the final say. In this case it was the Secretary of State for the Environment, and he announced his decision in March 1982. He refused to allow mining at Hose in the middle of the Vale, and asked the NCB to re-submit plans for the rest. He argued that more attention needed to be paid to environmental issues such as spoil heaps. Then in March 1983, he lifted his ban on mining at Asfordby which had been imposed after Leicestershire County Council accepted plans for mining there in October 1982.

The protesters in the Vale were hard-working and skilled in arguing their case both locally and nationally; and they had a number of advantages. They were defending the interests of people with the education, and the money, to support a powerful campaign. Pressure groups such as the Vale of Belvoir Protection Society usually disappear when such single issues as mining are decided but, in this case, it may not happen. Even though mining is coming to the Vale, the Society could stay active to make sure that NCB promises about limiting environmental damage are kept.

The case study of the Vale of Belvoir illustrates how people can be drawn into political activity through a pressure group. In the Vale the issue was mining but, in other areas, it could be the building of a power station, a factory, an airport, a prison, or a site for gypsies.

Pressure groups also raise the question of what we mean by the 'national interest' – and how we decide between the national interest and the interest of groups within Britain. They may not always be the same. A government can claim that it is elected to office and that it has the right to decide the national interest. But what if it acts in a way which is seen to threaten the interests of individuals and groups? Trade unions have been consistently hostile towards attempts by governments to control their activities; they argue that government controls restrict the rights of each and every trade union member in general negotiations with employers. But how far should opposition be taken? Are unions trying to 'run the country' if they use traditional methods of industrial action against governments – or simply ignore the law? Would the people of the Vale be justified in lying down in front of bulldozers? Indeed, what happens if any pressure group, feeling deeply about an issue, uses disruptive tactics? Pressure group activity is also concerned with the way politics is conducted.

Discussion and essay questions

1. What is the difference between political parties and pressure groups? In what ways do parties and pressure groups help each other to get what they want?
2. Why is it argued that the noisiest pressure groups are the least effective?
3. If you were national organiser for a new pressure group trying to raise the school-leaving age to 18, how would you plan your campaign – assuming that you have reasonable financial support? How would your campaign be different if you were pressing for an increase in old age pensions?
4. Devise a leaflet or poster or newspaper advertisement for a pressure group you are in favour of.
5. Why are some pressure groups more powerful than others?
6. 'Trade unions are too powerful.' 'Trade unions are an essential part of the political system.' Outline the main arguments which might be used to justify these statements. Are the statements contradictory?
7. Have trade unions a right to be consulted more than other pressure groups?
8. Do you think that the people in the Vale of Belvoir would be justified in opposing mining if the government said mining in the Vale was in the national interest?

13 Politics and the media

The importance of the media

News, information and entertainment all come to us through a medium. The medium might be a book, a speech or even a conversation but the word – in its plural form: *media* – has become used as a general term for radio, television and the newspapers. It is through the media that we get a great deal of our information about politics – the work of pressure groups, political parties, our own and foreign governments, and so on.

Information is not just a factual account of political events. In Britain the media report the variety of views involved in political disagreements, including the speeches of opposition politicians in parliament, the activities of pressure groups, warfare both between (and within) political parties, the actions of governments and criticism of these actions. This last point is particularly important. The political information we get through the media does not depend on what the government wants to tell us. Because of the absence of government control over the media we can talk about a 'free press' and, less usually, a 'free television'.

The consequences of such control can be illustrated by looking at the experience of other countries. During the Polish crisis in the winter of 1981–82 for example, when the military took over power and suppressed the free trade union, Solidarity, all official information reaching the Poles was heavily controlled. They were told what the military government wanted them to know about events in Poland, and no more. For alternative facts and interpretation of events the Poles had to rely on word of mouth, the 'underground' press, or listen to foreign broadcasts such as the BBC.

However, the media go beyond reporting events and highlighting political controversy. Newspapers and television programmes often campaign actively on behalf of individuals and groups. *The Sunday Times*, for example, was at the centre of the campaign to help those children born with defects caused by the Thalidomide drug prescribed to their mothers when pregnant. Such investigative journalism in the press or on programmes such as Panorama, World in Action and T.V. Eye helps to make government accountable by a constant process of checking, criticising and suggesting alternatives.

These actions of journalists, although they are vital in making us aware of issues, must not be confused with the power to make decisions. It may be that a government or a large private company or a nationalised industry tries to put right a fault exposed by journalists.

But the media have no power to do this themselves. And the media, themselves often raise issues, but do not follow them through after the story has gone 'cold' and become less 'newsworthy'.

The selection of news

A huge volume of news descends on newspaper offices and television or radio newsrooms and it is quite impossible to expect them to be able to transmit all this information to us. There has to be some process of selection and filtering out the information which is seen as important. This is the job of various editors and sub-editors who might be thought of as 'gatekeepers'. In all newsrooms there are individuals who open the gate for some items, and close it firmly against others. In doing this they are helping to shape *our* ideas about what is important and what is not. Sometimes there can be widespread agreement about major stories, in others none at all.

What factors help to determine 'news'? One is the attitude that gatekeepers have about the interests of their readers or viewers. 'Pop Star Goes Bankrupt' may reach the front page of *The Sun* newspaper but is unlikely to be a major story in *The Times*! Foreign news is often very scarce in the popular press, with the exception perhaps of bizarre stories which may help to confirm our prejudices about foreigners.

Clearly if we rely on the media to decide such questions as: What is news? What is politically important? Our own answers to these questions can depend on which papers we read and which television programmes we watch.

The press

A visit to any large bookstall shows that there is a huge variety of papers and journals available for us to buy. Many of them will be concerned, at least partly, with political issues and, in total, a wide range of political views are represented. The circulation figures of the more political journals are not large but they can be influential within political groups. The *New Statesman*, for example, has been a major channel for communicating ideas within the Labour Party for many years. Its importance depends on the extent to which influential people on the Left read it, rather than on a mass circulation.

But it is the national daily and Sunday papers which dominate the world of the press. Over 14 million copies of the main national papers are bought each weekday and read by around 41 million. The circulation of Sunday papers is around 18 million with a readership of over 50 million. These figures are slightly deceptive because people may buy or see more than one newspaper, but they illustrate the extent of interest in the national press. Unlike many other countries, Britain's daily reading is still dominated by national papers which can be bought

National dailies	Controlled by	Readership (1985) (Millions)	Average circulation (Millions)	Party supported in 1983 election
Daily Express	United Newspapers plc	4.9	1.9	Con
Daily Mail	Associated Newspapers Ltd.	5.0	1.8	Con
Daily Mirror	Mirror Group	9.9	3.3	Lab
Daily Star	United Newspapers plc	4.4	1.4	Con
Morning Star	People's Press Printing Society	(not avail.)	0.03	Com/Lab
The Sun	News International Ltd.	11.6	4.0	Con
Daily Telegraph	The Daily Telegraph Ltd.	2.8	1.2	Con
Financial Times	Pearson plc	0.7	0.2	Con
The Guardian	Guardian & Manchester Evening News Ltd.	1.4	0.5	All/Lab
The Times	News International Ltd.	1.2	0.5	Con
National Sunday Papers				
News of the World	News International Ltd.	12.8	4.8	Con
Sunday People	Mirror Group	9.2	3.0	Lab
Sunday Express	United Newspapers plc	6.7	2.4	Con
Sunday Mirror	Mirror Group	10.7	3.2	Lab
Observer	Atlantic Richfield Co. and Observer Trust	2.2	0.7	All/Lab
Sunday Times	News International Ltd.	3.8	1.3	Con
Sunday Telegraph	The Daily Telegraph Ltd.	2.3	0.7	Con

(Readership figures from JICNAR for 1985)

Figure 13.1 National, daily and Sunday newspapers.

anywhere in the country and carry very little regional news. This appears mostly in evening papers and a few regional dailies such as the *Western Mail* in South Wales.

The circulation and readership of individual newspapers varies considerably from the so called 'popular' papers with a mass following (*Sun, Mirror, Express, Mail*) to the 'quality' papers (The *Daily Telegraph, Guardian, Times*). As with the *New Statesman* mentioned earlier, the influence of a newspaper may not depend on high circulation figures but rather on the type of person who reads it. This point is made in *The Times* advertising slogan 'Top people take The Times'.

It was argued earlier that the British press is free, in the sense that it is not directly controlled by government. But newspapers exist largely to entertain their readers and to make a profit. They are business enterprises with the same problems of costs which face all companies in private industry. Like companies, they can be bought or taken over. Many national newspapers have been identified with their owners. Early owners such as Lord Beaverbrook and Lorth Rothermere saw them as part business and part vehicle for propaganda. They decided the political character of their paper, including which party and policies to support. It used to be said of the *Daily Express*, for example, that journalists there had complete freedom to agree with Lord Beaverbrook.

Lord Matthews (former owner of Daily and Sunday Express, Daily Star) and Rupert Murdoch (Sun, Times, Sunday Times, News of the World) at one time controlled newspapers with a readership of over 40 million. They are both staunch supporters of the Conservative Party.

In the last few years other tycoons have bought newspapers and the power to decide their policies: people like Rupert Murdoch (*The Sun, News of the World*) and Lord Matthews (*Daily* and *Sunday Express, Daily Star*). Murdoch also bought *The Times* but on the understanding that he would not decide editorial policy. However, in 1982 he forced the editor, Harold Evans, to resign – apparently because he disliked the 'line' the paper was following. Private ownership of the press does not always mean that owners supervise the paper from day to day. But in the end, ownership can mean control.

A further consequence of newspapers being companies has been that those which could not make a profit from sales and advertising have gone out of business. Smaller circulation papers such as *The Guardian* or the *Sunday Times* can attract 'quality' advertising and readers willing to pay a relatively high price. But those aiming at a mass circulation can be struggling financially even with a circulation of hundreds of thousands because there is fierce competition in this part of the market. In the past twenty years, many have gone out of business and that means less variety of political information and opinion.

The political bias of the press

Figure 13.1 shows how the main national newspapers advised their readers to vote in the 1983 general election. Most papers, however, went well beyond merely giving advice and some threw all their resources on the side of either the Conservative or the Labour parties. Headlines, choice of news stories, photographs, cartoons were all used in support of their case with no pretence at impartiality – a point illustrated in Figure 13.2. In this election, the bulk of the press supported the Conservative Party with only the *Mirror* and the *Sunday People*, of the mass circulation papers, on the side of Labour. This pattern has been true of Fleet Street for many years. The question really is whether

	Sun	Mail	Express	Mirror	Total column inches
Pro-Tory	282	332	234	–	848
Anti-Tory	–	–	–	325	325
Pro-Labour	41	–	23	221	285
Anti-Labour	429	514	302	–	1245
Neutral	222	276	185	171	854

This kind of judgement is bound to be subjective but complimentary adjectives and phrases, and the reverse, are not difficult to spot. (*New Statesman*, 4.5.79)

Figure 13.2 Press coverage of the 1979 election – how some newspapers used their column inches.

the pro-Conservative bias of the press matters; here the evidence is none too clear.

First of all, the majority of readers are already supporters of the party their newspaper favours. In 1979, for example, 64 per cent of *Express* readers, 68 per cent of *Mail* readers and 62 per cent of *Mirror* readers voted for the party supported by their paper. From that it appears that people tend to choose a paper which reflects political values and attitudes they *already* hold. Yet an important minority of readers still voted for the party that their paper did not support. The major exception in both surveys was the *Sun*. In 1979 it was vigorously pro-Conservative and yet 50 per cent of its readers voted Labour and only 38 per cent Conservative. In 1983, the vast majority of newspaper readers were found to be well aware of the political stance of their paper – when it had one – although 20 per cent of *Sun* readers got the political stance of their paper wrong.

Secondly, in spite of the pro-Conservative bias, the fact is that the two parties won the same number of elections between 1945 and 1983. Of course, this is not conclusive evidence because election victories come about for a range of reasons and Labour might claim that they could have won even more. But it does show that a Conservative dominated press is not necessarily a critical factor in deciding elections. According to Derek Jameson, editor of the *Daily Express* during the 1979 election: 'mercifully for the democracy of a healthy nation, the press, while it is biased towards the Conservatives, has had no real influence on the British public at large'. (Granada Schools programme, *A Free Press*).

Thirdly, the press is no longer as important as it was in terms of giving us political information. Television has come to dominate the way parties present their case at election time and this has, for example, compensated for the pro-Conservative bias of the press. This is equally true between elections and not just for views about political parties. The size of the audience, and the full range of television programmes from news to investigations of political issues, interviews, as well as party political broadcasts, all make television perhaps the most significant source of political information and influence.

But is there a danger of underestimating the influence of the press? The Left of the Labour Party argues that its views are rarely given fair coverage, even in pro-Labour papers. The *Daily Mirror* for example, which generally supports Labour, usually agrees with the centre right-wing of the party. And is it really likely that the praise of Mrs Thatcher and the Conservative Party by the *Sun*, the *Mail*, the *Express* and the *Telegraph* in the 1979 or 1983 elections had no effect? Given that elections can be decided, in marginal seats, by fairly small numbers of voters, the press can be influential in increasing the determination of wavering Conservatives to go out and vote.

The link between the political bias of the press and the ownership of newspapers is clear. But as the number of national newspapers declines and limits the range of political views, the way that their policies can be decided by a few people becomes a more important issue.

Television

As Figure 13.3 shows, the British are avid television watchers. Almost every family has a television set, and through it we get most of our entertainment. Many thousands of school children spend more time in a week watching television than they do in the classroom and the focus of most sitting-rooms is the box in the corner. The 'television personality' is almost as familiar as a close friend and will often have a huge personal following. For long-running serials like Crossroads and Coronation Street, audiences often rise to well over ten million, but they can be six or seven million for serious programmes, documentaries and the news. What effect does this have on politics?

First, the ability of television to reach a mass audience is its chief attraction for politicians, who can talk to, and be seen by, more people in one broadcast than in a lifetime of public meetings. But we view programmes in the relative calm of our own houses and one effect of television has been to change the way politics is presented to us. Television does not lend itself to the dramatic public speaker but to a more relaxed, conversational style of talking. Calm, sweet reasonableness are the qualities aimed at, for example, in party political broadcasts and political interviews.

Secondly, television has come to dominate the way parties and leaders fight general elections. It was shown in Chapter 4 that maximum exposure on television, quite apart from the party election broadcasts, is considered very important by party managers. Speeches and press conferences are timed, so that extracts can be shown on television news, and 'events' are deliberately staged for the camera.

Elections highlight a third effect of television. The Conservative bias of the press is countered by the access that the Labour and Alliance parties have to television. It also enables all parties to put their case as they would like. In party political broadcasts we can hear and see politicians arguing their point of view without it being filtered by anyone.

A fourth effect of television is more controversial. Programmes on politics, especially during elections, can be presented in a way similar to popular entertainment, with the emphasis on personalities. Of course, people can be presented more dramatically than policies, but should politics be reduced to a head-on confrontation between political leaders? This kind of criticism is not, however limited to television because the popular press does the same. And party battles have always been concerned, at least in part, with the view we have about politicians. Are they honest? Do we trust them? Do we like them? Policies may be rejected because we do not like the people putting them forward. What television has done, rightly or wrongly, is probably to strengthen our belief that we can answer such questions more accurately by seeing politicians on television. The concentration on leaders of the main parties has strengthened the 'presidential-style' of elections; the choice is then about which prime minister we want rather than which party and which policies.

Age group	Average weekly hours viewed (*Feb 1980*)
5–15	22.5
15–19	16
20–29	23
30–49	17.5
50–64	19
65+	22

(*Social Trends*, 1981)

Figure 13.3 The viewing public.

Lastly, there is no doubt that television has expanded our sources of political information, though some might argue that the visual presentation of politics seems more trivial than the written word. For example, a television news programme cannot carry the same volume of news as a paper like *The Guardian*. However, programme makers have become highly skilled in the way they present even complex issues; the full range of programmes available on BBC and ITV, now offer us considerable opportunities to gain access to a great deal of political knowledge.

Television and political bias

The Charters which set up both the BBC and ITV require them to be politically impartial and, unlike the press, they are forbidden to have any particular editorial line. They are able to produce programmes concerned with political controversy but they cannot emphasise any political opinion of their own. They are expected to be concerned, as far as possible, with maintaining a political balance. In addition, ITV, which raises its money largely through advertising, cannot allow political organisations to buy time for commercials.

But television offers a great range of programmes which could be described as 'political' and it is quite impossible to arrive at 'political balance' in every single one. The notion of balance has to be taken over a longer term. An in-depth profile of the prime minister, followed by an interview, does not need the same immediate treatment of the leader of the opposition to maintain balance. However, if the leader of the opposition never appeared on television then the existence of balance would rightly be questioned. The same applies to documentaries, drama productions, special reports, and so on.

Bias always depends on a point of view. In 1982 and 1983 many programmes examined the development of the Liberal and Social Democrat Alliance. Was this part of a 'plot' to gain public sympathy or a proper examination of an important new feature of British politics? At the same time TV gave a lot of attention to deep divisions in the Labour Party. Was it done by anti-Labour producers or was this part of the public's right to know? Criticisms of the general political bias of television sometimes appear to be based on the feeling that not enough emphasis is given to the bias which people prefer to see!

Bias can be at a more unconscious level, and there have been criticisms especially of the way news is selected and presented. News programmes are part information and part entertainment, as both the BBC and ITV want high viewing figures for their news programmes. And, of course, they face the problem of selection. Television is a visual medium and the existence of film to go with a story is bound to be a consideration in deciding whether to run it, and for how many minutes. There are also technical factors to consider. BBC and ITV have easy access to news from North America and Europe by satellite, but not from other parts of the world. Pictures from Asia or South America take longer to arrive and, by the time they do, the news story may be considered too old.

Violence flared on the picket line at Tilmanstone Colliery, Kent when miners returned to work during the 1984 coal strike. Did television news concentrate on peaceful picketing or the rarer violent clashes?

Another problem is language. The use of words such as 'terrorist' (freedom fighter?), 'moderate' (good?), 'extremist' (bad?) have been criticised because of the hidden messages they contain. The Glasgow Media Group has pointed out that workers are usually said to 'threaten' or 'demand' while employers and governments 'offer'. During strikes, workers are frequently filmed in outdoor meetings which can be noisy and turbulent, whereas management is interviewed in the calm of an office. In defence of television news producers it must be said that they have become very much aware of such issues, no doubt partly as a result of these criticisms. As Bob Hunter, one of the daily editors at ITN, has argued, 'Today's terrorist can be tomorrow's prime minister.' (Granada Schools programme, *What's News*'.)

The media, government and the law

Nearly two hundred years ago Samuel Taylor Coleridge wrote, 'In an

enslaved state, the Rulers form and supply the opinions of the people.'
For all the criticisms which can be levelled at the press and television
the fact is that they help to keep us from slavery by giving us access
to a wide range of information and opinion. They are also a protection
against the abuse of power by all types of organisations. But are there
limits, and should there be limits, on the freedom of the press and
television to publish what they want? In particular are they, in any
sense, controlled by government?

To begin with, there is a form of self-censorship. If articles were
written or programmes made in favour of drug abuse there would be
a public outcry. One limit is bound to be defined by what is generally
acceptable in society. The problem does not lie in these 'obvious' areas,
but in others where agreement is less easy to reach. Should television
give publicity to the aims of the Provisional IRA and interview its
leading members? Is it acceptable to put forward a case for abolishing
the monarchy? Indeed, how far should the actions of members of the
Royal Family be criticised? A further problem lies in the area of investigative journalism. Finding out news stories and digging into issues can
frequently mean that people are harrassed and their private lives are
ruined. Stories may be written which contain a damning half-truth (or
half-lie, depending on your point of view).

Politically the most sensitive area is investigating the actions of
government. Is there a danger that really necessary secrecy will be
destroyed? Would it be against the national interest to publish details
of British Army plans to deal with a Russian invasion of West
Germany, or should this be a matter which is part of our normal
political debate? What limits should there be on our 'right to know'?

At this point the idea of self-censorship breaks down simply because
there will be different views on what is meant by the national or public
interest. Supporters of CND, for example, are likely to believe that any
real debate on defence must be based on a wider knowledge of our
plans and capabilities. On the other hand, civil servants and military
officers may believe these should be kept secret. There is no doubt that
quite apart from defence, governments are obsessed with secrecy –
frequently in areas where it is hard to justify. How are such problems
resolved? Firstly the media is not free to publish everything it may
want to. It must take into account libel laws which penalise those who
expose individuals to hatred, ridicule or contempt. It is also unlawful
to stir up racial hatred. It is possible for the media to be in contempt of
court – for example by publishing any comments about a trial in progress. These limits on the freedom of press and television to publish can
usually be sorted out by a good lawyer. What is far less clear cut are
the powers of government to decide what is to be made public,
especially about its own activities.

Central to the power of government is the Official Secrets Act of
1911 which has few supporters – at least while they remain in opposition. Under this Act it is an offence for those employed in government and who have signed the Official Secrets Act to pass on
information to 'unauthorised persons'. If this covers all information,
government could become a closed book for most of us. In the past,

newspapers have been brought to court over disclosures they have made, although governments have not always been successful in the prosecution. The *Sunday Telegraph*, for example, was prosecuted over publishing a report on British policy towards the Nigerian Civil War in 1971 but the case was lost. More important for open government, an attempt to stop the *Sunday Times* publishing extracts from the diaries of Richard Crossman, former Labour Cabinet minister, also failed. In 1985 a civil servant, Clive Ponting, was charged under the Official Secrets Act with giving information to an unauthorised person on the sinking of the Argentine battleship *General Belgrano* during the Falklands War. The government admitted that he had not given away any information which threatened national security. In the event the jury found Mr Ponting not guilty. Yet again the Official Secrets Act came under considerable criticism especially because it seemed that the government was less concerned with using the Act to protect security than with avoiding political embarrassment. In spite of these cases journalists in the press and on television have to tread very carefully in disclosing government 'secrets' because, in the end, there is uncertainty about how this may be interpreted by the courts.

Governments are also very fond of 'managing news' through giving journalists 'off the record' briefings or 'non-attributable' statements. These lead to news stories beginning with phrases like: 'Sources close to the government said . . . .' The media can be used to float an idea so that the public response can be judged, and if it is hostile then the idea can be dismissed as a rumour. And there is no doubt that the media is also used as a way of carrying arguments within the government, even at cabinet level, much further. This does not mean that the media is controlled by the government. However, it is certainly true that some reporters are given stories of this kind and others are not. For instance, some journalists are accepted as 'lobby correspondents' which gives them the right to be in parliament and available to be briefed by ministers as well as MPs. A lobby correspondent who broke the rules by revealing where confidential information came from would lose this right. Is this an example of the media being used by politicians for their own benefit?

Case Study: 'News at Ten'

Independent Television News (ITN) is responsible for producing the national and international news for all Britain's independent television companies. There are three main news programmes during the day (at 1.00 p.m., 5.45 p.m. and 10.00 p.m.) but News at Ten is the longest and most prestigious. Viewing figures for ITN vary according to such factors as the nature and seriousness of news, as well as which programmes precede or compete with the broadcasts. But audiences for the 5.45 p.m. news and News at Ten can be anything between 5 million and 13 million people. The BBC nine o'clock news and News

Last minute checks before Leonard Parkin reads the news for ITN.

Independent Television Authority (ITA)
Appointed by government. ITA does not exercise day-to-day control, but must approve Board's choice of Editor, and is ultimately responsible for all aspects of the ITN network.

↑

Board of ITN
Includes representatives of ITV companies Editor and General Manager. Board selects ITN Editor, approves major policy decisions

↑

Editor of ITN
Duty to see that all news is presented 'with due accuracy and impartiality'. Complete editorial freedom within this brief.

↑

Editor of the Day
Each news programme has its own Editor of the Day who is responsible for putting the programme together.

Figure 13.4 The structure of ITN.

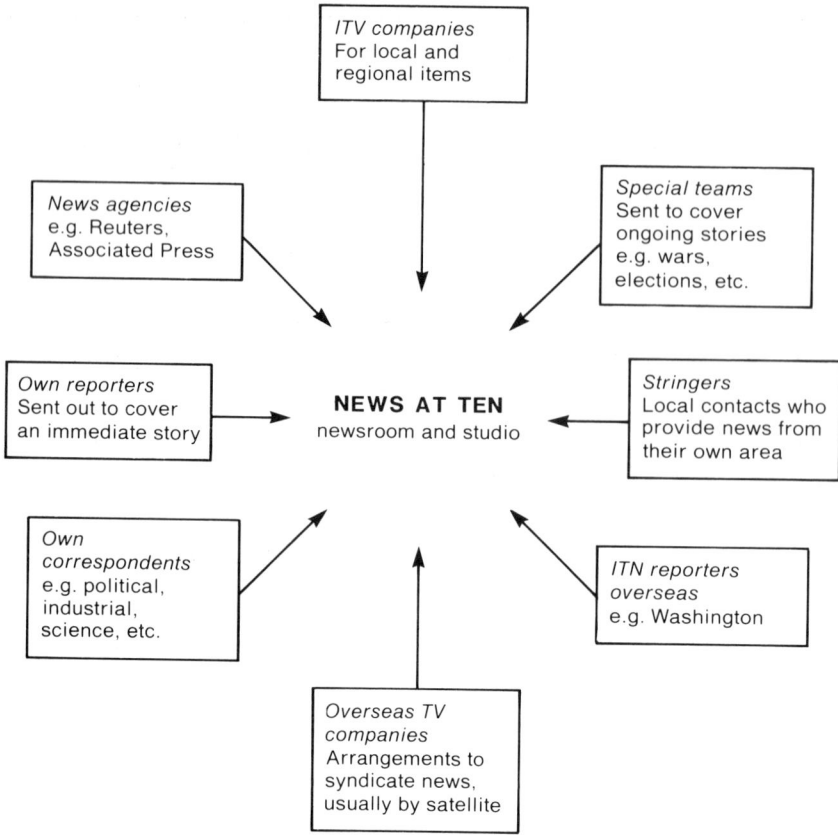

Figure 13.5 Sources of news for ITN.

at Ten will usually have combined audience figures of up to 20 million on any week day.

The presentation of news on television takes four different forms: direct 'live' news where an event is shown as it happens (outside broadcast or studio interview); news previously recorded on film or video tape; news in words spoken by the newscaster or reporter; and news in diagrams, maps and still pictures.

But where does news come from? Figure 13.5 shows the complex range of sources which can contribute towards a news broadcast. Immediately two points should be clear. There are a series of 'gatekeepers' at ITN who must continually decide whether a story is worth letting through or not. ITN, for example, receives all the news items from the various agencies continually through the day in the form of tapes. One 'gatekeeper' is the 'copy taster' whose task is to decide which agency news items should go forward. A second point is that, in producing television news, there has to be a much more rigorous selection of news than with a newspaper. News at Ten is unlikely to carry more than 20–25 news items at most. This will be reduced if there are one or two dominant news stories. With 20 seconds on television being the equivalent of 60 words there has to be considerable editing even when a news story is included.

4.00 p.m.	(previous day) 'Look ahead meeting' to consider known stories which include reports from teams overseas, 'known' events of the next day such as publication of employment figures, royal visits and so on. (Editor, Editor of Day, Specialist Editors).
10.30 a.m.	Meeting to consider overnight news. (Programme Editor, News Editor, Foreign Editor, Sports Editor, etc.).
1.00 p.m.	News.
3.15 p.m.	Meeting to 'firm up' stories and visual material. (Now include Chief of Film, Script Writers and Newscasters.)
5.00 p.m.	Meeting to decide provisional running order. (Same people as 3.15 p.m.)
5.45 p.m.	News.
7.00 p.m.	Final meeting – running order decided, length of stories etc.
9.30 p.m.	Rehearsal.
10.00 p.m.	News at Ten.

All during the day new stories are coming in, existing stories are being trimmed (and perhaps discarded), film sequences are being prepared and each item is being carefully timed.

Figure 13.6 News at Ten; production countdown.

A further point about News at Ten is that, at no stage in the day, can the contents of news be assumed. Even during the broadcast itself some news items are being edited and, sometimes, other stories are being added. Producing a programme like News at Ten involves quick decisions and rapid script writing, often in a highly charged atmosphere as Figure 13.6 illustrates.

What does ITN attempt to do? According to David Nicholas, the network editor, 'We are out to give people at the end of the day an information survival kit, so that they have a reasonable idea of what's actually happened during the course of the day.' (Granada Schools programme, *What's News*.)

Discussion and essay questions

1. List the different ways in which we find out about political events. What are the problems we face, with each one, in terms of their reliability?

2. What do you think is the political bias of the paper or papers you read? How is this political bias expressed? Does such political bias matter?

3. How much air-time does your favourite radio station give to politics? What sort of political issues does it cover? How effectively does it (a) tell you what's going on, (b) encourage or represent your views?

4. Compare and contrast the ways in which the press and television cover politics.

5. Watch the main evening news on television on BBC and ITV. What were the main news items on both? Were the sequences of news the same? Can you account for any differences in the presentation and choice of news?

6. Look at two national newspapers published on the same day. What differences can you spot in the treatment of news? How would you explain any differences in news treatment?

7. How far do you agree with the idea that we have 'the greatest half free press in the world'?

8. Select items from the main news stories of the day. Write newspaper headlines in favour of (a) the government (b) the opposition. Do the same with a television news script.

9. In what ways has television affected the nature of party political conflict in Britain? What effect do you think TV cameras would have in the House of Commons?

10. Discuss the argument that the media communicate in one direction only, with little chance for the public to be heard.

Part Six: GOVERNMENT IN THE MODERN STATE

14   The welfare state

The expansion of government

In the last century, governments concentrated on a very limited range of activities mostly concerned with the armed forces and internal law and order. The amount of money they needed to raise was tiny compared to the present day and that meant a very low level of taxation. Industry and commerce was left largely free to organise itself as it wished, and the government took no responsibility for trying to control the economy. During this century, and especially over the last fifty years, the role of government, and the way it affects our lives, has been transformed. Why has this happened?

Government responsibility for welfare

Firstly, governments have accepted a wider view of their responsibilities for the well-being of people. The development of the welfare state illustrates how the *purpose* of government has changed. It is now thought a proper function of any government to look after the interests of the poor and the sick, to help people at critical times, when they are children, parents, pensioners and to support them when disasters like unemployment strike.

This change did not happen suddenly. Some aspects of the present welfare state can be traced back to the beginning of the century; old age pensions, for example, were first given in 1908. But it took many years before governments accepted other responsibilities and this acceptance was influenced by a number of factors. The emergence of the Labour Party, with a powerful emphasis on social justice and a belief in the state as the means of achieving it, was of major importance. It was the Labour government of 1945–1951 which vastly increased the role of the state in social welfare. Conservative governments, although more suspicious of 'big government' have accepted the basic structure of welfare services as well. The two World Wars could only be fought successfully with governments having overwhelming

Statutory reforms

	Benefit	Applicable to
Old Age Pension Act 1908	One to five shillings per week	The over-seventies with annual incomes of less than £31.
Unemployed Workmens Act 1905	Small supplements; assisted emigration	Groups of unskilled casual workers
1910 Introduction of Labour Exchanges	Nationwide organisation of labour market	All workers.
National Insurance Act 1911	Seven shillings per week during unemployment.	Restricted to small groups of low wage trades only.
	Ten shillings per week sickness benefit.	Applied to all paying the fourpence weekly employee's contribution.

Poverty between the Wars
Between the two World Wars, poverty in Britain was particularly widespread. The British Medical Association set a minimum family income of 53 shillings per week for a 'healthy life' – and this allowed for absolutely no luxuries. At the peak of the depression some 15 per cent of the population were unemployed and nearly half of these were living below the BMA minimum. Half the families in the country were living on less than £3 per week and research revealed that approximately one fifth of working-class children were inadequately fed.

Figure 14.1 Britain before the welfare state.

control over all our resources. After both wars, such controls were considerably relaxed but they did not shrink back to the position before. We became more used to active government and had experience of how government actions could produce desirable results. In the Second World War, for example, there was a deliberate policy of supplementing the diets of children with free school milk, free vitamins, and so on.

Between the two wars the Depression, mass unemployment, and an increasing realisation of the levels of poverty suffered by millions of people again helped to change attitudes about the proper role of government. It became recognised that only government could ensure that the support people needed applied to *everyone*. The services found in areas such as health, education, housing were, in the past, one of the privileges of wealth. If they were to apply to the whole population then government needed to raise the money through taxation and borrowing, and provide the services itself. By becoming responsible for the organisation of all these activities government was bound to expand considerably.

The economy

Government has taken on many new economic responsibilities. To begin with it is, directly and indirectly, a major employer in the civil service, the forces, the health service, social security, nationalised industries, local government and education. This involves governments in issues such as employment, wage levels, investment, productivity and prices. Their decisions can have a significant effect on the economy as a whole.

Governments have also attempted to 'manage' the British economy in order to achieve certain overall objectives such as low unemployment, low inflation, economic growth. This has happened first of all because governments now have a much greater knowledge of how their own policies can affect the nation's economic performance. A key figure in this development was John Maynard Keynes. He argued that the problem of mass unemployment as seen in the 1930s was caused by too low a level of demand in the economy. There was a need to *raise the amount of spending* so that people would buy more goods and, as a result, encourage firms to expand production. This would lead to new factories being built, more people being employed, more spending and so on. To Keynes, government policies were the key. Public expenditure, for example, should be increased if unemployment rose and

An old people's ward in a hospital. Looking after the elderly is going to become more expensive as more people live longer – and we will be the elderly one day.

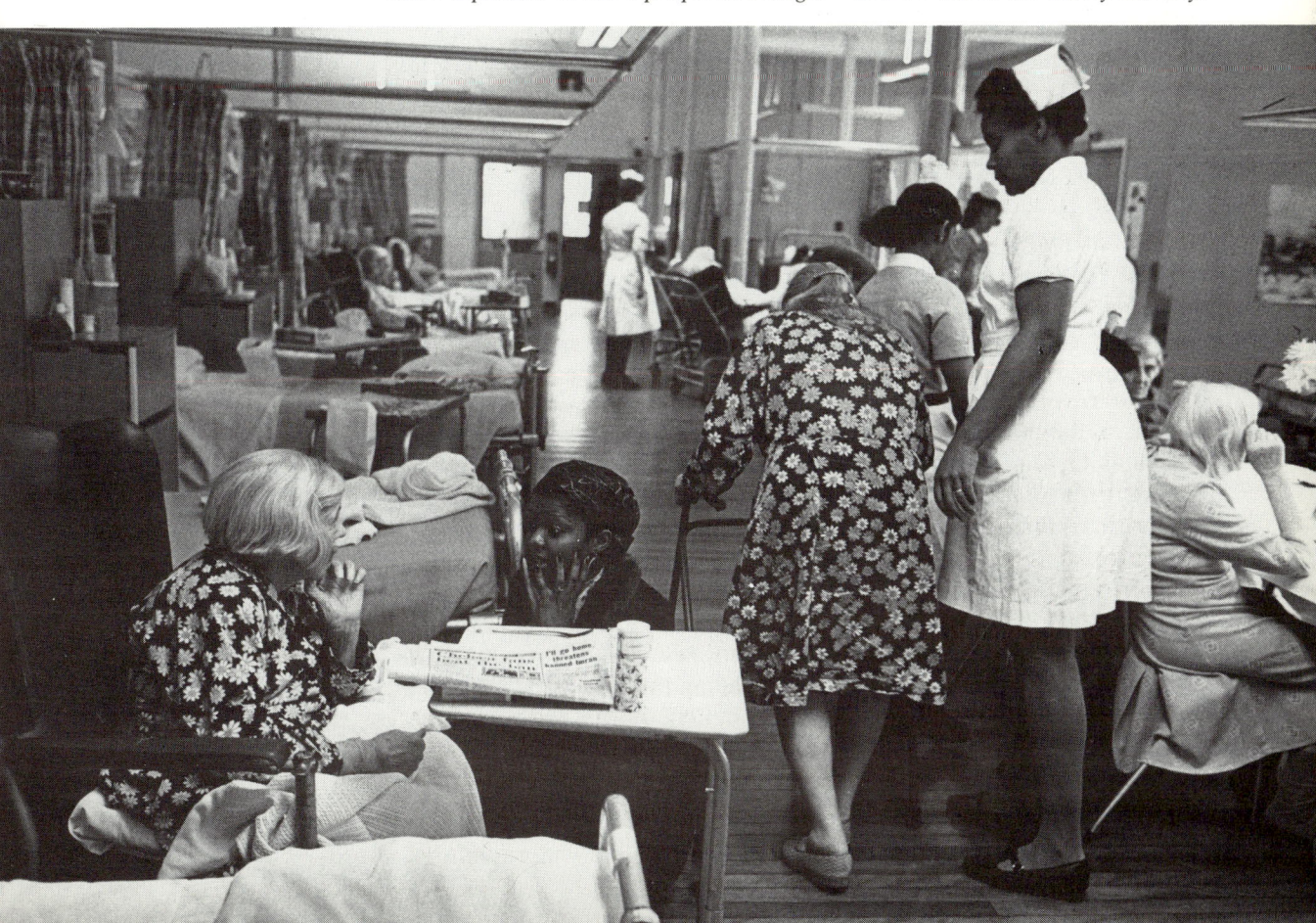

governments should be prepared to go into debt in order to finance it. The **'Keynesian revolution'** placed governments in the central position in terms of economic policy. It showed how changes in public expenditure, interest rates and taxation could affect the economy as a whole.

Ever since the 1920s Britain has experienced clear regional differences in prosperity. As the older industries such as coal, cotton and shipbuilding declined after the end of the First World War, problems of unemployment and social deprivation became acute in South Wales, parts of Northern England, Scotland, and Northern Ireland. Encouraging economic growth in these regions has involved a whole variety of schemes to attract new industries, most of them government financed.

The need to preserve or develop industries was another reason for expanding government activity. In most cases this took the form of nationalisation which brought coal, railways, electricity, gas, airlines, and so on under the control of government. The nationalised industries are not meant to be run by governments on a day-to-day basis (see Chapter 15) but government does retain the right to decide major issues of policy.

Science and technology

Modern governments have also been faced with a mass of changes which may not have originated in the world of politics but ultimately needed a political response. The invention of the internal combustion engine, for example, created new industries, led to vast road building programmes and brought the need to devise safety regulations. All this involved legislation, new government departments and agencies, extra expenditure and new forms of taxation. The list of scientific and technological discoveries seems endless – a good starting point is to think about the objects in our houses which did not exist in 1900.

Such advances have led to huge rises in the *scale* of expenditure. Modern military equipment, for example, is vastly more expensive than its equivalent in the past. Fifty years ago a battleship might have cost £150 million at current prices. Today one Trident nuclear missile submarine costs around £1.5 billion – in this case bought from the United States. The same kind of escalation in costs is true of many other areas of government activity, ranging from introducing computers in schools to the building of a new hospital. Such increases in government spending create many difficulties. Many people have objected to paying the taxes needed to finance this level of spending. In April 1981 the average married man paid 30 per cent of his total income in tax and National Insurance contributions and this figure excluded the taxes paid on goods and services such as VAT. Tax cuts have become a popular policy, as the Conservatives found in 1979. We appear to have rising costs, a reluctance to pay more in taxes, and a poor economic growth rate which does not increase the nation's wealth as fast as others.

Expectations

In the 1950s Britain was in the top ten richest nations in the world and our income per head was 25 per cent higher than West Germany and 500 per cent higher than Japan. Today we rank in the mid-twenties. West Germany's income per head is 200 per cent higher than ours and Japan's is 50 per cent higher. Nevertheless we are still a wealthy country and, although we may have been overtaken by others, living standards in Britain have risen sharply since 1945. This is reflected in the ownership of cars, washing machines, refrigerators, telephones, television sets, as well as the money spent on leisure.

This general increase in living standards has in turn raised our expectations about our own life styles still further. We have greater expectations about what government ought to provide – something that recent governments have been acutely aware of, and have in part encouraged by the expansion of their activities. And so the process still continues. Promises about solving our economic and social problems, and raising living standards, have meant that elections are won and lost on issues such as employment, inflation and the welfare state. Governments may prefer to blame high levels of inflation or unemployment on factors outside their control. But, by taking credit when things go well, and arguing in elections that they have the best policies to put matters right, it is not surprising that they have raised our expectations about what government can provide.

The results of the increase in government activities are seen in a variety of ways. In 1983, for example, the public sector, which includes local government, employed 34 per cent of the working population and public expenditure was £115 billion. It may be popular to argue that government should be 'taken off our backs' but a large public sector is the price paid for the kind of services which governments provide and which we appear to want. Civil servants can be a popular, if unfair, target but the public sector also includes teachers, doctors, nurses, the armed forces, workers in nationalised industries, social workers and the police.

Another result of the expansion of government is the need to regulate. It may seem that our lives are dominated by laws and rules but, as was argued earlier, it does not follow that they limit our real freedom. Administering social security, for example, is bound to involve rules about how, when and to whom different benefits apply and a large number of officials are needed to see that the rules are applied fairly.

The steps to a welfare state

Before the Second World War there were a number of benefits which people could claim, and services which the state provided. In 1911, for example, unemployment insurance was introduced. Employers and employees paid money into an insurance fund which financed those who were unemployed. To begin with, it was limited to just a few occupations considered most vulnerable to unemployment. In the same

1911 Act the first medical insurance scheme was also started. It enabled workers to get medical and sickness benefit. Specialist treatment was not included, however, and the scheme did not include workers' wives and children.

In 1920 unemployment insurance was expanded to cover most jobs. Unfortunately it was put under immediate strain by the rise in unemployment in the 1920s and 1930s. In some areas unemployment never fell below 20 per cent in these years and the 1920 scheme, which only allowed fifteen weeks of benefit for the unemployed, was hopelessly inadequate.

To fill the gap, extended benefits, soon called 'the dole' were introduced and, as the depression grew worse after 1929, these became 'means tested'. The amount received depended on the earnings and savings of everyone in the family which led to great bitterness among the unemployed.

In the 1920s council houses, built by local authorities and partly subsidised by the government, were first built, and slum clearance was started in the 1930s. But housing conditions for many people were still dreadful. The most effective form of slum clearance, in places such as London's East End, came tragically with the 'blitz' in the Second World War.

Education expanded after the 1918 Education Act with the school-leaving age fixed at fourteen, but there was no secondary school education for all children. Most working class children stayed in 'all age schools' with only a small proportion going to grammar schools after the 'eleven plus' entrance examination.

The Second World War solved one problem. Unemployment disappeared. And the need to maintain a healthy population at a time of great shortages led to government action on diet, welfare provision for children, and other measures. The war also brought people together in a way which is rare in peacetime. There was an increasing determination that Britain, after the war, should never return to the 'bad old days'. At the end of 1942 a government inquiry on social insurance published its report. The mood of the public can be judged by the fact that it became a best seller. The chairman was Sir William Beveridge.

The Beveridge Report and the creation of the welfare state

Beveridge was concerned with how best to fight the 'five giant evils' of want, disease, ignorance, squalor and idleness. He proposed a universal system of national insurance which would finance pensions, illness, unemployment, maternity, widowhood, and funeral expenses. Family allowances were also included. Contributions would come mainly from employees, employers and, only partly, from government. As a temporary measure only, there was to be a system of means-tested benefits to help those who were in danger of poverty and were not properly covered by insurance.

Central to Beveridge was the idea that the services would be provided equally and that, apart from the temporary scheme, there would be no means test. In effect Beveridge argued that there should be a form of 'national minimum' standard of living below which people should not fall. And Beveridge, by talking about the five giant evils, pointed out the need for a comprehensive health service, more and better schools and houses, and for governments to take measures to keep unemployment as low as possible. These were as necessary as national insurance if a **welfare state** was to be constructed.

The war in Europe ended in May 1945 and the wartime coalition broke up. A 'caretaker' Conservative government under Winston Churchill was then heavily defeated in a general election by the Labour party led by Clement Attlee. The new government was committed to a major reconstruction of Britain's social and economic structure. Between 1945 and 1951 the modern welfare state was created.

Social security: development and problems

Family allowances had become law just before the 1945 election and were financed out of general taxation. The National Insurance Act became law in 1948. It was compulsory for everyone of working age, except married women – although the rates paid varied according to whether people were employed, self-employed or unemployed. The benefits which could be claimed under the Act included sick pay, unemployment benefit, pensions, maternity grants, death grants. All this closely followed Beveridge and it remains the basis of our social security system today.

But, in important ways, the social security system has changed considerably since 1948 and has moved away from the Beveridge ideal. The most important of these changes has been the failure to cover all needs by one scheme of insurance. The National Assistance Board, set up in 1948, was intended only as a temporary safety net. It was hoped that there would be fewer and fewer people whose insurance benefits did not cover their needs. In 1966 'national assistance' became 'supplementary benefit' but the problem didn't disappear with the change in name. Means-tested supplementary benefits have become an integral part of our social security system because other benefits, for example pensions, have not been high enough. Supplementary benefits also provide a 'passport' for help such as free prescription charges, free school meals and a clothing allowance.

Governments could avoid the need for people to apply for means-tested supplementary benefits by increasing the size of the funds which are to pay national insurance. They would have to come from a very large increase in contributions or as a rise in taxation. Either way would be unpopular. There are also many people who argue in favour of a selective system of welfare which means that extra help goes not to all but only to those who need it. The only way to define 'need' is first of all to have some kind of accepted level of income below which people should be helped, a 'poverty line'; secondly, to have a system of means testing; thirdly, to put the responsibility for getting help on the poor themselves. Each one of these conditions creates its own problems.

Establishing a poverty line is difficult because of the different conditions people find themselves in. Parents with large families need more help than those with fewer children or none at all. Disabled people have certain costs which do not apply to others. Because there are different poverty lines for different circumstances the regulations on benefits are complex. The poverty line has become the level below which a person is entitled to claim supplementary benefits. However, families just above the line are hardly that much better off. Indeed we have reached a position where families in need may even find themselves *worse off* when they earn more income, go above the poverty line, and lose supplementary benefit and other 'passport' benefits. This problem is called the 'poverty trap'.

Some people will not apply for benefits because it involves being questioned or 'tested' about their means and because it has to be specially claimed and doesn't come as a right. To some it makes supplementary benefits seem charity and acceptance of it a mark of failure which is not helped by stories about 'social security scroungers'.

A second major change from the Beveridge Report has been the move away from the principle of equal contributions and equal benefits for all. It became clear that this system could not give full security for people when their income was interrupted, for example by illness or unemployment. It was found, for example, that higher paid workers faced huge problems if, when they lost earnings, they had to fall back on subsistence-type benefits. The system was changed in 1978 so that both contributions and benefits became 'earnings related', but under more recent economic pressures the Government has placed a time limit on earnings-related unemployment pay. So, the problem still remains, and the unemployed find that the level of 'Beveridge' type benefit they get from paying national insurance is too low.

A major change in social security came in 1972 when Family Income Supplements (FIS) were introduced. It had been found that some low paid workers could actually be better off leaving their jobs and living on social security, especially if they had large families. FIS was given to *employed* people whose incomes were low in relation to their family commitments. A further change in 1978 was that family allowances and the tax concessions given to fathers were merged into a new Child Benefit Scheme. This is usually given to the mother who claims the money from the Post Office.

Social security has moved a long way since Beveridge and 1948. To some extent the original plans were optimistic but changes since then have produced a maze of benefits and regulations. There are, for example, so many leaflets describing different benefits that the DHSS local offices produce a leaflet which catalogues leaflets. Certainly the problems have been made worse by inflation, which has meant that many benefits do not keep pace with the rise in prices.

In the last ten years a considerable rise in unemployment has also increased the difficulties of paying for a welfare state. An extra 100,000 unemployed cost the government about £438 million. This includes the cost of paying out benefits, loss of income tax and loss of taxes paid out when goods are bought. By 1985 the number of unemployed was well over 3 million.

Employment exchange in London. The increase in unemployment has added considerably to the problems faced by the 'welfare state'.

The National Health Service

The National Health Service (NHS) came into operation in July 1948. It was a fully comprehensive system which covered all forms of medical treatment. No one was charged directly for any of its services, including prescriptions, and no one was forced to use it. Patients could still pay for private treatment and doctors could practise in both areas. All hospitals, apart from teaching hospitals, were brought under government control.

Initially it was hoped that as preventive medicine developed, and the welfare services gave people a better chance of a healthy life, the strain on resources would ease. Today it is more common to talk of a 'crisis' in the NHS and waiting lists for treatment in hospitals appear to be an increasing problem. What, if anything, went wrong?

First of all people's expectations about medical care altered. We have become accustomed to having the best possible treatment for all our illnesses which is hardly a matter of complaint. Secondly, the frontiers of medicine have been pushed forward and the cost of modern treatment can be very high. One example of the 'problem' was illustrated by a Wolverhampton surgeon:

We can now save a limb crushed in a traffic accident but it may take four or more operations, five months in hospital and cost £20,000. A few years ago we would have cut the leg off and it would have cost £100. (*Sunday Times* 14.2.82).

A third cause of the crisis is simply that the welfare state has done its job well. The age structure of the population is changing as more and more people live longer. In 1951 there were 5.3 million aged over 65 – in 1981 there were 8.1 million, and more now live beyond 75. This increase in the number of old people has meant that more space has had to be used in hospitals for geriatric care. And again expectations are important. One key operation for many old people is hip replacement but waiting lists for this fairly new technique are growing.

The problem of an ageing population have been made worse by the scattering of families since the war so that pensioners are less likely to be geographically close to their children. Increasingly, the state has had to take old people into care, either in hospitals or homes, because there is no one to look after them. But hospital beds in geriatric wards have

High rise flats were seen as a solution to housing needs. Today they are often considered as simply a new problem. Why do you think this has happened?

their own waiting lists and state homes are full. Another effect is on NHS costs. It is estimated that a man aged between 25 and 44 costs the NHS £82 per year. People over 75 cost the health service on average, six times more than those between 25 and 45.

In many ways the health service is paying the penalty for success but there have been changes in the original intention. There are now charges for a range of services including prescriptions, treatment by dentists and opticians, and for hospital beds with special amenities – single rooms or in small wards.

Secondly, there has been a massive increase in the number of people who have private medical insurance. In 1985 this totalled approximately 4 million. Many companies use private medicine as a 'perk' for their employees and it has become a way of avoiding NHS waiting lists. Politically the Conservative Party sees private medicine as a symbol of freedom of choice. The Labour Party, while not prohibiting private medicine, argues that it drains resources such as trained staff away from the NHS and means that health care increasingly depends on income. They also fear that we will see two health services develop, with the NHS left to cope with the difficult and expensive problems of looking after the old and the chronically sick for whom private medicine is far too expensive.

The NHS, like social security, has moved away from its original conception – partly because we have either not been willing or able to finance it as intended. Yet it provides a very comprehensive medical cover for the vast bulk of the population, with services ranging from the family doctor to the best possible specialist help. It still remains a major achievement of British social policy.

Housing

Although local authorities started to build council housing for rent after the First World War and there was a huge increase in building private housing (and the beginning of slum clearance) in the 1930s, the housing problem in 1945 was desperate. House building ceased in the war years and bombing damaged or destroyed nearly one house in three.

At first the efforts of government were concentrated almost entirely on council housing of different kinds, including building new towns. In the 1950s private house-building expanded considerably and was one sign of developing prosperity. By 1984 56 per cent of the population lived in owner-occupied housing, 31 per cent rented from local authorities and new towns and 13 per cent rented privately.

Housing, like other social policies, highlights the different approaches of the two main parties. The Labour Party has traditionally emphasised the need for more council house building and supports subsidies for workers living in them. The Conservative Party, with its vision of a 'property owning democracy', has placed more emphasis on private house building and has argued that the privately rented sector needs to be encouraged.

But the most bitter battle has been over whether local authorities should allow council tenants to buy their own houses. The Conservative Party sees this as a way of extending house ownership and giving people a stake in the community. They also argue that it relieves local authorities of maintenance costs on their estates and will improve the quality of housing because people will look after them. The Labour Party largely opposes the scheme. They believe that it will reduce the stock of housing which local authorities can give to less well off families and argue that the system is unfair because certain council houses – for example those on small estates, or with larger gardens – are far more attractive to buy than others. By 1985 750,000 out of 6.5 million council houses had either been sold or were in the pipeline for sale.

One feature of housing policy followed by all governments has been to subsidise the private and the public sector. Most people buy their houses by means of a mortgage – borrowing money from building societies or banks on which they pay interest. But, on a mortgage up to a limit of £30,000 (1985) the interest paid is tax deductible. This means that borrowers can claim just under a third of their interest back. This is a considerable *subsidy* for the private house buyer who also knows that he is getting an asset which, since 1945, has increased in value often far more than the rate of inflation. Council house tenants have been subsidised as well by not having to pay back to councils the full cost of building and maintaining council houses or flats. However, in recent years, council house rents have risen substantially and many now pay more than those who have a mortgage – without the satisfaction of knowing that their house will some day belong to them.

There is no doubt that the steady increase in the percentage of people who are buying their own houses has important political conse-

	New units (built or acquired)	Sales (no of units)	
1978/79	24,000		
1979/80	16,000	5,425	
1980/81	22,000	5,747	94% houses
1981/82	16,000	10,849	6% flats
1982/83	9,000	18,556	

	Inner London	Outer London
% total sales	24	75
% housing stock sold	3	9

(Source for statistics GLC report *Council House Sales*) *May 1984*

Figure 14.2 Council housing in Greater London: how sales and building programmes affect housing stock levels.

quences because they now form the majority of households in Britain. A rise in bank interest rates usually means an increase in mortgage interest rates, so a government must be cautious about using interest rates as an economic weapon. Parties have been acutely aware of the need to devise policies which help people such as first-time buyers who face considerable expense. Any reduction in the tax allowance on mortgages would be politically disastrous even though it could be argued that it simply helps the better off. The huge increase in house prices has given house owners another advantage. It has concentrated more wealth in their hands. This can be seen quite simply by comparing the wealth which a council tenant and a house owner leave to their successors when they die. Another result of the division in housing is that council tenants, compared with house owners, find it very difficult to move. This can be critical in areas of high unemployment where, even though workers may want to leave they cannot simply walk into a council house somewhere else. Their only hope, often, is to join a waiting list.

Education

The 1944 Education Act was a landmark because·it declared that everyone was entitled to free secondary education. This meant an end to the 'all age schools' of the past. Local authorities were given the duty of providing schools according to 'age, aptitude and ability'. At first this meant that, for the vast majority of children, an examination at the age of eleven determined whether they would go to grammar, technical or secondary modern schools. Hostility to this system of separating children grew in the 1950s and 1960s. Many disliked the stigma put on children of failing the 'eleven-plus'. They argued that it was unrealistic to force such a decision at an early age and that such a separation was socially divisive. Such criticisms found a political home in the Labour Party, whereas Conservatives tended to support the maintenance of grammar schools. The grammar schools, to them, had fine academic records and worked well. A further concern was that the brightest children would be held back in comprehensive schools.

However, by the mid-1970s Labour controlled local authorities and pressure from Labour governments changed the secondary school system. In 1966 there were 1,273 grammar schools and 387 comprehensives. By 1977 the pattern was reversed with 407 grammar schools and 3,083 comprehensive schools as well as the remaining secondary moderns. Political conflict over education shifted instead towards the private sector where the battle lines of the two main parties are most clearly drawn.

In 1984 approximately 6 per cent of school children were educated in the private sector and although school fees have risen steadily (they can cost as much as £4,000 a year) there is no shortage of demand for places. And education, like health, is a good example of the way the basic values and attitudes of the political parties are related to actual policies. The Conservative Party sees private education, like private medicine, as an option which people should have if they wish. Otherwise there is no real freedom of choice. They argue that if parents are prepared to make financial sacrifices for their children then they should be allowed to do so. After all parents send their children to private schools for a range of different reasons. Some may want an emphasis on activities which a school specialises in, such as music. Other parents may be attracted because a school has a strong academic record. But the most obvious reasons for sending children to private schools are to do with resources. Most private schools have very small classes and many have superb facilities for teaching and other activities such as sport, music, drama. Money can buy educational advantage.

The Labour Party objection stems from the view that private schools do not just raise issues about education. Advantages later on in life especially in careers, can depend on the mere fact that a person has been privately educated or possibly went to one particular school. In effect private schools help to maintain a class structure. It also follows that from the very earliest age, the children of the wealthy have no contact at all with people of their own age group who go to state schools, so private schools can be seen as socially divisive as well.

Socialists in the Labour Party believe that their ideal of social and economic equality can never be achieved as long as wealth continues to buy educational privilege. Ideally, the standard of state schools should be high enough to ensure that private schools are less attractive educationally; a great deal has already been achieved in this respect. But so long as private schools carry social and economic advantages they will be supported by those who share these values and priorities. The socialist solution to this problem is to abolish private education. The first stage of abolition, proposed by the Labour Party, is to weaken the financial base by changing tax laws and the charitable status of such schools.

This section has looked at different problems associated with four of Beveridge's giant evils – want, squalor, disease and ignorance – and the methods used by governments to deal with them directly. But it is important to recognise that there is also a need to tackle the *causes* of crisis, and government is involved in this as well. These include, safety at work; preventive medicine (such as the campaign to discourage smoking); maintaining proper water and sewage facilities (an urgent problem in cities like Manchester); education about balanced diets and bringing up children; control of pollution (one example is the need to eliminate the lead content in petrol); and many others. Decisions in these areas can be vital for the long-term health of a nation, even though their immediate effect is often not very apparent.

In the end governments, and ourselves, face the harsh reality of choosing how scarce resources should be allocated in the very complicated field of social policies. The truth of politics is that choices must be made by governments, for instance between different social policies, and by electors, for instance about how much they are willing to pay. Social policies provide the sharpest example of the importance of choice because they are concerned with the clear issue of what kind of society do we want? It can be argued that one way of judging a civilised society is to see how it deals with those least able to look after themselves.

Discussion and essay questions

1. What are the arguments for and against the idea that help should only go to those that need it?

2. What problems are created for the welfare state by having an increasing number of elderly people?

3. Outline the main arguments for and against private medicine.

4. Should people be allowed to buy their own council houses?

5. Outline and explain the main differences between the Conservative and Labour parties in social security, housing, and education.

6. Dealing with different kinds of 'crisis' is one aspect of the welfare state but how can crisis be avoided?

15 Government and the economy

Britain can be described as having a **mixed economy**. The bulk of industry and commerce is in private hands but there is also a substantial section which is financed and controlled by government on behalf of the nation and the most important part of this are the **nationalised industries**.

What is a nationalised industry?

A National Economic Development Office study published in 1976 defined nationalised industries as being *public corporations* which have the following characteristics. Firstly, there is no private shareholding so the assets are publicly owned and are vested in a corporation. Secondly, members of the board are appointed by a secretary of state. Thirdly, the board members are not civil servants. Fourthly, such public corporations are mainly engaged in industrial or other trading activities.

Nationalisation since 1945

The reasons for nationalisation

Clause 4 of the Labour Party Constitution commits the party to the common ownership of 'the means of production, distribution and exchange'. When Labour won the 1945 election it started a programme of nationalisation which, although not as comprehensive as Clause 4, did transform whole areas of industry. The first group of reasons for nationalisation were essentially therefore political, and bound up with the idea of socialism itself. A socialist society could hardly be achieved while capitalism dominated the economy generally, and especially the key areas of industry and public service. Without public ownership, governments could not plan to use the nation's resources as they thought best.

Socialists had a traditional dislike of the profit motive as the main way of deciding what should be produced, how production should be organised, and where it should take place. If industries were in difficulty it was necessary to take a more sympathetic attitude than the profit motive would allow. It was also argued that some activities should not depend on the profit motive at all. Railways in rural areas or air links in the Scottish Islands might not be profitable but they were socially necessary – and could be economically vital for these areas as well.

	Turnover (£ m)	Capital employed (£ m)	Workforce ('000)	Profits before interest & tax (£ m)
British Aerospace	894	322	70	67
British Airports Authority	162	348	7	30
British Airways	1640	793	58	110
British Gas	2972	2181	103	443
British National Oil Corporation	432	751	1	11
British Rail	1979	1743	243	56
British Shipbuilders	810	72	82	−61
British Steel	3288	4020	186	−142
British Transport Docks Board	120	177	12	21
British Waterways	12	13	3	
Central Electricity Generating Board	4047	4237	62	363
Electricity Council	5116	6801	160	675
National Bus	437	199	64	31
National Coal Board	2989	1733	235	122
National Freight Corp'n	394	91	36	11
North of Scotland Hydroelectric Board	173	556	4	49
Post Office	4619	7469	411	827
Scottish Transport	106	80	14	2
South of Scotland Electricity Board	463	713	14	70
Total	26606	28062	1703	2685

(*Economist* 15.3.80)

This marks the high point of nationalisation before the process of de-nationalisation began in 1979 under the new Conservative government. At this time nationalised industries employed 7 per cent of the labour force, accounted for about 14 per cent of total fixed investment and contributed 10 per cent to total output. They dominated four strategic sectors of economic activity: energy, public transport, communications.

Figure 15.1 Nationalised industries in 1979.

Lode, Cambridgeshire – a disused railway line and station. Although nationalised industries run some activities at a loss for several reasons, this was not true of many small branch lines on the railways. They were 'axed' in the 1960s.

Economic reasons for nationalisation were just as important. Many industries, such as gas, steel, coal mining, had a large number of small and inefficient plants. To make them more efficient it was necessary to have larger units so that economies of scale could be achieved. But, to do this, a great deal of investment was needed. Some industries, such as the railways, were run down after the war when they had been over-used, and they had to be modernised. This investment was not likely to come from private sources because of the sheer size of the investment needed, nor was there much chance of any profit for some years.

Investment was also needed in newer industries such as nuclear power. Here it was argued that the cost of development was so high that research and expansion could only take place through nationalisation. Another argument, which was not entirely economic, was that worker-management relations in some industries had broken down to such an extent that a new start was necessary. The coal industry was an example of this.

Nationalisation: intentions and reality

The problems facing many nationalised industries go right back to when they were first set up. No clear objectives were planned from the

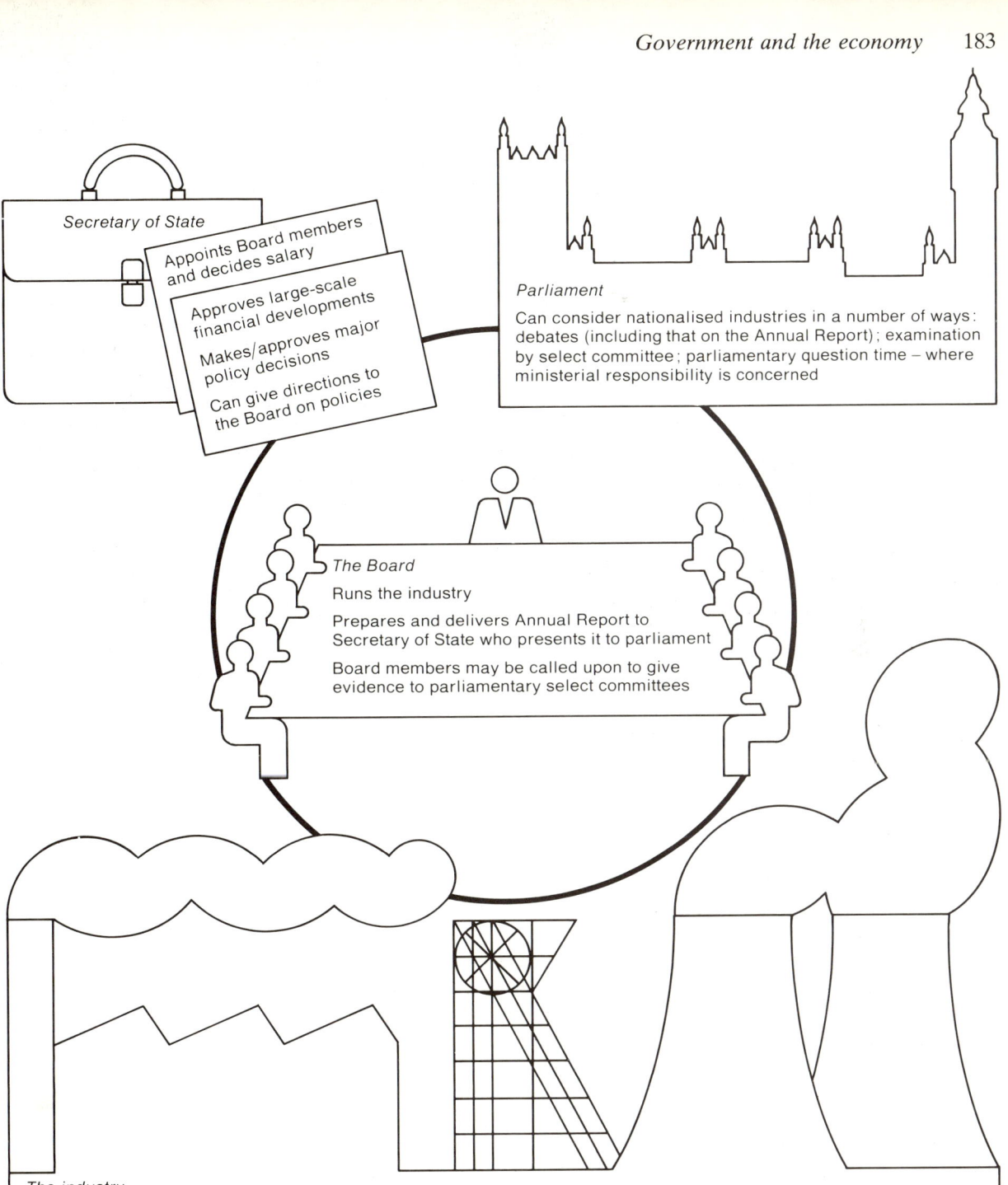

Secretary of State

Appoints Board members and decides salary

Approves large-scale financial developments

Makes/approves major policy decisions

Can give directions to the Board on policies

Parliament

Can consider nationalised industries in a number of ways: debates (including that on the Annual Report); examination by select committee; parliamentary question time – where ministerial responsibility is concerned

The Board

Runs the industry

Prepares and delivers Annual Report to Secretary of State who presents it to parliament

Board members may be called upon to give evidence to parliamentary select committees

The industry

Organised internally according to its functions (e.g. manufacturing, research, distribution etc.) and to location (e.g. regional services such as those of British Gas)

Figure 15.2 The structure of a nationalised industry.

outset, and this has led to more recent arguments regarding their purpose. Nationalised industries were not meant to be entirely commercial with, for example, the highest possible profits as one of their aims, rather they were expected to 'break even'. Yet the success or failure of a nationalised industry is now often judged by politicians and the public on profitability alone. On the other hand, if they do act in a commercial way and, for example, British Rail closes unprofitable lines, they are then criticised for not being socially responsible. Nationalised industries are forced to face two ways at the same time. They must be profitable and yet must carry out activities which are not.

Secondly, when they were set up the industries were expected to operate at arm's length from government but not completely independently. Ministers had clear responsibilities over such matters as appointments to the board. In some cases they had the power to make final decisions. But they were not expected to interfere except by giving general directions over policy.

An alternative structure could have been to run nationalised industries as government departments. But all the work of departments, down to the last detail, *can* be examined in parliament, because the minister is responsible. The departmental structure would have made it very difficult to avoid characteristic civil service reliance on precedent and the slowness, carefulness, of decision-making. Nationalised industries needed the freedom to act quickly and commercially. Herbert Morrison described the hope as follows: '. . . we are seeking a combination of public ownership, public accountability, and business management for public ends'.

The relationship with parliament was also intended to be fairly distant. Although ministers take final responsibility in certain areas and are accountable to parliament as a result, parliament is not able to challenge the detailed, day to day running of the industries, unlike government departments.

However, all governments have intervened in the running of nationalised industries to suit their own policies. Nationalised industries have been given limits and directions for their capital expenditure on major new developments. Their borrowing and the wage levels of their employees have been controlled. In short, they have become part of the way that general economic programmes of government are carried through. A key area is prices. Governments have held down nationalised industries' prices as part of a counter-inflation policy (in the late 1960s and early 1970s), and actually forced some industries to raise their prices when they did not want to (British Gas, 1981) as part of government policy on energy saving. Ministers' orders can go much further than 'general directions' and can concern the detailed running of an industry. For example, the Parliamentary Secretary to the Minister of Transport said in November 1979, 'the Minister of Transport has made it clear to the British Rail Board that we will not approve any fare increases weighted against the captive London and South East commuter'. (*Hansard* 22.11.79.)

A third problem follows from the way that governments have controlled nationalised industries. As we saw earlier, ministerial responsibility means that a minister can be held to account by parliament where a clear responsibility is established. Sometimes ministers

Modern digital telephone exchange. Vast investment has been needed by many nationalised industries to keep up with, or originate, technological change.

have been quite open about their instructions to the management of nationalised industries – and these actions can then be questioned in parliament. But on many occasions it is not at all clear whether the minister has given instructions or not. Wage negotiations in national-ised industries, for example, are supposed to be between the industry management and unions concerned. The government may *seem* not to be officially involved. But have they put pressure on the management to hold wages down? Discussions between the chairmen and ministers are not necessarily formal but can include lunch together and other unofficial contacts. Sir Peter Parker, Chairman of British Rail (1976–83) called all this, 'Government by nudge and fudge'. The result is that it is difficult for the *responsibility* for failure to be pinned down to management or government.

Nationalisation and party politics

Ever since 1945, the Conservative and Labour Parties have disagreed over nationalisation. Just as public ownership is a central part of socialist thinking, so is private enterprise to Conservatives. The result is that virtually each change of government has meant either more nationalisation or de-nationalisation, with the steel industry, for example, being nationalised twice and de-nationalised once.

The Labour Party

Between 1945 and 1951 the Labour government nationalised coal, railways, gas, steel and road haulage as well as bringing airlines and electricity into full public ownership. Steel and road haulage were de-nationalised by the Conservatives (1951–1964) who were prepared to keep the rest under state control.

The 1964–1970 Labour government re-nationalised steel and parts of road transport through the National Bus Company and the National Freight Corporation. But otherwise it did not extend nationalisation. However, the Labour government of 1974–1979 set up the British National Oil Corporation (BNOC), nationalised shipbuilding, and the aircraft industry. It also established the National Enterprise Board (NEB) which had the power to buy shares in private companies. NEB investment saved British Leyland from bankruptcy but it was not, strictly speaking, nationalisation because British Leyland was not run as a public corporation.

The issue of nationalisation began to divide the Labour Party. The Left wanted more nationalisation and the centre-Right doubted if it was either desirable or politically popular. In 1976 the Left's strength on the party's National Executive Committee meant it came out with a programme for nationalising the major banks, insurance companies and agricultural land, with state control of a leading company in each industrial sector. However, the 1979 Labour manifesto, considerably influenced by Prime Minister James Callaghan, did not contain any of these policies.

The attitude of the Labour Party to nationalisation since 1979 has been very much influenced by Mrs Thatcher's policy of, where possible, de-nationalising (or 'privatising') parts or all of nationalised industries. In the 1983 election, Labour promised that it would take these industries back into public ownership. Nationalisation continues to be one of the issues which divides Left and Right in the Labour Party. The Right are more committed to a mixed economy and fear that extensive nationalisation proposals would be unpopular even with the majority of Labour supporters. The Left see nationalisation as a vital part of any socialist society.

The Conservative Party

Conservative attitudes towards nationalisation have varied a great deal since 1945. To begin with, each Conservative government has been responsible for running nationalised industries and helping them to succeed. Some industries have been de-nationalised but the Conservative Party, until 1979, never made any real effort to bite deeply into the nationalised sector. Indeed it was a Conservative government

The financially attractive Jaguar car business was sold to the public in August 1984, previously having been a subsidiary of the British Leyland Group.

which, in 1954, created a new public corporation, the Atomic Energy Authority. Conservatives did however try and inject more competition into some areas by breaking up the **monopoly** which nationalised industries had been given. For example, private airlines were encouraged. Between 1970 and 1974 Edward Heath's Conservative government de-nationalised Thomas Cook and the state-controlled breweries in the north-west. Then in 1971 it faced a crisis over Rolls Royce. The company was on the verge of bankruptcy and, as it was important for its defence engineering, the government decided to step in and give it financial support. It effectively took over the shares of Rolls Royce but did not nationalise it, stating that it wanted Rolls Royce to act as if it were a private company.

In 1979 the Conservatives, under Mrs Thatcher, were heavily committed to selling off part or all of nationalised industries back to the public. In 1981 a half of British Aerospace was sold and a half of Cable and Wireless (which had come into public ownership very early in the century). The National Freight Corporation was sold to employers, managers, and bankers for £50 million. The Post Office was broken up into two sections by the formation of British Telecom which was made responsible for telephones and communications and was privatised in 1984. It lost its monopoly to supply telephone equipment to consumers. These decisions reflect a determined attempt to reduce the nationalised sector, but there is a major problem in following this policy. For shares to be attractive, the parts being sold off need to be profitable. The more parts that are sold, the more the government loses the chance of earning profits itself and the more it is left with the loss-making industries.

These de-nationalisation, or privatisation, policies illustrate the deep gulf between the values and attitudes of the Conservative and Labour parties towards the whole idea of state involvement in the economy. The Conservative Party has argued that efficiency depends on the existence of competition. It might be true that some of the nationalised industries, for example those concerned with energy, compete with one another and with oil. But the Conservatives argue that state industries are shielded from the realities of competition in a number of ways. For instance, they can never go bankrupt while they have the government behind them. This means that high wage increases can be made and given much more easily than in the private sector. There is also far too little pressure for modernisation and moves away from old, and inefficient, work practices.

Conservatives go further and point out that a number of nationalised industries are monopolies which do not face competition at all. And, as monopolies, there is less incentive to become efficient. Consumers, for example, have no choice but to accept what they are given. This was true of the Post Office. The destruction of the Post Office monopoly in supplying telephone equipment has meant that people now have a wider choice of telephones. This may not be an earth-shattering change but it does illustrate the advantages, as Conservatives see it, of healthy competition. When competition was introduced in the inter-city bus services there was a massive fall in prices.

The Conservative Party has never been happy with the idea that it should be one of the state's responsibilities to become involved in industry. It might be that some industries, such as the railways, could never be run at a profit. But where a nationalised industry, or part of it, does make a profit then the Conservative policy is to de-nationalise it and let it face the discipline of the market place.

Has nationalisation succeeded?

To some extent the answer to this question depends on party preference. But success or failure is difficult to judge because it could be due either to nationalisation itself, or to the particular conditions in each industry, or to the actions of government. This last point may be especially relevant when governments force industries to adopt policies against their wishes. If a government tells an industry to hold its prices down then it is hardly fair to judge its success by the size of profits, or the size of a loss.

Another problem is that many of the original nationalised industries, such as coal and the railways, and later ones such as steel, already had enormous financial and economic problems when they were first nationalised and continue to do so. Indeed one of the arguments for nationalisation has been that the government must take over such firms and industries if they are considered vital for the economy. Even the Conservative Party found this essential with Rolls Royce. But this has not helped the public image of nationalisation, which is often associated with failure.

Nevertheless each nationalised industry can point to areas of economic success. Productivity in the coal industry has risen sharply as pits have been modernised, bonus schemes introduced, and manpower cut. Between 1960 and 1975, for example, the industry lost 389,000 men. British Rail has successfully electrified many of its main lines. The gas industry was able to change from town gas to oil-based gas to natural gas in little more than ten years and each change needed new technology; British Airways is one of the world's largest passenger carrying airlines. None of this should disguise the fact that nationalised industries still need to solve a number of problems – such as over-manning and the introduction of new technology. Nor has the balance between accountability to government and parliament and commercial freedom been satisfactorily sorted out. With privatisation under the Conservative govermment of Mrs Thatcher, and nationalisation still a central part of Labour Party policy, state control of industry will be on the political agenda for many years.

The management of the economy

Few things are more central to the intentions of government than its economic and financial policies. Questions about education, the health service, pensions, and defence almost invariably come down to choices about how financial resources are going to be distributed.

It might be assumed that such problems of choice can be broken down to two basic questions – firstly, how should governments distribute their resources between competing alternatives? One government might put welfare state spending before defence and roads, another might put law and order before expanding education. Secondly, how much money should be spent and how should it be raised? Some governments prefer to limit either the total of expenditure or parts of it and prefer to see taxation cut. Other governments might want both increased.

But government economic policy is not just a book-keeping exercise with a list of projects in order of priority on one side, and a list of fund-raising ideas on the other. Governments attempt to *manage* the economy in order to achieve objectives such as low inflation, high employment and economic growth. Decisions on spending and raising money are central to these objectives.

A further problem is that these objectives can conflict. Policies for reducing unemployment, for example, can mean an increase in inflation, and vice versa. Governments therefore have to decide which of their overall objectives must come first. In 1979, for example, Mrs Thatcher's government clearly made reducing the level of inflation its major priority. This not only affected its taxation and expenditure proposals but also meant that economic growth and employment levels were likely to suffer.

How is economic management attempted?

There are three main weapons which governments use to control economic activity. These are **fiscal** policy, **monetary** policy and **direct controls**.

Fiscal policy

Fiscal policy is concerned with government finance and includes taxation, government expenditure, and borrowing. The centrepiece of fiscal policy is the Budget.

The use of fiscal policy as an economic weapon owes a great deal to the 'Keynesian Revolution' (see Chapter 14). Budget proposals for taxation and expenditure will affect the general level of demand in the economy. If there is unemployment, a cut in taxes and an increase in government expenditure puts money into people's pockets to spend. This raises the level of demand and decreases unemployment.

If the level of demand is too high, which can mean rising prices and people buying many goods from abroad, then government expenditure can be cut and taxes raised. But taxes can be altered more quickly than

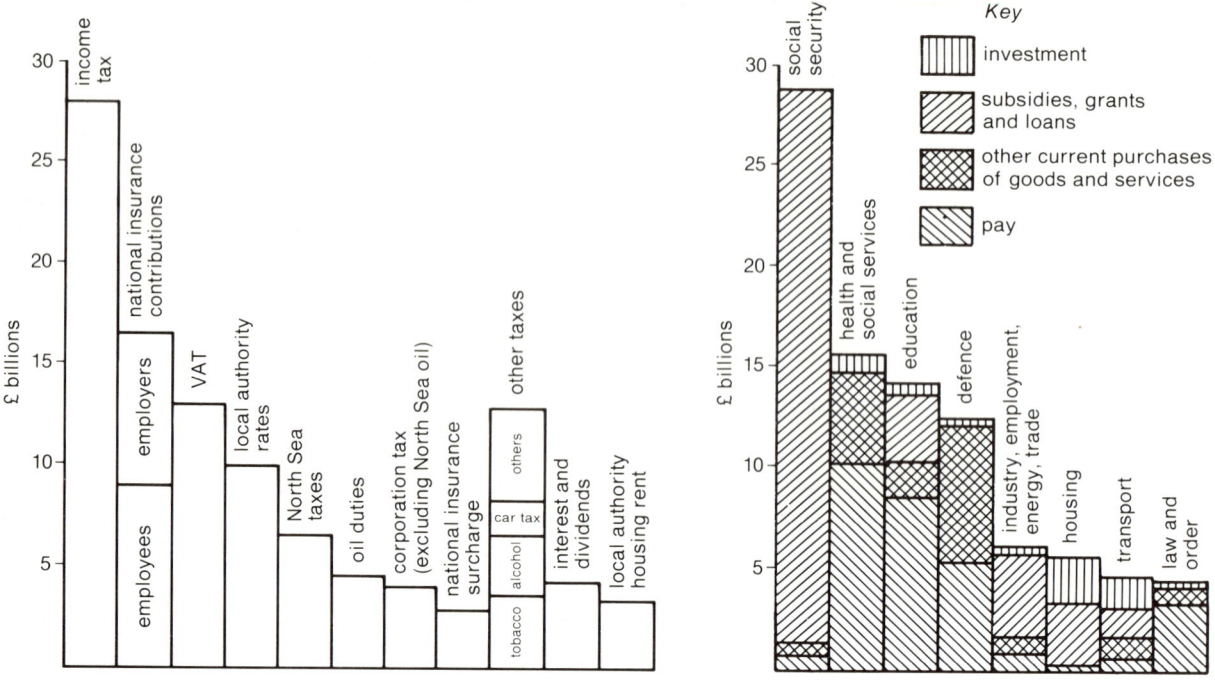

Figure 15.3 Public expenditure: where the money comes from: where the money goes to.

government expenditure as spending plans are fixed over some years and are difficult to change.

Governments do not raise all the money they need through taxation, they also need to *borrow* money to cover the difference between revenue and expenditure. This gap is called the Public Sector Borrowing Requirement (PSBR). Money can be borrowed in two ways. Firstly over the long term, which can raise interest rates because the government has to make any loan attractive to lenders. Secondly, in the short term by selling Treasury Bills; but if banks buy these Bills, they can use them as a security to lend customers more money – and this will in turn increase demand. It follows that any government anxious to reduce the level of demand, would prefer not to borrow and will want to cut the PSBR. To do this, it must cut expenditure.

Monetary policy

Spending depends on how much money people (or firms) have and how much credit they can get from lenders. If money and credit are easily available, this encourages spending on goods and services so that the level of demand will rise. This might reduce unemployment but would probably put pressure on prices, and again there is a danger that more foreign goods will be bought.

Monetary policy is aimed at controlling the activities of banks, credit companies, and building societies. To do this the government acts through the Bank of England. The main method is to change the price of getting credit; in other words to alter interest rates. If interest rates rise, money is more expensive to borrow. Another way is to change hire purchase regulations, for example, so that either more or less needs to be put down as a deposit. Governments will be especially concerned to control the ability of banks to lend to their customers. The danger is, of course, that restricting the supply of money and credit may reduce the pressure of inflation but it is likely to increase unemployment because people can buy less and firms find it expensive to borrow the necessary money for expansion or development. Very high interest rates can force businesses to the edge of bankruptcy, or beyond.

Direct controls

Fiscal and monetary policy have an effect on the economy but they still allow a certain freedom of choice. High interest rates, for example, might discourage people from borrowing but they do not stop anyone doing so altogether. As a result governments have also used more direct controls. In recent years they have attempted to use direct controls in areas such as pay and price policies, limiting the amount of money people could take abroad for holidays, and so on. They have also given special help to certain regions of the country.

Some politicians have favoured direct control over the amount of imports, such as foreign-made cars, to protect British workers' jobs. For over a hundred years there have been politicians in favour of using customs duties, or tariffs, to reduce imports. But if we impose controls on imports, then the same might be done to our exports to other countries.

Economic policies

Managing the economy, then, is no easy task. How have governments used these economic weapons? Three economic problems, inflation, unemployment, and regional development illustrate the way economic policies have been applied.

Inflation

Britain's inflation rate was, on average, 3.2 per cent in the 1950s, 3.8 per cent in the 1960s and 12.0 per cent in the 1970s. In 1975 it reached 27 per cent and had become, without question, the central economic problem facing government.

What causes inflation? To begin, there are certain factors which are outside the control of any British government. An example of this was the decision by the major oil producing nations to raise the price of oil four times in 1973. Inside Britain, one explanation is that inflation has been caused by excessive wage demands, especially when they are greater than any increase in productivity. As a result one approach to inflation which has been tried in different forms since 1961, is to try and reach agreements on limiting pay increases.

Successive governments have introduced a 'pay pause' (1961), a 'guiding light' of increases around 3 per cent (1962), voluntary restraint (1965), a pay freeze (1966), severe restraint with a zero norm (1967), pay freeze (1972), £1 plus 4 per cent (1973), a social contract with unions, giving £6 maximum (1975), then guidelines of 10 per cent (1977) and 5 per cent (1978), limits on pay rises in the public sector (1980–83). The mixture has varied from voluntary restraint to a statutory or compulsory policy. Each attempt has helped to reduce the inflation rate, but the incomes policies have also had certain disadvantages. To begin with, any **percentage** increase in incomes gives the better paid more cash than the lower paid. Secondly, various anomalies develop because some groups such as powerful unions or very profitable firms can use their industrial strength to gain or give larger wage

'The Winter of Discontent 1978–1979' was a time when the Labour government faced large wage demands from, and strikes in, public sector industries like health and local government.

Deserted housing block. Birkenhead 1979. Local authorities have been forced to cut back their spending – which means that they have great difficulty dealing with their own problems such as housing.

increases than weaker groups. Thirdly, governments, as employers, can usually control wage increases in some parts of the public sector more effectively than in others. The result can be a build-up of resentment. In the winter of 1978–79 this led to strikes by government employees in such areas as the health service.

Labour governments have also tried direct controls on prices by forcing manufacturers to justify price increases before various bodies such as the Prices and Incomes Commission and both parties deliberately held back price increases in nationalised industries as part of their inflation policies in the late 1960s and early 1970s.

The Conservative government after 1979 rejected the use of direct controls on prices and incomes. In the public sector, they used 'cash limits' as a way of limiting pay increases. Departments and nationalised industries were given ceilings on how much cash they could spend. They could choose to give modest pay increases for everyone, or cut employment and give the survivors more. But these cash limits were not kept. In 1981–82, for example, the government wanted pay increases of around 4 per cent. But miners, firemen and water workers received around 9 per cent and the police were given 13 per cent. Workers in the first group have industrial strength, and the government put a high priority on law and order which favoured the police. Nevertheless, wage increases in many parts of the private sector were severely affected by the survival problems which firms faced, and by the rise of unemployment itself. Workers were reluctant to use their industrial power because this could endanger the future of their companies, and there was little chance of finding alternative work.

The second major policy used since 1976 to tackle inflation has been to reduce the supply of money and credit in the economy. It involves cutbacks in government borrowing, which limits increases in credit, and in public expenditure. This was applied with increased effort by the Conservative government after 1979. Cutbacks in public expenditure meant severe cash limits on central government departments and on government rate support grants for local authorities. Services were cut back as economies had to be made, and virtually every activity of local government felt the pinch.

Interest rates were raised and one effect was to make Britain an attractive place for foreigners to invest their money, which strengthened the pound. But it also meant that firms which needed to borrow money had to pay very heavily for it, and mortgage rates went up as well. Overall, the effect of these policies was also to raise the level of unemployment.

These attempts to control inflation helped to reduce the rate from 21.8 per cent in May 1980 to 10 per cent by early 1982 and just under 5 per cent in 1985. But, according to critics, the cost was very high. Economic growth fell, unemployment reached well over 3 million by 1985 and there were record levels of bankruptcies. The position was worsened by a general economic depression in the industrialised world until 1983 which made it more difficult to sell our goods. And it is worth remembering that during this period inflation rates in countries such as West Germany and Japan were still below ours.

Unemployment

In the years after 1945 the unemployment rate was very low in Britain. In the 1950s it averaged 1.5 per cent of the working population, and it was only 2 per cent in the 1960s. Yet the size of the working population increased by almost 2 million over the same period. At that time one of our problems was a shortage of workers. By 1969 we had a workforce of 25.4 million and there were only about 450,000 out of a job.

In 1973 the fourfold increase in oil prices marked the beginning of a recession in the world, and from then on, unemployment gradually rose. By 1985 there were over 3 million unemployed – the highest total since the 1930s. What is more, the length of time people stayed out of work increased as well. Some groups in Britain have been very badly affected. By the beginning of 1984, for example, almost 25 per cent of those under eighteen who were looking for work could not find it.

Types of job	Category	Category total (*no. of jobs*)	Percentage (%)
Typists Telephonists Secretarial Accounts clerks Office jobs	Office staff	46	12.5
Engineering Motor trade Electricians Warehouse Building	Technical/ industrial	60	17
Hotel and catering Shops Security Drivers	Service industries	100	28
Representatives		19	5
'Today's vacancies' Young people Community programme		63 30 40	17.5 8 12

Figure 15.4 A list of jobs available in one local job centre over a week. What do the job categories tell us?

Unemployment can be caused by a general recession in the economy such as Britain experienced after 1973. But there are other causes as well. Although the level of unemployment was low after 1945 it was not the same throughout the country. Britain has a pattern of regional unemployment which goes back to the 1920s.

The decline of industries such as coal, shipbuilding, cotton at that time was caused largely by such factors as foreign competition and the development of substitutes such as synthetic fibres. The result was a permanent fall in demand for these British goods and the creation of localised, structural unemployment. Unemployment in towns such as Jarrow and Merthyr Tydfil rose to 75 per cent in the early 1930s and in the 'depressed areas' as a whole it was rarely below 20 per cent until war came in 1939.

The decline of the older industries would not have caused such a disaster if the new industries which developed, such as motor vehicles, electrical goods, had absorbed the unemployed. But these grew up in the Midlands and the south-east, not in the depressed areas. This regional imbalance in unemployment was always present in the 1950s and 1960s, although efforts were made to create jobs in the older industrial areas. After 1973 it became more apparent. However, by

Jarrow March 1932 and Peoples March for Jobs 1983. Marching against un-employment – 50 years apart. In both cases the intention was to draw attention to the scale of the problem.

Figure 15.5 Regional unemployment (1983). How do the unemployment figures relate to the location of the heavy, traditional industries? What reasons might there be to take a regional protest about unemployment to London?

1983, as the map (Figure 15.5) shows, even some areas which were prosperous a few years earlier, such as the West Midlands, now joined the list of regions with a higher than average unemployment rate.

Tackling unemployment

Both regional unemployment and mass unemployment are likely to fall if the level of demand in the economy rises. The problem in the 1970s and early 1980s for British governments was that policies which raised the level of demand, were certain to increase inflation. These included increased government spending, tax cuts, lower interest rates, and so on. The counter-inflation policies being followed were the reverse of these and actually increased unemployment. Curing inflation was clearly regarded as the main priority. Governments also argued that controlling inflation, and thus helping to make the British economy more competitive, was the only way to solve the problem of unemployment in the long run.

This was especially the view of the Conservative government after 1979 which argued that 'real jobs' needed to be created through greater competitiveness in the British economy. Unfortunately this is not as easy as it seems.· Modern factories which are more efficient because they use high technology, do not need the same number of workers for each process. Looming up in the future is the likelihood of 'microchip unemployment' to add to our problems.

However, governments did attempt to help the position of some of the most severely affected groups in the country. The young unemployed, for example, were offered Youth Opportunity Programmes and, in 1983, a Youth Training Scheme where all school leavers would either get work experience or training. This had the result of keeping down unemployment figures, but it could not be considered permanent help.

Since 1945, two types of overall policy have been used to attract new industries to the old 'depressed areas' now called 'development areas'. They have been described as the 'carrot' and the 'stick', assuming that moving firms is the same as moving donkeys! Carrots have included giving advantages such as investment grants and tax concessions to firms going to development areas. Advance factories have been built, ready for firms to move into them. Particular blackspots have been termed 'special development areas' with extra help given.

Government itself is a major investor and employer. The steel industry, for example, set up two of its most modern plants after 1945 in Port Talbot and Newport in South Wales, the Vehicle Licencing Centre was built in Swansea. In 1980 the government introduced eleven 'enterprise zones' in development areas. Firms opening up in these zones do not have to pay rates for up to ten years, and planning controls have been relaxed so that factories can be built more quickly.

How successful have these policies been?

One of the great problems of development areas was their dependence on only one major industry. Government policies have helped to change this. In South Wales, for example, the coal industry has declined sharply but the region now has alternative employment in steel, car components, chemicals, oil, as well as a range of smaller consumer industries producing goods such as washing machines, refrigerators, and vacuum cleaners. But, regional policy also had the effect of drawing firms away from the apparently prosperous regions such as the West Midlands. In the recession after 1973, and especially after 1980, unemployment in the West Midlands was only slightly better than in Wales and actually worse than Scotland as its own industries, such as car manufacturing, were hit by the recession.

For many years after 1945 the problem of unemployment was seen in regional terms. It was assumed that large-scale unemployment affecting the country as a whole would not return. The increasing scale of the recession after 1973, the need to control inflation, the push for more efficient and labour-saving technology, the lack of competitiveness of parts of British industry compared with some of our rivals, altered all this.

This deeper unemployment has considerable social consequences. Young people face the prospect of no permanent work and older people who lose their jobs after they are fifty may never be employed again. It also distorts government spending because of the cost of paying benefits. The solution may be found in a much more efficient industrial base, a moderate increase in public expenditure to create jobs, schemes such as work-sharing or early retirement, or a mixture of them all. The fact is that for the first time since the 1930s, solving the problem of large scale unemployment has once again become a major task of government.

Discussion and essay questions

1. How far do you think the problems facing nationalised industries are caused by 'too much political interference'?

2. What arguments do you think would be used by Labour politicians in favour of nationalising banks? What counter arguments might be put by Conservative opponents?

3. Compare and contrast the problems faced by the chairman of a nationalised industry (for example coal or the railways) and the chairman of a large private firm such as ICI.

4. What arguments can be put forward in favour, and against, de-nationalising industries? Apply these arguments in particular to the railways, British Airways, and the coal industry.

5. Why have governments attempted to manage the economy in recent years? What main methods have they used?

6. There has been a great deal of attention recently to the need to cut public expenditure. Why have governments wanted to do this? Which areas of public expenditure, if any, would you like to see cut? Give reasons for your choice.

7. What are the main social, economic and political effects of
   (a) inflation
   (b) unemployment?
   If you were in charge of the government which problem would you put as your priority to solve – and why?

8. What is meant by 'regional unemployment'? Why has it been caused and what policies have been used to try and deal with it? What do you think should happen to areas that have lost their economic strength?

9. How would you deal with the problem of unemployment among
   (a) school leavers
   (b) those who lose their jobs in middle age?

Part Seven: LOCAL GOVERNMENT

16   Why have local government?

The study of local government provides opportunities we have not really had before. When we considered the work of the Cabinet, parliament or pressure groups, we were largely limited to reading other people's comments about them. It is difficult to talk to a Cabinet minister, impossible to be at a Cabinet meeting and very expensive to make our own study of a parliamentary election. But local government is far more accessible. Instead of 650 members of parliament we have some 23,500 county and district councillors. Pressure groups, political parties, bureaucracies and political decisions can all be observed at local level. In many parts of the country there are local elections every year, while the wards which councillors represent are measured in terms of streets and neighbourhoods rather than towns and cities. The study of local politics can become an opportunity for observation and discovery. It is an odd thought that a county council is perhaps spending upwards of £300 million each year and yet many people who live in that area will be hard pressed to name a single elected member or which political party is in control of its affairs.

Local government and public services

One of the most important functions of government is to provide services to people in the community. As we saw in Chapter 14, this aspect of government has grown greatly in the twentieth century. These services have to be provided fairly and efficiently. While parliament decides the laws, there has to be some form of public bureaucracy which puts them into operation. This job can hardly be handled from London alone. The Department of Education and Science in London, for example, cannot directly run every school or college in the country. Nor can $3\frac{1}{4}$ million unemployed all collect their benefit in London. There has to be some sort of network of local offices which can provide local knowledge, and a point of contact for the public.

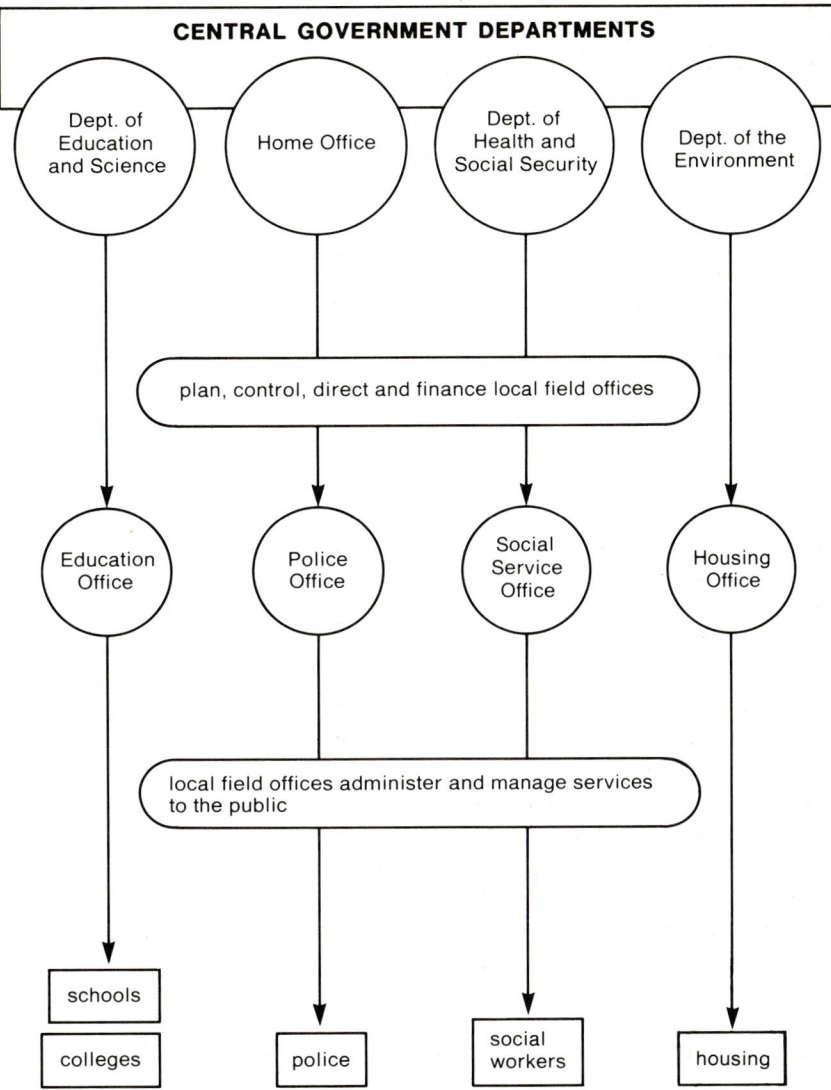

CENTRAL GOVERNMENT DEPARTMENTS

Dept. of Education and Science

Home Office

Dept. of Health and Social Security

Dept. of the Environment

plan, control, direct and finance local field offices

Education Office

Police Office

Social Service Office

Housing Office

local field offices administer and manage services to the public

schools

colleges

police

social workers

housing

Figure 16.1 A possible system of providing services using local field offices.

Figure 16.1 shows a possible way of doing this. All government departments might have a local office with local officials to see that their services were carried out according to the rules. This is in fact the method used in Britain to make cash payments to the sick, disabled and unemployed. But social work for the old, children, the handicapped is *not* run from local DHSS offices; it forms part of local government, along with the responsibility for running schools and maintaining or building many of the roads.

Figure 16.2 shows the system of local government. In some ways it is closely linked with the national government departments. The Home Office has a lot of influence over police work; similarly, the Department of Education and Science has to approve any reorganisation of local schools. But local government is not the same as a system of local

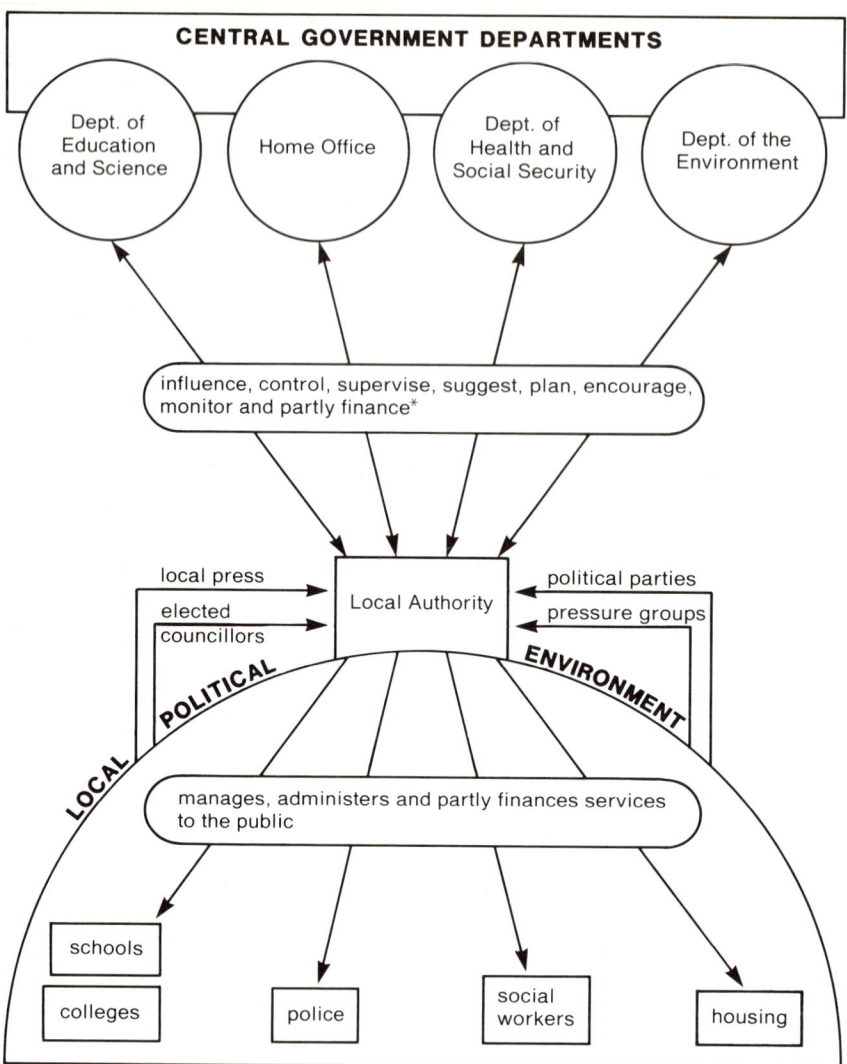

CENTRAL GOVERNMENT DEPARTMENTS

Dept. of Education and Science

Home Office

Dept. of Health and Social Security

Dept. of the Environment

influence, control, supervise, suggest, plan, encourage, monitor and partly finance*

local press

elected councillors

Local Authority

political parties

pressure groups

LOCAL POLITICAL ENVIRONMENT

manages, administers and partly finances services to the public

schools

colleges

police

social workers

housing

*This is a complicated relationship which is explored in more detail in Chapter 20. The important point to note is that local authorities are given a degree of choice to decide priorities and propose initiatives.

Figure 16.2 Providing services through local government.

offices for government ministries, because it has three characteristics of its own. First, local authorities provide a number of services, not just one. Second, powers of decision-making rest with locally elected councillors rather than civil servants. Last, local authorities have the ability to raise money through taxation in their own right.

Public services and social problems

Any form or organisation of public services will require full time professional staff who have been trained as teachers, policemen, architects or engineers. Yet many of the problems of society do not fall neatly under any one profession. An educational problem of poor attendance at school, for example, may be closely related to family problems at home. These in turn could be linked to poor housing conditions, or even unemployment. Similarly, many of the problems of inner cities involve professional staff in widely different fields such as public transport, roads, play facilities, planning decisions, employment, housing and police policy. Again links have to be formed between various professional services, if the problems are to be tackled effectively.

The running of public services often needs co-ordination and there has to be a constant interchange of ideas and information at local level. As we shall see in Chapter 19, local government finds it difficult enough to achieve effective co-ordination between its own various departments. But interchange between local government departments and the local offices of Whitehall departments can lead to even greater problems. Social workers from local government have to have regular contact with staff from the local office of the Department of Health and Social Security and frequent co-ordination with the staff of the National Health Service. Even local government itself is broken up between the services provided by the county council and those of the local district council. This concern for proper co-ordination is a fairly new issue in the development of administration in Britain but an advantage of local government is that it can help to solve this problem. However, this is only part of the argument.

The political basis of public service

It is simply impossible to meet all the demands for public services. There have to be priorities and rules to decide who gets what.

Consider the case of a proposal to build a new major road across a city. In recent years such projects have produced angry letters to the local newspaper, public meetings, petitions, and demonstrations. This conflict cannot be simply dismissed as some sort of game created by political parties or by the personal objections of those involved. On the contrary, the road proposal is bound to have very different results on people's lives. Car owners may approve of the scheme but those without cars may consider that the money would be better spent on public transport. The route of the road will suit some people more than others because it will affect the value of land and houses – and none of us want a new road outside our bedroom window. Some will oppose the scheme because it would involve the demolition of their home, while others may be delighted to be rehoused if this is the only way they can get to the top of a local authority list for a new council house.

These are genuine conflicts of interest which cannot really be solved by telling everybody to use their 'common sense'. Is it common sense to build the road or not to build it? Is the community interest better served by improvements to roads or public transport? The trouble with terms like 'common sense' or the 'community interest' is that they do not really help anybody to make the choice. Everybody wants to see decisions which are in the best interest of our towns and villages. But is that better served by a new school or a new home for the elderly? Is it served by an open-cast coalmine or sewage works? Unfortunately few of the choices which confront government have 'obvious' or 'self-evident' solutions. We are often just left with conflicting political judgements.

The importance of political choice

If public services were only organised through local offices of central government departments (Fig. 16.1), one important result would be that each office could only consider its own problems and priorities. The education office would consider educational problems while the highways office would consider the problems of transport. There would need to be central government machinery to decide whether a new school in Hull was even more important than one in Coventry. But it would be quite impossible to decide whether Hull's school was a more or less important priority than a new road through that same city to ease traffic problems.

This is not simply a theoretical problem. If a health authority decides to build a new hospital in your town it has taken this decision in the light of an assessment of national, regional and local health needs and available facilities. It will not, and cannot, consider other possible needs of your town. Bad housing conditions, old schools, congested roads, are all irrelevant to the decisions of the health authority.

The organisation of public services through local government therefore introduces an important dimension of *choice at local level* which could not be considered by isolated offices of central government departments. It also introduces politicians as decision-makers at this local level. Without these local politicans, choices and decisions would have to be made either by the Cabinet and government ministers or by professional civil servants at national or local level. From what we have discovered about the amount of work which already falls to the Cabinet and government ministers, it is quite clear that all the choices and alternatives could not be settled by central government politicians. They can and do indicate the major priorities as they see them. But there is a world of difference between deciding to allocate less national resources to education because of the fall in the birth rate, and recommending which particular school should be closed. That choice either has to be left to local politicians or local professional educational experts.

There are clearly many decisions that we are quite happy to leave to local professional experts. It is difficult to imagine a party political debate about the diameter of storm drains for a new road. Indeed, frequently there is criticism of local politicians for too much 'interference' in the work of professionals. A recent example was the attempt by local politicians to have a greater say in police policy in Manchester. Chief constables and the Home Secretary have firmly resisted any such move, arguing that professional judgement must form the basis of such policy decisions. While a professional judgement continues to receive widespread popular support, this can work satisfactorily. But when expert judgement is frequently challenged, the situation can become more difficult. We might be very happy to accept a civil engineer's judgement concerning the diameter of the storm drain, but that does not mean that we would be happy to accept his judgement that the road should be built in the first place.

As we shall see, the existence of local elections and elected councillors does not guarantee that the preferences of the public automatically decide policy choices. But they do give a framework for public debate, argument and decisions.

Local government and the community

A modern local authority does not control or even influence all that happens within its geographical boundaries. Company decisions to open or close factories may have a profound influence on the life of a community, but local authorities can often do little but watch and hope. The policy choices of local government are limited by local circumstances, by the actions of those who manage the different parts of local trade, industry or agriculture, and by the complexity of problems it tries to solve. In short, local government cannot be separated from its total socio-economic context, neither can it be divorced from

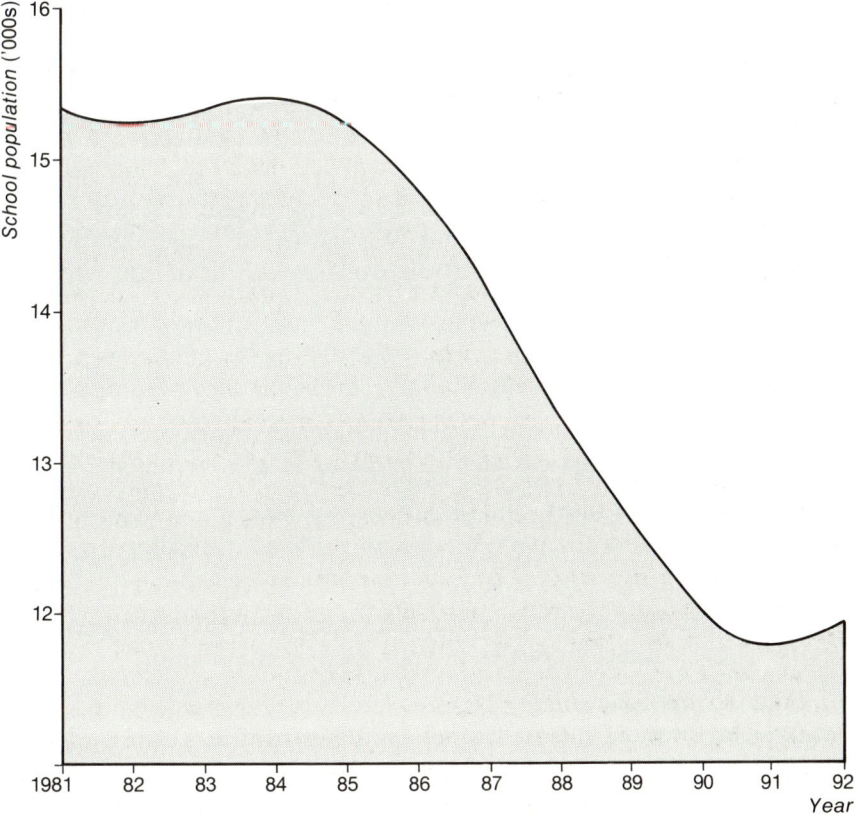

Figure 16.3 Projected high school population (Jan 1981–92) Stoke-on-Trent. Who is to decide which school to close?

(a) Where the money comes from

3.7% Other local authorities and County Balances		£15.54 million
8.0% People charged for services		£33.60 million
39.2% Ratepayers	21.4% Domestic	£90.09 million
	5.5% Private Industry	£23.14 million
	6.1% Commercial	£25.51 million
	6.2% Other	£26.09 million
49.1% Taxpayers	Government Grants and Reimbursements	£206.76 million
100.0%		£420.73 million

Figure 16.4 County council services in Staffordshire.

its legal and government context. Local government is only part of the machinery of the state. It is created by central government and parliament which decides its legal powers and, increasingly, the resources it has at its disposal. As we shall see this is frequently the major influence on the choices of local authorities.

In spite of these limitations, it would be a great mistake to underestimate the importance of local government. With a total expenditure in 1981–82 of £30 billion, it is not surprising that local authorities are crucial to the management of local affairs.

Figure 16.4 indicates the activity and range of services of just one local authority – Staffordshire County Council. No other single institution can have such an impact on community life. We can try to change the pattern of expenditure and priorities. We can and do frequently criticise the way that decisions are taken. But we cannot abolish politics in local government. We can try to change its form or its consequences, but we cannot remove the need to decide between competing demands – which is the basis of politics itself.

Discussion and essay questions

1. What are the differences between a national network of local offices providing public services and a system of local government?

2. How would you justify the importance of having a system of local government from the point of view of (a) local councillors (b) local residents?

3. Give an example of a recent conflict of interest which has occurred over local authority policies in your area or community?

4. Find out the following:
    (a) The location of your district and county offices.
    (b) The name of the political party which is in overall control of your county and district council.
    (c) The names and parties of your local county and district councillors.

(b) Where the money goes to — County council services

The following tables show estimated income and expenditure and numbers of people employed for each of the Council's main services and for the Magistrates' Courts and Probation committees.

	Gross Expenditure £ million	Number of Employees (whole-time equivalents) 1982/83 Number		Gross Expenditure £ million	Number of Employees (whole-time equivalents) 1982/83 Number
Education	258.936	19,738	Records and museums	0.688	50
Farms and agriculture	0.386	15	Social services	33.056	3,605
Fire and public protection	9.034	783	Waste disposal	3.748	145
Highways and transportation	38.891		Misc. services, precepts and other expenditure	4.475	130
Libraries	4.617	451	Contingency for inflation etc.	20.825	
Magistrates' Courts	2.268	187	Total	420.729	29,447
Planning	2.449	182	Employees in central departments dealing with all services		626
Police	38.063	3,012			
Probation	3.293	279	Total		30,073

(c) What is provided

Education

185,636	Pupils and
73,810	Students educated at
674	Schools and colleges
12,458	Teachers and lecturers
78,580	School meals provided daily
£618	is the annual cost of educating a child at primary school and
£886	at a secondary school

Social Services

2,087	Elderly people accommodated at a cost of £78 per week per person
512	Children under supervision
1,462	Children accommodated and boarded-out
9,400	Elderly people visited
37,200	Hours of home help support a week
1,590	Telephones for the disabled
39,500	Cases dealt with by social workers
10,670	Meals-on-wheels served weekly
1,031	Places in industrial training units, adult training centres and activity units
138	Places for blind and disabled persons in sheltered workshops

Libraries, records, museums

2,369,800	Books, music scores, maps, microfilms, records and pictures
9,591,300	Issues per year at an average cost of 44.1p per issue
45	Libraries full-time
7	Mobile libraries serving 1,000 places
5	Caravan libraries serving 18 places

Police

2,108	Police Officers
44	Cadets
156	School Crossing Patrols
40	Traffic wardens supported by
222	Manual workers and
442	Civilian staff

Fire and public protection

829	Firemen dealt with
8,216	incidents in 1980/81
11,263	Complaints dealt with in 1980/81 by trading standards and consumer protection staff
179,766	Goods examined or analysed

Highways

3,528	Miles of road
177	Miles of trunk roads
40	Miles of motorway

Waste disposal

590,000	Tons per annum at a cost of £5.99 per ton

Other services

Town and country planning
Country parks and picnic areas (4,180 acres)
Smallholdings (8,550 acres)
Magistrates' Courts
Probation

17 The structure of local government

When our present system of local government came into being on 1st April 1974 many people found that they now paid rates to a different local authority and that they lived in a place with a new name, in some cases invented for the new system. In this chapter we look at the system before 1974, why change was needed and at how the present-day structure came about.

The system before 1974

The origins of the 'country' or 'shire' stretch back into Anglo-Saxon times and names such as Yorkshire or Worcestershire, Essex or Northumberland are a thousand years old. When the last big re-organisation of local government was carried out in 1888 and 1894, it was decided that each county should have a county council to run its major services. Seventy years later, these services included the provision of education, new roads, and a police force. But the counties were also divided into districts, with rural district councils and urban district councils (for the thousands of small towns in Britain). They took care of less expensive and complicated services such as sewage, public libraries and baths, road repairs. This was a *two-tier system* of local government. However, another important tradition of local government was the 'borough'. Through the ages, towns and cities had acquired charters from the monarch of the time which granted them powers of managing their own affairs and certain rights such as holding markets. In the largest towns, the nineteenth-century legislation built upon this tradition by creating the all-purpose 'county boroughs'. These were quite independent of counties and provided all local services from a *single tier*. The smaller towns which had historic charters, but were not considered large enough to be able to run all their own services, were known as 'non-county boroughs'. They had similar powers to an urban district council.

Why was change needed?

First, the patterns of social life and work changed greatly after 1894. As transport developed, people moved away from town centres to new suburbs outside the town boundaries or even to villages which might then grow into towns. Industrial development sometimes meant the

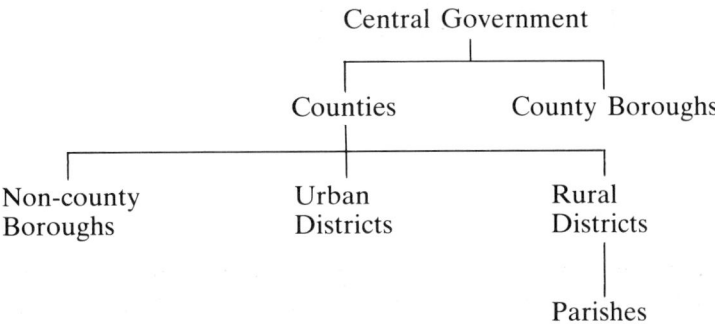

This structure of local government made an important distinction between the major urban areas (County boroughs) and the rest of the county. County boroughs provided all local authority services but in the counties the County Councils were responsible for some services while the second tier authorities (non-county boroughs, urban districts and rural districts) provided the rest. Town and country were rigidly divided with even relatively small urban areas having the status of independent county boroughs.

Figure 17.1 Local government system in England and Wales 1894–1974.

rapid expansion of cities, such as Coventry after mass production of motor cars began.

Such changes created difficulties for local authorities. Sometimes it was simply a matter of a county borough or urban district negotiating with a county for land on which to build new houses or a new sewerage works. In the case of the great conurbations it was impossible to tell where Birmingham, Liverpool or Manchester ended and another town began. This led to problems in organising transport, police and road-building because of the number of councils involved.

Second, there were difficulties in providing efficient, modern services. A modern fire service is very different from its nineteenth-century ancestor which used horse-drawn engines from fire stations dotted around the country and often manned by part-time firemen. It needs a centralised system to call on the nearest available equipment of the right sort; training schools to give firemen all the skills they need, co-operation with other services such as the police and ambulances and so on. It is a lot more expensive and a great deal more mobile, and only works well if one service covers a wide area.

Third, ideas about what local government ought to be doing and how it ought to be doing it, have altered. We have come to accept that local and central government should play an active part in planning the environment, and helping to free people from the tyranny of squalor, poverty and ignorance. As our ideas have changed, so have our expectations. Mass education, council housing, social and welfare facilities, recreational provisions have all become normal expectations of local government. Even those authorities which are the most enthusiastic in

Urban conurbation: an aerial view of Birmingham showing the size and spread of the city.

cutting public expenditure have found just how difficult it is to reverse these expectations.

Of course, even the strongest case for changing the system would meet with all kinds of opposition. Political parties, for instance, might fear a change in local government boundaries which would bring voters in a wealthy suburb into a Labour-controlled area, or break up a smart residential district with a solid Conservative majority. Council officials might fear for their careers if they felt that the council which employed them was about to be abolished. Among citizens there could be objections to the idea of their town or district being 'swallowed up' by a big neighbour, especially if rates were higher there or the services were thought poorer. In general, there is often a belief that it is easier to have a democratic voice in a smaller authority than a big one.

Greater London

Despite these doubts there was growing pressure for change in the 1950s, especially in the conurbations which included Liverpool, Manchester and Birmingham. It was generally agreed that these lacked a form of government which could consider the problems of the whole area. This was even more obvious for the London region.

The built-up area of London included about 8 million people and extended well beyond the area of the London County Council. Parts of Surrey, Essex, Hertfordshire, Kent and all of Middlesex were effectively part of the greater London area. In 1957 the government established a Royal Commission under the chairmanship of Sir Edward Herbert to consider the future of local government in the region. The Commission's report provided the basis for the subsequent system of local government in London. The London Government Act 1963 broke important new ground; and from 1965 the Greater London Council (GLC) took over important functions for London as whole, including transport, and the ambulance and fire services.

The Act also established the very important 32 London boroughs which became responsible for the remaining services of local government. There was however one important complication. The former London County Council had run the education service in what was by then inner London. Instead of splitting this service between the new inner London boroughs, it was decided to create the Inner London Education Authority.

Figure 17.2 Even by 1951 the socio-geographical pattern of London had spread into Middlesex, Hertfordshire, Surrey, Essex, Kent, and Buckinghamshire. Any planning and policies for London could only be achieved through negotiation with numerous authorities.

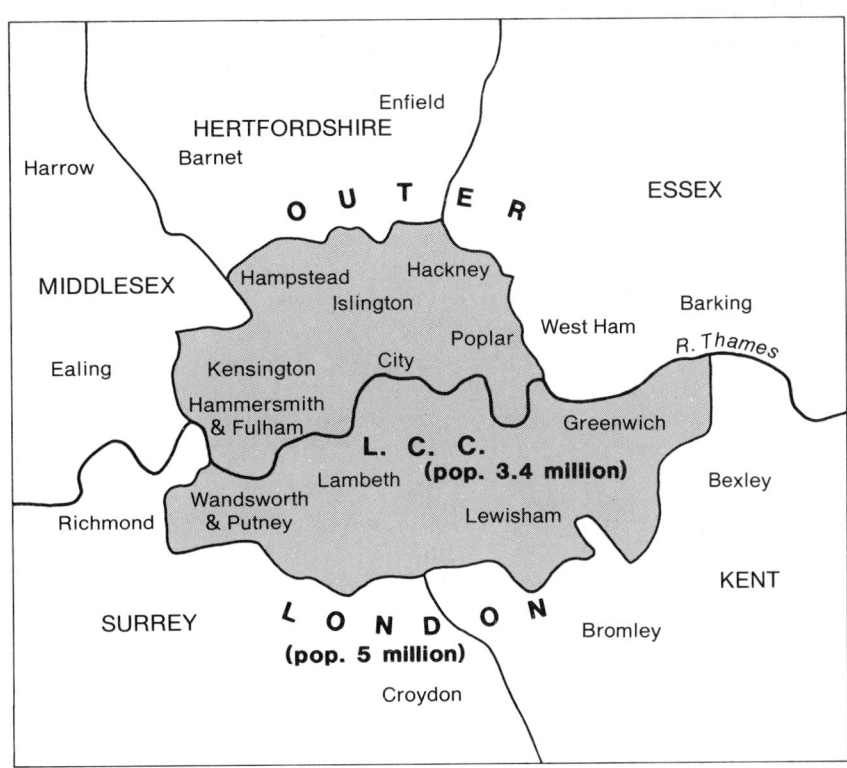

GLC: Greater London Council.
Covers an area of about 600 square miles, containing 8 million people. Responsible for development plan for Greater London; fire, police and ambulance services; main roads and transport; refuse disposal. Also shares powers in housing, open spaces, sewerage and drainage where these functions cut across or involves several boroughs.

32 London Boroughs (plus the city), each with an elected council.
Responsible for housing, health, welfare, libraries, non-major roads, education (except for Inner London Education Authority area, which has special GLC committee and representatives of each IL Borough Council), and local planning.

Greater London and London Boroughs

Greater London

Inner London Education Authority

Figure 17.3 Structure of local government in London.

Other English regions

Elsewhere, procedures for review, which had been introduced by the Local Government Act 1958, had made very slow progress. And in 1966 the Government finally decided to appoint a *Royal Commission* under the chairmanship of Sir John Maud (from 1967 Lord Radcliffe Maud) to examine the whole problem.

The long-awaited report was published in July 1969 and identified a series of major problems with the existing structure of local government. The major criticisms were as follows:

1. Many authorities were too small to provide the financial resources, qualified manpower and expensive capital equipment needed for many local services.
2. The areas of local government no longer fitted the pattern of life and work which made overall planning of land and transportation very difficult.
3. The services of local government were often split between different local authorities which was confusing to the public and made co-ordination very difficult.
4. The structure of local government was too divided and hence too weak to counter the power of central government which was increasingly dominating local decisions.

The Commission then laid down a set of principles for building a new system.

Firstly they argued that town and country districts were now socially and economically interlocked and should not come under separate local governments. Secondly they recommended that services could be provided most effectively if the future units of local government were between 250,000 and 1 million people. Lastly they declared that there were substantial advantages for having all services provided by a single unit of local government.

They recommended that this **unitary principle**, as it became called, could be applied everywhere in England apart from the three largest conurbations around Manchester, Liverpool and Birmingham, where two levels of government would be needed.

The major proposals of the report were accepted by the Labour government, but before they could introduce new legislation, they lost the general election in 1970.

It is not surprising that the new Conservative government did not like the idea of unitary authorities. County boroughs which the report wanted extended into the countryside tended to be dominated by the Labour party. Conservative strength traditionally was in the suburbs and countryside and the party was strongest in the county councils and district authorities. There was however more to the Conservative rejection of the report than party advantage. They felt that unitary authorities would be too busy and too remote from most citizens. Some services could be effectively provided on a smaller scale, they argued, and it was not necessary to force them to follow the pattern of large units needed for the others.

Figure 17.4 Metropolitan and shire counties of England.

The six metropolitan
counties and London

Counties (6)
Responsible for overall planning, transport, police and fire service.

Districts (36)
Responsible for education, social services, housing, local planning, environmental health and recreation.

Figure 17.5 Structure of metropolitan areas.

Counties (39)
Responsible for overall planning, transport, police, fire service, education, social services.

Districts (296)
Responsible for housing local planning environmental health and recreation.

Parish/Town Councils (about 7,000)
Responsible for local amenities.

Figure 17.6 Structure of shire counties.

The present structure

The Conservative Government passed the Local Government Act in 1972; and predictably, it did not create a unitary system. Instead, when the new local government authorities came into being on 1st April 1974 they were arranged in a two-tier system, for both urban and rural areas.

Six *metropolitan counties* (see Figure 17.4) were set up for the West Midlands, Merseyside, Greater Manchester, Tyne and Wear, South Yorkshire and West Yorkshire. They were given the tasks of government where it was felt that services would be best provided on a large scale, such as strategic planning, transport, emergency services and policing. However, the government thought that the metropolitan counties should not have charge of the personal services such as education, housing and social services (see Figure 17.5). These are also the biggest spending local government departments and it was thought important that decisions should not be made too far away from the people using the services. So they were given to the second tier, the five or six *metropolitan districts* inside each metropolitan county. So, in the conurbations, local government is 'bottom-heavy', with most spending being done by the smaller authorities.

Outside the conurbations, the government decided to have thirty-nine *shire counties* (see Fig. 17.6) as the first tier of local government in England. (There were different arrangements for Scotland and Wales, as we shall see later.) In most cases these were the old historic counties, but a few new ones were created, such as Humberside and Avon. Other new counties came about through amalgamation, such as Cumbria or the combined Hereford and Worcester. Many of the shire county councils set up in 1974 had bigger populations and more spending power than before, because they took over local government in the forty-two towns which had previously been county boroughs.

Perhaps the most obvious sign of change for most people occurred at the second tier of government. The government replaced about 1,000 former boroughs, urban and rural districts with 296 *district authorities*. These were drawn up by a Boundary Commission and it was these changes which were responsible for new names and boundaries which many people found so confusing.

The government's original intention was to create a very top heavy structure with nearly all major responsibilities, apart from housing and development control, resting with the counties. However, former county boroughs such as Portsmouth, Derby, Stoke-on-Trent, Southampton, Hull and Nottingham had a long tradition of providing all of their own local government services. As these towns and cities were to be down-graded to being district authorities they were to lose nearly all their powers to the county councils. It was not surprising therefore that the new 'districts' fought very hard in parliament to gain further responsibilities. They had some success, and gained powers to make local plans, operate building regulations and maintain unclassified roads. Their most controversial success was the so-called 'agency clause' under which districts, with the county's agreement, could operate certain aspects of a service on behalf of the county.

However, in spite of these changes, it is the shire county with control over such services as police, fire, education and social services, which is the dominant unit of local government in non-metropolitan England and Wales.

Local government reform in Wales

The reform of local government in Wales followed a rather different course from that in England. Before 1974 there was a top tier of thirteen administrative counties and the four county boroughs of Cardiff, Swansea, Newport and Merthyr Tydfil. As in England, the first moves towards reform started in 1958 but the issue became so controversial that in 1965 the new Labour Secretary of State for Wales decided to set up his own inter-departmental working party of civil servants to look at the problem. As this group was still at work in 1966, Wales was left out of Radcliffe-Maud's Royal Commission.

Figure 17.7 Scotland: regional and island authorities; cities and principal towns.

No fewer than six White Papers on the future of Welsh local government were published between 1958 and 1971. The problem was always the very uneven distribution of populations between the northern coastal strip, rural central Wales and the industrial South.

The 1972 Local Government Act eventually created eight new 'shire-type' counties to replace the original thirteen and the county boroughs. These had little or no relationship with the former boundaries and except for West, Mid- and South Glamorgan, they were given names which had some historical association with their new areas – Clwyd, Dyfed, Gwent, Gwynedd, and Powys. This Act also created a second tier of thirty-seven district councils.

One interesting feature of the Welsh legislation was that it required the creation of local community councils *throughout* Wales. In England, parish councils or meetings are only found in rural areas.

Local government reform in Scotland

Generalisations about the system of local government in England and Wales do not usually apply to Scotland. This distinctiveness of Scottish local government has remained, in spite of a reorganisation which is similar to developments in the rest of Britain.

The basic structure before 1975 consisted of four all-purpose authorities in Glasgow, Edinburgh, Dundee and Aberdeen and a variety of two-tier structures. The thirty-three county councils or joint county councils provided most of the services in the rural areas, but delegated some services to the small 'burghs', (town councils), and everything except for education to the large city councils.

Figure 17.8 Wales: shire counties, cities and principal towns.

Although the Scottish Office had made some progress towards reform in the early 1960s, the Labour government established the Wheatley Commission in 1964 to parallel the Radcliffe-Maud Commission in England. The Wheatley Commission Report led to many arguments before parliament passed an Act in 1973 to change the Scottish system on 1st May 1975.

The major institution of Scottish local government is now the *region*. There are nine first-tier regional authorities and three island areas to replace the counties and all-purpose city authorities. The fifty-seven district authorities provide housing, leisure and recreation amenities, libraries, and local planning, while all other local government services are provided at regional level.

Was reorganisation worthwhile?

Reorganisation was a confusing time for the public and for people employed in local government. New organisations had to be created, new jobs applied for, old departments brought together to work under new direction and leadership. In view of all the difficulties and problems, it is not surprising that many people, not least those working in local government, have wondered whether the whole exercise was worthwhile.

This is not an easy question to answer. How can we decide if children are better or more efficiently educated? How can we determine whether the system is more responsive to the public? Even if we could find ways of measuring these things, how could we be sure that any changes in performance were actually *caused* by the reorganisation rather than some other factors?

The most frequent objections tend to fall into three broad groups. Firstly, the boundaries of many authorities are thought to pay insufficient attention to present-day social geography and too much to historical boundaries.

Secondly, a two-tier structure divides responsibility. It makes co-ordination of policy just that little more difficult and may well add to public confusion as to who is responsible for which service. Lastly, arguments about size and public access still continue. Many are not convinced that greater size has led to greater efficiency and complain at difficulties in gaining access to the relevant councillor or official.

Although in the late 1960s and early 1970s there was perhaps, general agreement between the political parties about the future government of the large urban areas like Manchester, Liverpool and London, by the 1980s this agreement had broken down. In the Autumn of 1983 the Conservative government announced in a White Paper its intention to abolish the metropolitan counties and the Greater London Council. The government argued that the original legislation intended a relatively minor role for these authorities but as they have attempted to extend their activities they have not only come into conflict with the metropolitan districts and London boroughs but also increased public spending. The Conservatives therefore intend to transfer a number of functions such as planning, highways, waste disposal, libraries and recreations to the second-tier authorities and establish joint boards for police, fire, public transport and education in inner London. But as these are all Labour-controlled authorities it is perhaps not surprising that the opposition regards the White Paper as political attack upon their policies rather than a fresh attempt to come to terms with the major problems of big city life.

Discussion and essay questions

1. Identify and explain three aspects of changes in society which created pressure for the reform of local government.

2. What were the major conclusions and recommendations of the Royal Commission 1966–69? Why do you think the government rejected the conclusions of the Report?

3. What type of local authority exists in your area since reorganisation? How are the services of local government distributed? Draw a map of the boundaries of the authority.

4. Compare and contrast the Metropolitan and Shire forms of local government.

5. Compare and contrast the organisation of local government in either Scotland or Wales with that in England.

6. Find out what type of local authority existed in your area before the reorganisation of local government in the 1970s. Draw a map of the old boundaries of the authority. Why do you think they were changed?

18 The political context of local government

By mid-March each year all the local authorities have prepared their plans for the next financial year. As the results of their decisions become clear, the political argument starts in the local newspapers:

Sir – Regarding the proposed 30 per cent rates increase in Cheshire, I would suggest we have Whizz kids at the top of the County Council. If they had been running a normal business they would have been bankrupt years ago.

We need tens of thousands of Cheshire ratepayers who will refuse to pay any more than 12.5 per cent increase on last year's rates.

Come on folks, you are being conned.

(Stoke-on-Trent *Evening Sentinel* 3.3.82).

Staffordshire Council also came under attack in the same edition, and for that matter so did the whole idea of locally elected councillors.

Sir – As we all know, Staffordshire County Council have just announced the expected rates increase . . .

The people who control our rates are not capable of doing so. They are elected, only because they belong to the party which happens to be in favour in the area at the time and not because they are the best persons to be councillors.

Let us have financial experts planning our councils and spending our money. Instead of paying councillors to attend meetings to spend our money, let us spend it on professional people to do the job . . .

(*Evening Sentinel* 3.3.82.)

The time when the views of these letter writers can be put to the test comes in May when most local elections are held. In terms of democratic politics, local elections provide the key link between the public and government. They are the mechanism for translating the preferences of the community into action. The elected councillor represents a small area. He or she will constantly try to keep in touch with local opinion or risk the revenge of the constituents at the next election. In this way the councillor is held accountable for his or her past actions and is responsive to public wishes for future ones. However, as we shall see, the reality is rather more complicated. Indeed this simple 'electoral chain of command' view has to be seriously re-examined in the light of our knowledge of local voting behaviour.

The electoral system

All councillors are now directly elected for a four-year term of office using the same 'first past the post' rules employed in parliamentary elections. However, two different types of electoral systems are found

LOCAL ELECTION ARRANGEMENTS

(The normal day of election will be the first Thursday in May)

	5 May 1983 7 May 1987 etc.	3 May 1984 5 May 1988 etc.	2 May 1985 4 May 1989 etc.	1 May 1986 3 May 1990 etc.
Shire county councils			Whole council	
Metropolitan county councils			Cancelled (i)	
Greater London council			Cancelled (i)	
London borough councils				Whole council
Metropolitan district councils	One-third council	One-third council		One-third council
Welsh district councils	One-third council or whole council	One-third council or none		One-third council or none
Non-metropolitan district councils (England)	One-third council or whole council	One-third council or none		One-third council or none
Parish councils in metropolitan districts	Whole council			
Parish councils in non-metropolitan districts	Whole council (ii)	None (ii)		None (ii)
Community councils	Whole council (ii)	None (ii)		None (ii)

(i) The government has proposed to abolish both the Metropolitan County Councils and the Greater London Council in 1986. In preparation for this reorganisation, legislation was passed by parliament to cancel the elections which were due on 2 May 1985. The existing councillors will hold office for an additional year until abolition.

(ii) Where a Welsh district council or a non-metropolitan district council is elected by thirds, the year of parish or community council elections may be altered to coincide with the election of district councillors for the area in which the parish or community is located.

Figure 18.1 Pattern of local elections.

in local government. The first is the 'clean sweep' and when *all* the councillors retire from office together, and an election is held on the first Thursday in May. The full council then remains in power for four years, apart from any by-elections. This system, used by both the shire and metropolitan counties, is simple and clear. The electorate makes its judgement and the new council has a clearly defined period of office to put its programme into operation before it has to face the electorate again.

There is, however, an old tradition in local government of **partial renewal elections**, when only one third of the council is up for election at any one time. The system is used in all the metropolitan districts. They are divided into multi-member wards. Each year one of the members for each ward stands for election. He or she then remains in office for four years while a second member stands for election in the second year. For each of three years there is a district council election and in the fourth year they all take a rest while the metropolitan county councillors have their turn.

The picture is a little more complicated in the shire districts because at the time of reorganisation they were given the opportunity to choose which pattern of electoral system to adopt. One third of the shire districts opted for partial renewal while the rest hold a clean sweep election in the year which is mid-way between county council elections.

Partial renewal systems mean the electorate is asked to go to the polls every year. Local political parties value elections because they keep the party machine ticking over. The system does however have two disadvantages. Firstly multi-member wards have to be larger than the single member wards which would be needed if the same authority had used a clean sweep election. Secondly, the meaning of electoral results can sometimes be rather unclear. It is quite possible to have a situation where a party has a disastrous election, loses seats everywhere, yet still retains control of the council because of the seats which it had won in earlier years. Studies of local elections show up two main trends. In most cases only a minority of voters turn out and national party political policies are more important in deciding the result than local questions.

The level of electoral activity

The general level of turnout at local government elections has remained at about 40 per cent, both before and after reorganisation. The contrast with parliamentary elections is highlighted by the elections of 1979. In that year the general election was held on exactly the same day as the local elections and this is reflected in the higher local turnout figures for that year. But in 1980 and 1981, local turnout figures returned to normal. Various explanations have been offered for what seems to be a general lack of interest in local elections. Many elected councillors, not surprisingly, tend to interpret the figures as meaning that most people are broadly satisfied and see no reason to come out and vote. Others have taken a rather more critical view. For example, a recent survey showed that about 26 per cent of those asked could not

	Percentage of seats uncontested							Percentage turnout in contested elections						
	'73	'74	'75	'76	'77	'78	'79	'73	'74	'75	'76	'77	'78	'79
Shire Counties	12				12			43				42 51		
Welsh Counties	19				21			55				51		
Metropolitan Counties	4				1			37				43		
GLC	0				0			37				43		
Scottish Regions		15				26			50				45	
Shire Districts	12			16		7	19	39			44		42	76
Welsh Districts	18			21			27	50			53			77
Metropolitan Districts	3		1	2		1	1	33		33	39		36	74
London Boroughs		1				0			36				43	
Scottish Districts		20			22				52			48		

The relative lack of interest is highlighted by the surprisingly large number of seats which are not even contested in local elections. (From 1980 onwards, local election statistics were no longer collected on a national basis. The figures here are adapted from T. Byrne, *Local Government in Britain*, pp 106/7)

Figure 18.2 Local authority elections 1973–79: percentage turnout, and percentage of seats uncontested.

Poll question: Can you tell me any of the services which are provided wholly or at least partly from the rates?

Service named	*Percentage of those taking part in poll, who were able to identify services*
Refuse collection	43
Local roads and paths	27
Schools	26
Police	19
Libraries	15
Street lighting	14
Fire services	13
Public parks	12
Ambulances	10
Old peoples' homes	7
'Don't Know'	26

The absence of 'housing' is perhaps explained because it was not seen as a service. Similarly ambulances may be a source of confusion because whereas the ambulance service is run by health authorities, there are also social service ambulances used to pick up people for day centres etc.

(Gallup Poll for *New Society* and BBC Radio 4, *New Society* 4.3.82)

Figure 18.3 Public knowledge of local authority services.

name a single service provided by local government. How can people pass judgement on the quality of the services if they do not even know what they are? Of course, some voters may know but still decide that it just does not matter to them who runs the council.

Some researchers have looked at the difference in turnout between different wards or local authorities. They have shown that the percentage vote can be affected by such factors as the degree of party activity, the number of party candidates and the possible closeness of the result. However, it is still very unusual for the turnout to approach that of a parliamentary election.

The significance of national political factors

Every May, political writers survey the results of the local elections and try to decide what they would mean for the government if they were repeated as a general election. Local elections are used as a test of national opinion. The value of these calculations is strongly supported by research findings. The ups and downs of party fortunes in the local elections in Reading and Birmingham followed almost exactly the results of *national* opinion polls. It would seem that voters do use local elections to express their feelings about the national government. The rise of the Social Democrat/Liberal Alliance, the economic policy of the Conservative government, the 'Falklands factor' and the quarrels amongst the leadership of the Labour party in the early 1980s were all national issues, yet they affected local election results.

It would seem that we pay almost no attention to what our local leaders have actually been doing since the last local election. Far from either rewarding their efforts on our behalf, or ejecting them from office if we are dissatisfied, we simply ignore their actions and vote on national issues. When there is a swing from one party to another in a local election, it is remarkably consistent from one authority to another, regardless of any local differences in terms of policies, politics or problems. Of course, once citizens have the vote it is not possible to tell them how it should be used. We have a perfect right to ignore local affairs if we so wish, but it can be argued that it seriously weakens the local accountability of local government.

The political parties

Local government is dominated by the major national political parties. The vast majority of elected councillors are recruited, selected and assisted by the local organisation of these parties. Indeed until the recent revival of the Liberal Party and the founding of the SDP, the Conservative and Labour parties shared about 95 per cent of the metropolitan county seats and almost 90 per cent of the shire county seats. Even in the smallest of district councils, the two parties controlled on average about a quarter of the seats. Most of the remainder are held by independent or non-party councillors. Before reorganisation in 1974 these non-party members had a much stronger position in the counties and the smaller authorities, particularly in the countryside.

The major function of the constituency and ward organisations of the national parties are the selection of candidates, the fighting of elections and the generation of ideas and support. In fighting elections, before and during polling day, they act in the same way as in general elections (see Chapter 4). Low turnout is not thought of as a threat to local democracy but as a possible obstacle to winning.

The parties have also shown an increasing interest in developing political ideas, proposals and policies at the local level. The old local election manifesto contained little more than a photograph of the candidate, preferably surrounded by a family and a dog, and a vague promise to do the best for everybody. This is changing, particularly among urban Liberal and Labour parties. Increasingly, party members want a greater say in council policy. Sitting councillors are expected to attend ward meetings. Frequently the party manifesto is a long and detailed policy statement which is expected to form the basis of council policy if the party wins the election. The traditional fund-raising activities of party members, and the politics of personal influence and patronage, are being replaced by ward newsletters and 'surgeries' for constituents.

One of the interesting aspects of the development of party politics in local government is the consequent development of party systems. At local government level there is a tremendous variety of party systems. Indeed, perhaps only a fifth of all authorities have a two-party system when either main party has a reasonable chance of power. A large number of authorities are effectively one-party systems, as in South Wales where the Labour Party dominates. At the other extreme there are authorities with a multi-party system where no party has an overall majority.

Pressure groups

The operation of pressure groups at local level has received little attention until recently. One problem is that they are often identified with the activities of national pressure groups. This view of pressure group activities is not really true at local government level.

One of the methods used by local government to provide certain public services is the creation of a sort of partnership between the authority and a voluntary association. The local authority makes a financial grant to the association which in turn provides the service, using voluntary labour and private fund-raising. In this way the advantages of self-help and voluntary work are reinforced by a cheap and flexible method of providing public services. These sorts of arrangements are particularly important in the social services and in the arts, recreation and leisure fields.

Normally perhaps such groups would not think of themselves as pressure groups, yet in many ways they are. They bring to the attention of the authority the needs of their particular clients and press their case for resources. Simply because the groups provide services themselves, rather than demand them from others, they are often well received. And they are often brought closely into the system local authorities use to decide policies by being co-opted to council committees or joint planning teams. The more well-established the group, and the more favourable the image of their clients amongst councillors and officials, the greater is their potential influence.

A second group of voluntary associations fits more easily into the traditional idea of a pressure group. These are formed to represent the views of people who use a local government service such as the houses on a council estate or a school. Council tenants associations or parent teacher associations, can have a rather uneasy relationship with the authority and particularly with its professional staff. Demands by parents to be involved in school policy or by tenants who want a say on repair programmes may be the reason for forming such groups. In the end their success seems to depend upon establishing a working relationship with school teachers and housing managers.

The third and fourth groups of voluntary associations are much more like many national pressure groups. These are the local interest and cause groups. Perhaps the longest established are those linked to the various economic interests of the community. Market traders, shop-keepers, local businessmen, taxi drivers and trade unionists all have local organisations which try to protect their members' interests. Like all economic interest groups they tend to become involved in political issues only when they feel that their interests may be helped or threatened by council policy.

These economic interests are most regularly voiced directly by elected councillors who frequently have contact and friendship links with different parts of the local economic community. The groups themselves are usually most active in town and country planning issues. The progress of a pedestrian precinct scheme will be closely followed by the local Chamber of Trade, and a proposed out-of-town hyper-market may well produce a political outcry from local shopkeepers.

However, the role of economic interests raises wider and more controversial issues. Local government itself is big business. It becomes involved, for example, in massive construction programmes and urban redevelopment projects. These projects have changed the whole shape of city centres right across the country. Often they are the result of a kind of bargaining process between property development and construction companies on the one hand, and local authority planning departments on the other. The councils want to see the replacement of old and decaying properties with schemes which will provide new jobs, offices, homes and shops. The private companies want opportunities for profitable investment and construction contracts. For these they need planning permission from the local authority and this often produces public arguments. Locally the first moves are made by the private companies who put up a proposal for redevelopment and the council then has to decide its views on the scheme. Objectors to a development project sometimes feel that they are fighting the combined interests of the development companies *and* the council.

Economic groups are by no means the only organised interests in the community. Some, such as churches or sports organisations, may have only an occasional interest in council policy. But for others the activities of local government may be their main concern. Residents' associations and ratepayers' associations in recent years have become some of the loudest and most active of these groups. Some have even organised as political parties to get councillors elected. They tend to see the activities of local government as a threat to their interests, either through proposed changes to the neighbourhood of the residents' association, or through levels of expenditure which ratepayers consider too high.

The last category of pressure groups is the cause group. The most obvious examples are amenity and environmental groups. Some of these may stem from a particular conflict over a new road proposal or redevelopment project. Their starting point is therefore often the protection of the interests of those who feel threatened by the scheme. If such groups are to establish themselves on a permanent basis, they have to widen their membership. They need to attract others interested in the protection of the countryside or preservation of old buildings, and take up new issues.

All pressure groups have to operate in a political setting which is likely to be more responsive to some than others. A group which defends the interests of old people and is prepared to raise money on their behalf is more likely to be taken seriously than a public demonstration by a group of squatters or gypsies.

Pressure group activity is becoming an important avenue of public participation in local government. Many have argued that this is bringing a new life and vitality into local government in a period of declining political party membership and a low level of electoral activity. But it is not without its dangers to democracy. Successful pressure group activity needs certain skills and resources. Holding meetings, duplicating papers, arguing with committees, understanding the law, writing letters, knowing the right people are all important. Yet these skills and resources are by no means evenly distributed throughout the community. It could be argued that the poor, the old, the less educated are those who are least able, or willing, to take part in pressure group politics and yet most need local government services.

Elections, parties and pressure groups, together create a **political environment** for the work of a local authority. Councillors and local government officers must be constantly aware of this environment because some of their decisions have a political impact. They may try to anticipate a hostile reaction and change their decisions as a result, or just decide to weather the political storm. Although much of their work is routine and uncontroversial, politics can be rather like lightning and can strike unexpectedly. However, councillors and officials also have to consider other factors – including their relationship to central government and the practical problems of providing services.

Discussion and essay questions

1. Explain clearly the distinctions between partial renewal and clean sweep elections? What are the advantages and disadvantages of each type of system?

2. What are the major types of local pressure groups? Illustrate each type with an example from your locality.

3. What problems are there for local government if the election of councillors is decided mainly by national factors?

4. Why are some local pressure groups more successful than others?

5. At the time of next elections for your local authority:
   (a) Collect the manifesto for each candidate delivered to your home. Compare and contrast their ideas and proposals. What sort of political image are they trying to create?
   (b) Collect the results from your local newspaper. Compare the turnout and proportion of votes for each candidate in each ward or electoral division. Is there a *national* trend in these election results?
   (c) What is the party composition of your local authority? How would you classify the party system?
   (d) Why do you think the turnout at a local election is lower than that at a general election?

19 Decision making in local government

The people involved

Elected councillors

Final decisions in local government are the responsibility of directly elected local councillors. As a social group they are hardly representative of the general population. Like members of parliament they tend to be male, middle-aged and middle class. The national averages set out in Figure 19.1 however do not show the important differences between local authorities. For example, the social background of elected councillors of an industrial urban authority are likely to be rather different from those of a predominantly rural and agricultural area. However, one problem which faces all councillors is the demands of council work on their time and energy.

In 1976 a study of local councillors suggested that on average they spent 79 hours per month on work associated with their local authority. The demands on council leaders – that is to say the chairmen and vice-chairmen of committees and other office holders – was even greater. They spent on average 100 hours per month on council work. (Figure 19.2.)

Professional staff

Local authorities employ about 2.7 million people (1.8 million full time) covering a very broad range of work. Teachers, dustmen, gardeners, solicitors, engineers, architects, accountants, planners, carpenters and social workers are just a few of the jobs and professions found in local government. The vast majority of this total workforce are directly involved in providing services to the public rather than dealing with councillors, or the work of administration that goes on in council offices.

Perhaps the most striking characteristic of local authority staff is their professional nature. Local authorities are usually organised on the basis of separate service departments such as education or planning, and each one has a professionally qualified staff. The top jobs in the planning department, for example, are held by professionally qualified planners and the top highways officials will be engineers.

This form of organisation contrasts sharply with the organisation of the civil service where traditionally those recruited as general administrators and not as professional economists or scientists were most likely to achieve senior positions (see Chapter 8).

All of the information is from research done for the Committee of Inquiry into Systems of Renumeration of Members of Local Authorities, Vol. 2 1977. All figures are percentages.

Sex	Councillors	Population
Male	83	48
Female	17	52

Age	Male councillors	Male population	Female councillors	Female population
21–34	9	30	8	27
35–44	17	18	16	16
45–54	24	19	27	17
55–64	29	16	32	16
65 and over	21	17	16	25

Occupation (*economically active males only*)	Councillors	Population
Manual	33	60
Clerical, sales, service	23	22
Administrators and managers	14	6
Professional and technical	27	10
Other	3	2

Level of formal education	Councillors	Population
Higher education	50	8
Other qualifications	13	25
No qualifications	37	67

Figure 19.1 The background of local councillors (1976).

The involvement of professionals has two important results. First, it has meant that the staff of local government departments are relatively isolated from each other. Teachers, firemen, police, social workers are all trained in different ways, have quite separate organisations for their work and their chances of promotion. Each is more likely to know about how their job is done in another local authority than about the work of other professional staff in the one which employs them. One important check on this isolation is the unions. NALGO (National Association of Local Government Officers) represents many white collar workers (but not teachers, policemen or firemen).

	All councillors	Leaders*	Back benchers
Council and committee meetings:			
Attendance at	23	30	21
Preparation for	13	16	13
Travelling to and from	8	10	7
Party meetings	5	6	5
Meeting officers	5	9	4
Other duties:			
Electors problems	13	12	13
Meeting organisations on behalf of councils	8	11	7
Other	4	6	4
All duties	79	100	74

* Leaders are councillors who have positions as mayor, chairman of the council or committee chairmen.
Source: Committee of Inquiry into Systems of Renumeration of Members of Local Authorities Vol. 2 1977)

Figure 19.2 The work of local councillors; average time spent on council duties by leaders and members (hours per month, 1976).

NUPE (National Association of Public Employees) and one or two other general workers' unions represent most of the manual workers. These unions negotiate nationally with the Local Authority Association about pay, grading, and conditions which are standardised throughout the country. But having standardised pay grades does not bring a social worker and a clerk in the rates office any closer together in their working lives.

Secondly, the task of managing the staff of the authority and presenting policy advice to the elected members falls upon the professionally qualified staff. Yet their background and training was as lawyers, accountants, engineers or social workers, with little or no emphasis given to policy making or management. Only since the 1960s have training courses tried to include these sorts of topics and issues.

The framework of decision making

Decision making in local government is organised mainly through a parallel structure of professional departments and council committees of elected members. The Housing Department, for example, is mirrored by the Housing Committee, and the Planning Department by the Planning Committee. The normal method is for each committee to consider policy proposals and problems raised by the Department and then to send its recommendations to a meeting of the full council. Each committee usually meets once during the 'cycle' of council business. This cycle is the time period between full meetings of the council. It can be as long as three months, in which case the committee will meet more than once. But in urban areas it is usually about five or six weeks. The most important institutions in making decisions are, therefore, the full council meeting and the committee meeting.

This picture is complicated by the frequent use in local government of the party group meeting. The majority of elected councillors are members of political parties, and it has become usual for members of the same party to meet on a regular basis to co-ordinate their decisions. In many authorities the party group meeting has become the third part of the structure of decision making.

The full council meeting

The full council meeting is presided over by a mayor in boroughs and former boroughs, and a chairman elsewhere. In a city the title of Lord Mayor is used – although both city status and the name are given by the monarch and have no practical significance. There are different conventions which apply to the work of a mayor and the chairman of a county council. Both are elected at the annual general meeting of the council but the mayor is expected to leave the cut-and-thrust of party politics for a year and to act as 'first citizen'. He or she attends civic functions and opens shows and is not a political leader of the authority so much as the social representative of the community. Political leadership rests with the chairmen of the major committees and the leader of the majority party group.

By contrast, the chairmanship of an authority such as a county council is thought of as a more political job. It would be unusual in large authorities for the chairman to be elected from the minority parties on the council. Often he or she is re-elected for a number of terms of office.

The mayor or chairman usually sits at the front of the council chamber flanked by the chief executive and perhaps the chief legal officer of the authority. These are the only professional officers of the council who normally take part in a full council meeting and even then they tend to limit themselves to sorting out points of procedure or law.

Although the main business of a council meeting is to consider the reports of the local authority's committees, the 'standing orders' which regulate the conduct of the council often provide two further types of business. The first is the chance for question time. The extract below from the minutes of a meeting of Lambeth Borough Council in London illustrates the use of question time to raise matters of ward interest and to check on the progress of the work of the council.

Question: Is the Chairman [of the committee] satisfied with the Directorate [Department] of Civil Engineering and Public Services' handling of the requests to prune trees outside George Beare Lodge, Notre Dame Estate?

Answer: I thank the Councillor for his question which is similar to one he asked six weeks ago [at the last council meeting], but in a different area and unfortunately the situation has not changed any way in our favour in as much as we have not been able to get any more trainees or people who are tree pruners to do the job.

This particular tree or trees in this particular area were scheduled to be dealt with in October but we have got that far behind that they are now scheduled to be pruned in January. Until the situation improves in relation to staff that is the best estimate I can possibly give. What I will say is that the experts have inspected the trees and they are safe at this particular time.
(Council minutes 29th November 1979, Lambeth Borough Council)

Sometimes question time can take on the bitter flavour of parliamentary question time. The following exchange took place at the same meeting of Lambeth Borough Council:

Question: Since the Chairman of the Policy Committee is prepared to extend political rights to the Conservative Party and since by no stretch of the imagination could he be considered a supporter of ours, otherwise he would be on this side of the Chamber and not on that side, will he therefore admit that when he accused me of being a member of the National Front because I supported rights for them, that he was making a deliberate slur and will he withdraw that accusation or alternatively produce evidence to support it?

Answer: At no time in this Chamber or anywhere else have I stated that you were a member of the National Front. What I said is that you are advocating the freedom of the NF to prolificate and propose its evil propaganda of racism and fascism. That is what I said and I think that is exactly what you did. You did propose the use of facilities of the Council for fascists and in no way will we tolerate fascists using the premises or the facilities of this Council and I certainly owe you no apology at all and you're certainly not getting one.

(Council Minutes 29th November 1979, Lambeth Borough Council)

A second way of introducing business is by using a formal motion proposed by a councillor on a matter of topical interest. The Conservative opposition proposed (without success) the following motion at the same meeting as the earlier exchanges:

That this Council supports the [government's] fight against inflation and will strive to limit the burden on Lambeth rate payers by a maximum increase of 10 per cent in 1980–81.
(Council Minutes 29th November 1979, Lambeth Borough Council)

Not all council meetings involve debates on such controversial matters and it has to be said that many meetings of the full council can be very dull affairs indeed. The greatest proportion of time is given over to considering reports or minutes of committees. Here is an example:

Recreation and Amenities Committee 18th November 1981
1059 SHELTER – JUNCTION OF WHITMORE ROAD/SEABRIDGE ROAD/WEDGWOOD AVENUE

A scheme for the improvement of the shelter incorporating the provision of a seat along its back wall was submitted for consideration. The seat which was to be provided by the Council at an estimated cost of £150 was to be constructed from an angle iron and hardwood and was to be bolted to the back wall and floor of the shelter.

RESOLVED: That consideration of this matter be deferred and reconsidered along with the Revenue Estimates for 1982/3.

(Committee papers for meeting of Borough of Newcastle-under-Lyme District Council, 19th December, 1981)

Increasingly, councils delegate routine matters to their committees whose reports are presented simply for information. The major part of each committee's report tends to be accepted without discussion or debate. It is quite possible, if unusual, for a full council meeting to get through a hundred pages of reports in under an hour.

This form of business has two results. Firstly, any matter on the agenda will have already been considered in detail by a committee. Secondly, in all but the smallest or non-partisan authorities, party group meetings will have already decided their attitudes to the issues under consideration. This can lead to a rather formal debate at the full council which is directed at the press and public, rather than helping councillors to make up their minds. Often the majority party starts a debate simply to explain in public a new proposal or decision. Similarly the minority party or parties can demonstrate their public opposition when they attempt to 'move back' a decision for further consideration by the committee. The full council meeting only becomes of crucial importance in determining council policy when there are no party groups on the council or the majority group is divided or no single group has an overall majority.

The committee meetings

The committee system is central to decision-making in local government. Committee membership is voted on at the annual general meeting of the council which follows the local elections. But in practice the party groups decide membership in proportion to party strength on the full council.

The most obvious difference between a committee meeting and a full council meeting is the key roles of two people – the committee chairman and the professional officer who advises the committee. The chairman will come from the 'ruling' party if there is one, and is very much the political leader of the committee and its public spokesman. He or she is regarded as part of the collective leadership of the authority and is frequently re-elected as chairman for a number of years. Professional officers usually brief committee chairmen before a meeting about the problems and issues on the agenda. Clearly there is a real danger that full-time officers, because of their experience, knowledge or personality, can dominate committee chairmen. Many of the items for discussion come from problems which arise in the day-to-day running of departments. Often they involve difficult, complex and technical considerations. Officers report directly to the committees, and it would be surprising if frequently they did not influence their deliberations and decisions.

However, committee chairmen are usually experienced local politicians who often jealously defend political control. Their status and reputation amongst their colleagues can depend on how well they handle politically sensitive matters, something which is also appreciated by professional chief officers. If chairmen simply seem to be the mouthpiece of officers they may find their political leadership undermined.

The party group meeting

The existence of party group meetings has been one of the more controversial issues in local government. They have been accused of undemocratically taking decisions behind closed doors in the absence of advice from professional officers. These decisions are then pushed through the council on party lines, thus introducing a wholly unnecessary element of party conflict into council business.

However, just as it is difficult to prevent people voting for party candidates at election time, so it is difficult to see how to stop party councillors working together after the election. It can be argued that, if a party seeks election and wins, then it can only be held responsible for the actions of the local authority if it has the power to co-ordinate and control the decisions of the council. Furthermore, party groups are far better informed than is usually thought, especially if they are the majority party providing the committee chairman. Often committee chairmen are well briefed by their own departments before the group meeting takes place, and even council chief executives may attend them in the larger urban authorities.

Party group meetings usually take place after the cycle of committee meetings and before the full council meeting, to decide how to deal with controversial matters and to settle any conflicts within the party group. Although perhaps one result of such a development is to emphasise party politics, it is important to recognise that there are vital differences of ideas and interests between the parties on local government matters. Attitudes towards education, housing, public transport and, above all, the overall level of expenditure and taxation are all sources of conflict between the parties.

The pattern of internal organisation

In 1967 the government published the Maud Report on the management of local government. It identified two fundamental weaknesses in the traditional structure of decision making. Firstly, the report argued that local authorities continually create extra committees and departments in response to new legislation or new demands and problems.

Secondly, council policy was too fragmented. The parallel structure of committees and professional departments tended to emphasise the separateness of each particular service. There was no clear managing body for the council as a whole, either among members or officers. After the report, many authorities reduced the number of their committees and amalgamated some departments. But the question of integration and co-ordination did not go away. On the contrary, by the early 1970s, the subject of **corporate management**, as it had become known, was one of the most discussed topics in local government.

Corporate management

The first basic idea of corporate management is that a local authority should undertake a comprehensive review of the physical, social and economic trends and needs in its area. Then, each year, the authority should establish the objectives and priorities of policy covering their activities as a whole. Lastly, the impact of council programmes should be monitored and systematically reviewed.

Nearly all authorities have since tried to strengthen the links between departments and create a rather more integrated structure. However it has proved difficult to define clearly the objectives of policy and then to see what progress has been made towards achieving them. So the main effect of corporate management has been a reorganisation of committees and departments, mostly at the time of local government reorganisation in 1974.

During 1973, 'shadow' councils were elected to the new authorities with the task of setting up a new committee and departmental structure which would be ready to take over the provision of services on 1st April 1974. The key influence on the decisions of these shadow councils was the report of the Bains Committee (1972) which had been set up by central government. The report supported a corporate management approach, although it had little to say about how this approach could actually be put into operation.

The Bains Report continued the trend towards reducing the number of committees and departments by grouping functions together. However, it also introduced two important new developments. The first of these was the idea of a 'policy and resource committee' responsible for the central direction of council policy. The Report recommended that the central committee should have four key sub-committees. Three of these would look after the resources of money, land and staff, while the fourth would be responsible for reviewing the performance of the authority. The other committees created by the authority would manage and control the services of the council, but within the overall framework of the council's corporate policy.

The second innovation was the recommendation that all but the smallest authorities should appoint a chief executive. This official should be free from the responsibility of running a department and would be the chairman of a 'chief officers management team'. This

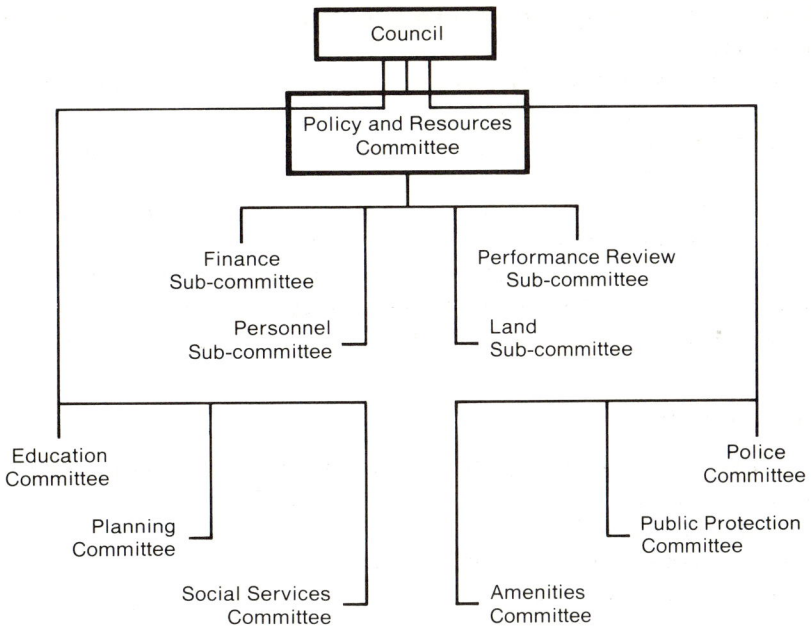

Figure 19.3 Committee structure (shire county). Source: Bains Report.

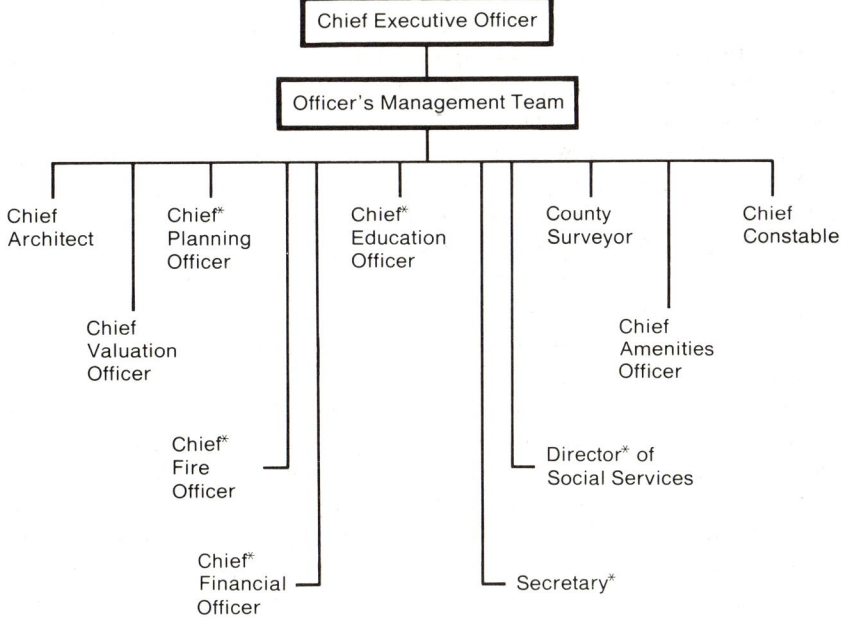

Figure 19.4 Departmental structure (shire county).

team would consist of the heads of all or some of the major departments and was designed to try and achieve a corporate approach.

Before many of the ideas and changes could be fully developed, local government, from the mid-1970s onwards, was confronted by a rapidly deteriorating financial situation. In some authorities this led to a return to older, tried and trusted methods of organisation, while for others it marked a search for new ones.

Discussion and essay questions

1. Compare and contrast the function of a committee meeting with that of the full council.

2. Describe the work and role of a local councillor. Why do you think councillors tend to be 'male, middle-aged and middle class'?

3. What similarities and what differences are there in the work of local councillors and MPs?'

4. What are party group meetings in local government? Why are they important?

5. Try to attend a meeting of your local authority and from your own observations answer the following questions:
   (a) What issues were the subject of debate and voting?
   (b) Prepare a list of the major full committees of the council. Compare your list with the appropriate recommendations of the Bains Report.
   (c) Cut out the reports in your local paper concerning the meeting you attended. Would you have reported the meeting in the same way? Write your own report of the meeting for the local press.
   (d) What evidence did you find of party politics in the council meeting?
   (e) Which professional officers took part in the meeting and what was their contribution?
   (f) Identify the different forms of business at the meeting.

20 The relationship with central government

A source of confusion?

There is little doubt that the relationship between central and local government is not working particularly well. The Department of the Environment complains about the 'overspending' of local authorities, while they in turn argue that central government 'interferes' in local affairs. Meanwhile everybody complains about the financing of local services – and particularly about the increasing cost of local rates.

The fundamental problem is that the relationship between local and central government was never planned – it simply evolved piecemeal to deal with changing problems as they emerged. Another problem is that the relationship itself has to deal with three rather distinct sets of needs and issues. The conflicts between these needs is the origin of much difficulty in medium and long-term planning over recent years.

The needs of a unitary state

Britain is a unitary – not a federal – state, and parliament, in a legal sense, is supreme and sovereign. Local government exists because Acts of Parliament have given councils the power to take certain decisions and carry out public services which are named in law. Indeed, whereas you and I can do anything which is not stated to be illegal, local authorities can only do those things where they have been given authority by one or other particular law.

The national government is politically responsible for the affairs of the state and this must include the activities of local government. This responsibility arises because only a few local government activities are important for just one locality. Roads and transport are part of a *national* system for moving people and goods. Planning decisions involve economic issues concerning the structure and location of industry. Even theatres, parks, museums and leisure facilities often have a regional importance and need a catchment area made up of several local authorities if they are to be used effectively.

These national considerations apply to the costs of services as well as the arrangements for their provision. Almost 30 per cent of total public expenditure is actually carried out by local government, and almost half of this is directly financed by central government itself. No chancellor of the exchequer in his struggles to manage the national economy can ignore this expenditure because of its effect on such issues as unemployment and inflation.

Ken Livingstone campaigning for London Transport 'Fair Fares'. In 1980 Ken Livingstone put forward a system of subsidies for public transport. This is not unusual in many European cities, but the GLC's decision to launch cheaper fares led to conflict with central government who maintained that the GLC had overstepped its powers. The final judgement from the law lords went against the GLC. Fares had to be increased and rate payers given a rebate on their tax bill.

Even more important than questions of economic management are the issues of equality and social justice in providing public services. Local independence means the chance to make local choices, which may lead to considerable variation in public services between different parts of the country. But to what extent should the people of Cornwall receive a different quality and range of public services from those living in Wigan? Should your chance of further or higher education depend on where you live, or on your academic ability? Just as the state has taken powers to try to regulate the overall levels of public expenditure, so it has had to limit the variations in public services. The central government cannot ignore some responsibility for the care of the homeless, gypsies, or one-parent families, simply because local elections have produced a council which considers that this care costs their ratepayers too much money. The needs of the unitary state require important elements of central control.

The needs of the local area

Britain may be a unitary state, but this does not mean the priorities and policies which are right in Liverpool will also work in Bristol. Each local authority is faced with its own particular problems and issues. The social, racial and age structure of the population; the patterns and conditions of houses and schools; the availability of sports facilities; the adequacy of the roads – all vary from one community to another. The relationship between the central and local government has to take into account these variations. While the unitary state creates pressures towards uniformity, differences between areas, or the idea of 'locality', create pressures towards variations in policies.

But there is more to the idea of 'locality' than simply the recognition that Guildford is not Gateshead. Local authorities are democratically elected political organisations. Supported by their professional staff, they are not only equipped with local knowledge, but they have a powerful claim to *represent* their locality. Direct election gives a degree of legitimacy to this claim.

This degree of legitimacy produces two results for the relationship between local and central government. Firstly, local authorities have a *right* to be heard. Secondly, there is the possibility of *political conflict* with the central government. Each has a claim to decide priorities. A particular authority may feel it has the right to challenge the central government. On the other hand, the central government could consider that it has the right to override the decision of a local authority. The result is that the relationship between central and local government has to provide machinery to prevent or resolve such conflicts.

The needs of public service provision

Another difficulty in working out a clear relationship between central and local government is the problem of putting policies into operation which involve a large number of different organisations. The Departments of the Environment, Education and Science, Health and Social Security, the Home Office, the Treasury and the Ministry of Transport, all have some interest and involvement with local government. These government departments each have different legal, policy and professional connections with their counterparts in local authorities. It is very difficult to get a clear relationship when there are so many different people involved. However, there is an important common interest between civil servants working in London and the teachers, planners, architects and social workers employed in local government. The civil servant in Whitehall, for example, needs to know what is happening on the ground. The local professional is interested in what is happening elsewhere. The relationship has to provide machinery for this exchange of professional and technical information.

Control and influence over local government

Central government has a large number of powers and ways of influencing and controlling the decisions of a local authority. A balance must therefore be struck between too much control and too little control if central and local government are to have a working relationship. This balance must mean that each recognises the role and authority of the other. But it is not a static balance. Changes in policy at either central or local government level constantly run the risk of reopening the debate and questioning the nature of the balance.

Local authorities are **statutory** organisations and, as we have seen, they exercise powers which have been granted by parliament. Their powers are not arbitrary and they are subject themselves to the rule of law. One of the fundamental legal principles of local government is that it must have clear legislative authority for any actions. If a local authority exceeds those powers and acts *ultra vires* (Latin for 'beyond one's powers'), then these actions can be declared illegal in the High Court. All local authorities are required to have an external audit of their accounts and the Audit Commission appointed by the government can refer cases of *ultra vires* expenditure to the High Court. The Court can then disallow this expenditure and may order repayment, or surcharge councillors who authorised the expenditure in the first place. Local authorities have only the power to spend no more than the product of a 2p rate (see p. 245) in ways that they decide locally. All other expenditure needs specific legal authorisation.

Ultra vires provides a framework for the activities of a local authority. But it is the central government departments rather than the courts which operate the most continuous kind of control and influence. This is based on the various Acts of Parliament which created the services of local government. Sometimes this legislation grants very wide powers of supervision to the central government. Perhaps the most famous example is the 1944 Education Act which granted to the Education minister (now the secretary of state) the powers 'to secure the effective execution by local authorities, *under his control and direction*, of a national policy for providing a varied and comprehensive educational service in every area'.

Frequently the legislation gives ministers the power to issue regulations and make orders which fill in the *details* of legislation in particular aspects of policy. The most dramatic form of ministers' power occurs when the legislation goes so far as to give them *default powers*. Under such a clause they may take over directly the running of a service if they are dissatisfied with the way a local authority is doing it. This clearly gives one way of sorting out any conflict between the central government and a local authority. But this kind of direct action, rather like cases of surcharge, is rarely used. It acts as a deterrent on local authority behaviour rather than a way of solving the problems of conflict.

The day-to-day running of local government, broadly speaking, involves four types of interaction with the departments of central government. Firstly, Whitehall supplies a steady stream of circulars, discussion papers, information bulletins, conferences, meetings, and even ministerial speeches. Sometimes these messages have statutory force but often they just contain advice, information and suggestions. Secondly, there is the formal machinery of inspection. The Department of Education and Science makes use of Her Majesty's Inspectors (HMIs) to gain information about the work of schools, colleges and local education authorities.

Thirdly, local authorities are often required to submit plans of future action for ministerial approval before they are put into operation. These sort of controls apply for example to transport and housing policies, land use plans, educational reorganisation plans and building programmes. In recent years this has become a very important way of linking central government and local authority policies.

The fourth type of interaction is the most important because it involves the way that local government is financed. Every year, local authorities are required to provide a range of services for which they have absolutely no hope of collecting enough money locally. This has become perhaps the single more important influence on the whole direction and scale of operation of local government.

Local government finance

The expenditure of local government

In 1980 local government spent £29,611 million. This represented slightly less than 30 per cent of total public expenditure. In order to understand the financial problems of local government it is necessary to distinguish between revenue or current expenditure and capital expenditure. Broadly speaking, **revenue expenditure** covers such things as salaries, wages, heating, lighting, postage and materials which are used during the year. **Capital expenditure** is spending on such things as buildings, land, schools and council houses whose useful life is much longer than just one financial year. In such cases it is argued that the full cost of building a new school or museum should be shared by future generations. This is done by borrowing the money and paying back the loan and interest over a period of time which corresponds roughly to the life of the building.

As Figure 20.1 shows, different services of local government need different mixes of revenue and capital spending. The greatest proportion of capital spending occurs in housing, while education alone consumes almost 40 per cent of the revenue budget, largely through wages and salaries. Significantly the second largest item of revenue expenditure is actually repaying the interest due on the loans taken out to pay for capital spending in the past.

Even ignoring the effects of inflation, local government expenditure grew almost continually between 1945 and 1975–76. But between then and 1981–82 it declined by about 20 per cent in real terms. Indeed, the

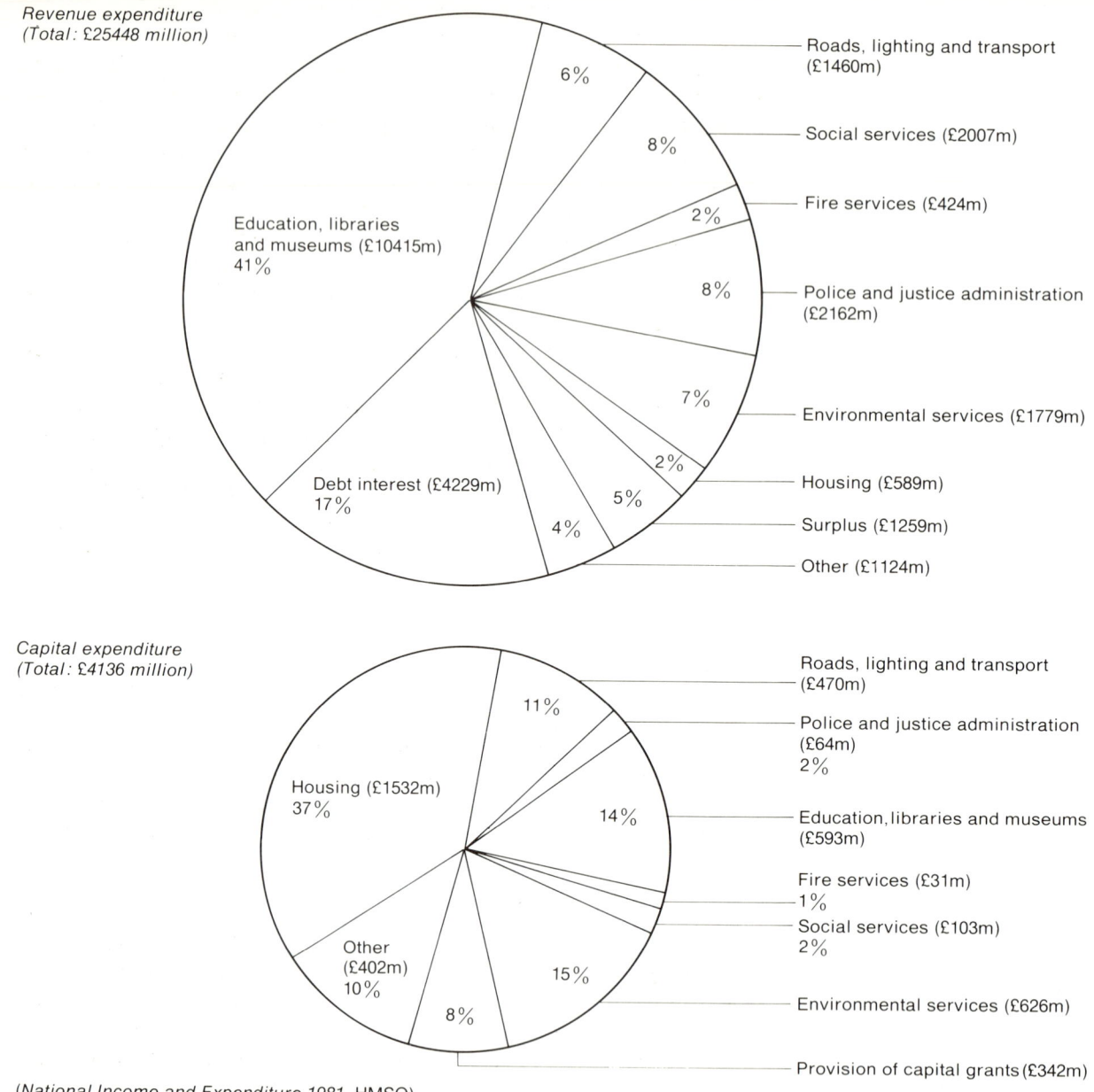

Revenue expenditure
(Total: £25448 million)

Education, libraries and museums (£10415m) 41%

6%

8%

2%

8%

7%

2%

5%

4%

Debt interest (£4229m) 17%

Roads, lighting and transport (£1460m)

Social services (£2007m)

Fire services (£424m)

Police and justice administration (£2162m)

Environmental services (£1779m)

Housing (£589m)

Surplus (£1259m)

Other (£1124m)

Capital expenditure
(Total: £4136 million)

Housing (£1532m) 37%

Other (£402m) 10%

11%

14%

8%

15%

Roads, lighting and transport (£470m)

Police and justice administration (£64m) 2%

Education, libraries and museums (£593m)

Fire services (£31m) 1%

Social services (£103m) 2%

Environmental services (£626m)

Provision of capital grants (£342m)

(National Income and Expenditure 1981, HMSO)

Figure 20.1 Local government expenditure 1980.

level of *capital* expenditure fell by no less than 60 per cent during this period. This change had a major impact on local government. The decline was partly a direct result of central government policy but it was also due to the effects of inflation. Local government work is labour intensive and there are few opportunities to introduce technology to improve the productivity of teachers or social workers. The result is that local government has found it difficult to cut costs without reducing the services themselves.

The central government does not have the power to interfere directly in the contents of the budget of a local authority, although it has always kept tight control over borrowing for capital expenditure. The present system for this control came into force in April 1981. Each authority makes a bid for an allocation of capital spending under five headings: Housing, Education, Social Services, Transport and Others. The total of these five allocations gives a fixed ceiling to capital spending on all items and projects over £6,500, regardless of how the spending is financed. Although each authority has some freedom to switch money from one heading to another, the total capital expenditure in any particular year is under the direct control of the Department of the Environment.

There has been more controversy about central control over revenue expenditure. This is understandable. Cutting capital expenditure can be fairly painless – at least in the short-term. If a planned new school is not actually built then the old one can always be made to last just a little longer. No jobs are lost and only the construction industry is placed in a difficult situation as building contracts disappear. However, since 1975 we have seen the central government attempt to apply increasing pressure to revenue spending as well.

The income of local government

Local authorities have three major sources of income which are used to finance their services along with their borrowing for capital spending. Firstly they have their own form of taxation, the rate. Secondly they make charges for certain of their services, such as council house rents. Lastly, they get considerable grants from the central government. This last item represents about 52 per cent of total revenue expenditure, and gives the government considerable influence over local revenue expenditure.

The **rate** is a form of property tax. Payment is based upon the results of two calculations. Firstly, the Inland Revenue fixes a rateable value for every type of property (except agricultural buildings, crown properties and churches). This valuation, where possible, is based upon the rent that a property might be expected to command. The second calculation is that of the local authority. Each March, local authorities announce a 'rate poundage' for the next financial year. An announcement of a rate of 115 pence in the pound means that for each pound of rateable value, the ratepayer is required to pay £1.15. The tax is actually collected by the district councils but county and metropolitan councils are paid a share for the services they provide.

Local government is rather unlucky in that the rating system is unpopular. There are many demands for complete reform even after the effects of rates have been eased by allowing payment by instalments, rebates to low income ratepayers, and a general subsidy of 18.5 pence in pound from central government to reduce domestic rate bills. In some ways this opposition may seem odd. Rate demands on average equal only 2.2 per cent of personal disposable income (the amount of money people have to spend after tax), and this is a smaller demand

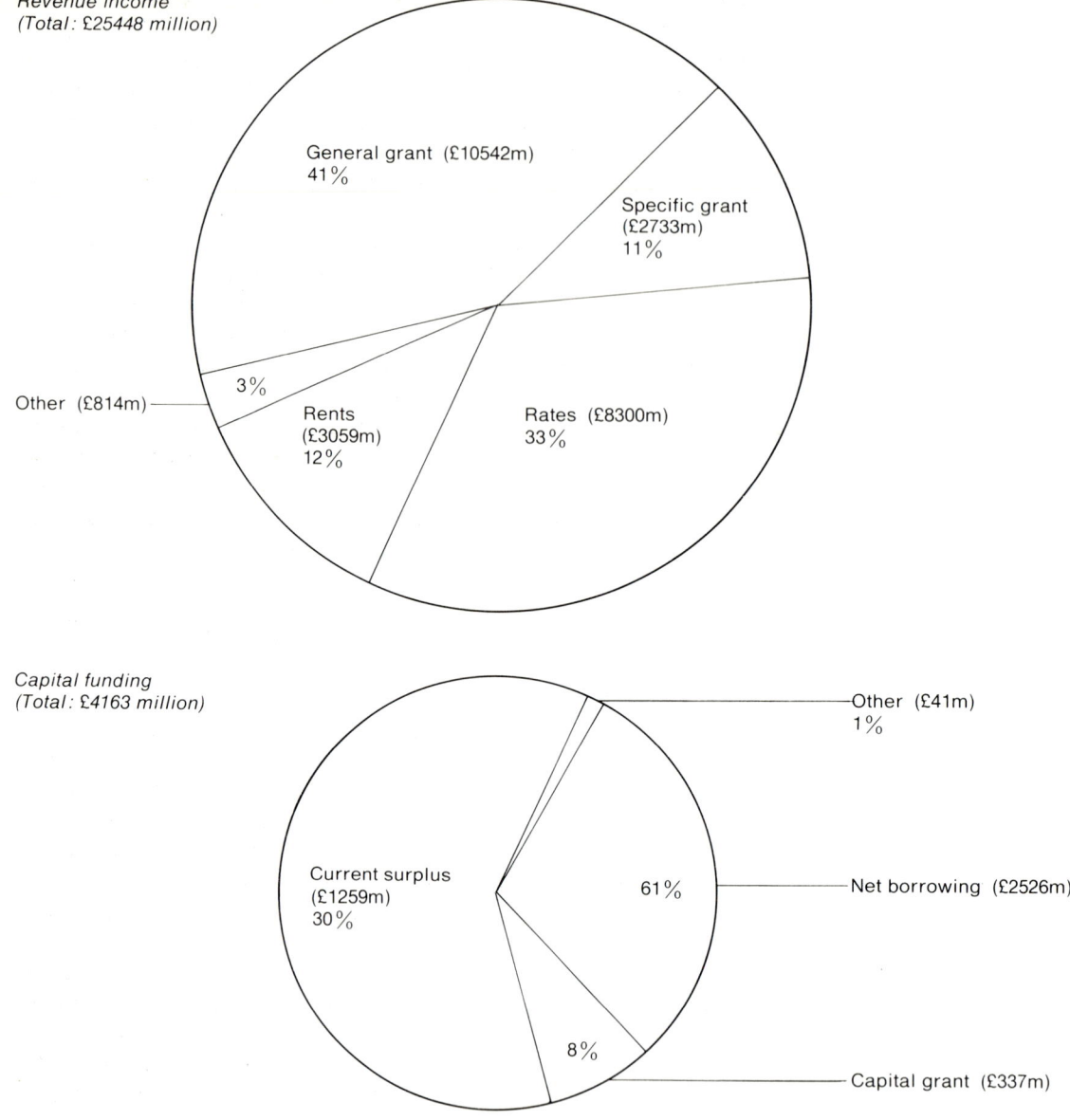

Revenue income
(Total: £25448 million)

General grant (£10542m)
41%

Specific grant
(£2733m)
11%

Other (£814m)

3%

Rents
(£3059m)
12%

Rates (£8300m)
33%

Capital funding
(Total: £4163 million)

Other (£41m)
1%

Current surplus
(£1259m)
30%

61%

Net borrowing (£2526m)

8%

Capital grant (£337m)

(National Income and Expenditure 1981, HMSO)

Figure 20.2 Local government income 1980.

on household budgets than in 1938. Furthermore, the rate accounts for
for only about a tenth of our total tax payments. It is a cheap and easy
tax to administer and collect as property is distributed right across the
country.

However, it does have serious disadvantages. One problem is that,
unlike income tax or VAT, the revenue from rates does not rise automatically with changes in price levels. Local authorities have to take
the unpopular political decision to raise the rate of tax simply to collect

as much real spending power as the previous year. Secondly, even paying by instalments rather than a lump sum does not hide the burden of rates from the ratepayer. Thirdly, the way rates are calculated seems to be mysterious compared with other taxes. Finally, rates on business and commerce do not take account of the profitability or otherwise of the company or enterprise.

The main problem for those who would like to abolish rates is that it would need an increase in the basic rate of income tax of about ten pence in the pound, or a 10 per cent increase in the rate of VAT. This is a great deal of money and collecting it would make any of the ideas for replacing rates just as unpopular. Among schemes for an alternative to rates have been proposals for a sales tax or a local income tax, perhaps on each earning member of the household (which is why it is sometimes called a 'poll' or 'head' tax).

The second source of funds available to a local authority is the many different types of charges it collects. These vary from council house rents to car parking fees, payments for home helps and rents for hiring civic halls. Some of these charges are related to the cost of the service while others amount to a token contribution from the user. There has been considerable encouragement from central government for an expansion of charges which cover the full cost, which raises the question of whether the service could not be provided by a commercial organisation in the first place. This clearly involves an important political judgement about the role of public services and the scope of government. It must be remembered that for some public services like the police there never can be a real private market and that many other services are made available to those who are least able to buy them for themselves. Raising charges is always unpopular and in the case of council house rents central government has actively intervened to force the council tenant to pay a greater proportion of his or her housing costs. But there is no way that the long-term future of local government is going to be based upon full cost charging.

We are left therefore with the key issue of the grants paid by central government to local authorities. Although grants fell as a percentage of revenue spending from 58 per cent in 1976 to 52 per cent in 1980, this still represented £13,255 million. There are two types of grant. The first is a *specific grant* paid to support a particular service, for example the police grant. But much more significant is the *general* or *block grant* which is paid in aid of local expenditure generally. This totalled £10,542 million in 1980.

The total block grant available is decided by the central government in light of their own review of all of public expenditure. Since 1975 it has been government policy to reduce in real terms the value of this total grant and since the passing of the 1980 Local Government and Planning Act, the government has introduced a new formula for distributing it. If the budgets of all the local authorities in the country indicate a level of spending greater than the Secretary of State for the Environment considers that the country can afford, a proportion of the total grant is 'clawed back' by the government. For example, the total grant was reduced by 3.5 per cent in 1981–82.

Since then the government has gone further and given each local authority a specific spending target. If the authority takes no steps to bring its spending into line with the target then part of its grant may be 'held back', thus putting further pressure on the local authority. Faced with these grant reductions one legal alternative for an authority determined to stick to its own spending decisions was to levy a further or supplementary rate. This power has now been abolished, and in early 1984 the Conservative government proposed new powers for the Secretary of State for the Environment to determine the level of the local rates for local authorities which consistently overspent government targets.

Although many observers have supported the principle of the new distribution formula, the operation of these conditions has been widely seen as an important change in the overall balance between central and local government. Put simply, should it be the local authority which decides the right level of local spending or the Department of the Environment?

As we saw in Chapter 15, both Labour and Conservative governments have made cuts in public expenditure as part of a counter-inflation policy. After 1979, the Conservative government also showed a clear determination to change the balance between the public and private sectors of society. Through de-nationalisation and other policies they set about reversing the trend of expansion in the scope and role of the state. But during the 1960s and 1970s this expansion had been most apparent in the services and expenditure of local government which, as we have seen, has important traditions of local political control. The arguments about central/local relationships have become a debate about the role of the state.

Discussion and essay questions

1. If you were Chancellor of the Exchequer how would you argue the case that national government should control local government spending? What might be the reply of the leader of a metropolitan authority such as Birmingham?

2. In how many different ways can central government control or influence the activities of local government

3. How does local government receive its income? What are the advantages and disadvantages of the present system? Suggest ways in which you would change it.

4. Have a look at the rate demand which is sent to your home in April each year:
   (a) What is the rateable value of your home?
   (b) What is rate poundage of your district and county council?
   (c) Make a list of the services of your local authority in order of their financial cost.

Part Eight: BRITAIN IN EUROPE

21   Britain and the European Community

What is the European Community?

The EC originally consisted of three different organisations which brought together France, West Germany, Italy, Holland, Belgium and Luxembourg. In 1952 these countries formed a European Coal and Steel Community (ECSC). In 1957 they signed two Treaties of Rome, one to set up the Atomic Energy Community (EURATOM) and the other to found the European Economic Community (EEC) which was often called 'The Common Market'. In July 1967 all three communities were merged into a single European Community or EC.

Economically the EEC and then the EC set out to establish common policies in certain key areas of activity. Firstly, all countries would place the same **tariffs** (or import taxes) against goods imported from other parts of the world. Secondly, tariffs between member countries would be abolished so that a huge 'common market' could be formed. In effect, this would give the EC a 'home market' for its goods – as large as the United States. But not only goods could move freely. The same would be true of labour and investment so that people could work, build factories, or invest their money anywhere within the EC. To make this common market possible there would need to be common policies towards industries such as agriculture, steel and coal.

Many other industries would need to be 'harmonised' so that countries did not have different regulations about products or weights and measures which would stop goods moving freely.

Harmony had a political meaning as well. A more unified Europe was seen as the best chance of avoiding the rivalries that had led to two world wars. To many, the EC had an even greater objective – the creation, in time, of greater political union.

The 1939–45 war produced total devastation in many urban areas, especially in Germany. After 1945 the United States lent huge sums of money to rebuild the West European economy but it became increasingly accepted that recovery needed a high degree of co-operation between the countries themselves. At the same time the Soviet Union controlled Eastern Europe and a large part of Germany itself. The 'Cold War' between East and West began. It made rivalries

View of Hamburg taken from the tower of St. Michaels Church, showing the bomb damage to the town caused by the RAF raids.

Re-built Hamburg from the tower of St. Michaels Church. Germany's economic recovery since the war's end in 1945 has made it a strong European partner.

Russian military strength paraded in Moscow. Since 1945 Europe has been at the centre of the 'Cold War' which is one reason why Western European nations have drawn closer together.

A line of United States Air Force Boeing B-52D Stratofortress bombers glitter with steely menace in the sunshine: a symbol of close ties between Western Europe and the United States.

between West European countries seem irrelevant. Better relations between them was also helped by the fact that they were losing their colonial empires in Africa and Asia and thinking of themselves more as European, not global, states.

Why didn't Britain join the EC at the beginning? Although invited, the British showed little interest in the idea. To a great extent, this was because we still had a view of ourselves as being a world power. The empire had been replaced by the Commonwealth, and there were strong economic and emotional links with the member countries. Moving closer to Europe seemed to many like a kind of withdrawal from our history. However, British ability to be a world power was undermined by economic weakness after the war and the importance of the 'super powers' such as America, China and Russia. Common-

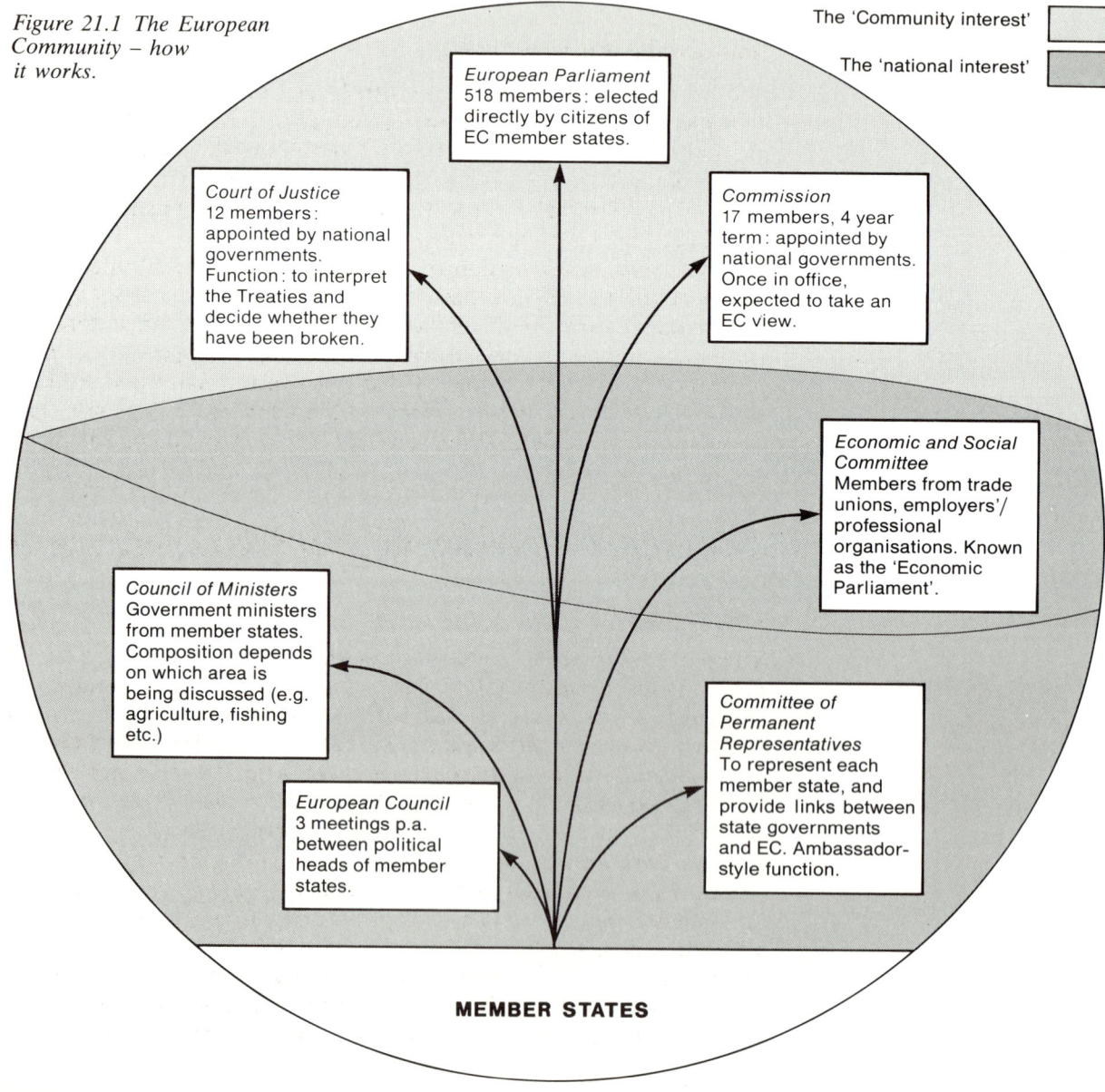

Figure 21.1 The European Community – how it works.

The 'Community interest'

The 'national interest'

European Parliament
518 members: elected directly by citizens of EC member states.

Court of Justice
12 members: appointed by national governments. Function: to interpret the Treaties and decide whether they have been broken.

Commission
17 members, 4 year term: appointed by national governments. Once in office, expected to take an EC view.

Economic and Social Committee
Members from trade unions, employers'/ professional organisations. Known as the 'Economic Parliament'.

Council of Ministers
Government ministers from member states. Composition depends on which area is being discussed (e.g. agriculture, fishing etc.)

Committee of Permanent Representatives
To represent each member state, and provide links between state governments and EC. Ambassador-style function.

European Council
3 meetings p.a. between political heads of member states.

MEMBER STATES

wealth countries increasingly pursued their own interests which did not always match ours. On top of this, the original members of the EC experienced greater economic growth than Britain in the 1960s. A new, and very powerful economic force was being forged in which we had no voice and with whom we were forced to compete. Industrialists began to argue that our future lay inside the EC tariff walls, not in having to climb over them. Britain applied to join twice in the 1960s (1963 and 1967), but was turned down on both occasions as a result of French objections to the terms of entry. By the time Britain finally became a full member of the EC (in January 1973, along with Ireland and Denmark), the political structure of the EC had been decided, the Common Agricultural Policy (CAP) was in operation, and the close ties between France and Germany established. British interests had not been considered in shaping these matters.

How does the EC work?

The major problem of the EC – in 1957, and now – is clear. What kind of balance should there be between the national interests of each state and the wider Community interest? After all the EC brought together twelve nations after Spain and Portugal joined in 1986. They may all be European but there are wide differences between them in culture, language, and economic structure, and the way they organise their political systems. Each country is likely to have different interests to defend, but if the EC is to have any meaning, common policies need to be hammered out. The institutions of the Community reflect this tension between national and Community interests as Figure 21.1 shows. A further problem which the EC has to solve was that there are considerable differences between some of the member states in size, and economic wealth. The EC has never been a partnership of equals.

The institutions of the EC: the Community interest

The Commission

There are seventeen commissioners who are appointed by national governments. France, Italy, West Germany, Spain and Britain have two each and the rest one each. They are all appointed for four years and to support their work there are over 9,000 officials employed in the Commission. Each commissioner is given a 'portfolio' which means that they cover the main areas of EC activity – agriculture, industry, the budget, and so on. But although they are chosen by national governments they are not national representatives. They are expected to make the 'community interest' their main concern. To do this, the Commission has three main functions. Firstly, it puts together policies which are then sent to the Council of Ministers for final approval. It is only the Commission which can *propose* legislation. Naturally before it does this, the Commission is involved in discussions with a wide range of different groups including national governments. Secondly, it is responsible for putting the agreed policies into operation and administering the various funds for special purposes. These include agriculture, regional development, and help for developing countries which have an association with the EC. Thirdly, the Commission is the 'guardian of the Treaties'. It is the watchdog of the EC and tries to make sure that member states follow their legal obligations. For example, the Commission can take individuals, companies or even governments to the European Court. A number of expert advisory committees are attached to the Commission. They have the right of consultation about proposed legislation and give technical help.

The Court of Justice

There are twelve judges, one from each state, appointed by the national governments. Their task is to rule on the interpretation and the enforcement of the different Treaties and the legislation which comes under them. Cases can be brought by individuals, national governments or by the Commission.

The problem facing the Court, however, is that it has to rely on each national government and national courts to enforce its decisions. For Britain a Court of Justice of this kind is a new experience because it has a constitutional meaning. For example, it could decide that legislation passed by the British parliament breaks EC Treaties and, as a result, is unlawful. In joining the EC we accepted that where EC law was established it takes precedence over our own law.

The European parliament

In 1979 the first direct elections to the European parliament were held. In this election each country decided for itself which kind of electoral system was to be used, and Britain kept to a 'first past the post' system, although a form of proportional representation was used in Northern Ireland which enabled the Catholic minority to elect a member. In the European parliament, members (MEPs) sit in loose party groups rather than forming different national blocks. Socialists, for example, are the largest single group coming mainly from France, West Germany and Britain. But there is nothing like the tight party organisation found in the House of Commons. British Labour Party MEPs may vote with British Conservatives on some issues. Of course, there is no 'European government' which depends on keeping a majority in the European parliament, as we have in the British system.

The European parliament can question commissioners and call for reports. On average around 2,800 questions, written and oral, are tabled each year. It has the right to be consulted before Community laws are made and, in 1980, the European Court ruled that a directive, agreed by ministers, was illegal because this had not happened. In fact about two thirds of amendments to European legislation proposed by the European parliament have been accepted.

The European parliament also has the right to reject the EC Budget as a whole on a two-thirds majority and to amend the 'non-obligatory' parts of the Budget. In 1979 the Budget was actually thrown out as a

	% vote ('79)	('84)	% seats ('79)	('84)	No of seats ('79)	('84)
Con	50.6	40.8	70	58	60	45
Lab	33.1	36.5	21	41	17	32
Lib ('79)/All ('83)	13.1	19.5	–	–	–	–
Total turnout	32.1	32.1				

The system used in Britain almost inevitably meant that the two main parties virtually shared the seats between them. In 1979 and 1984 Britain was the only country to use the first past the post system. Membership of the European Parliament as a whole was divided up in the following way:

European MPs		Electors (per seat)
		(000s)
France	81	435
W. Germany	81	520
Italy	81	505
UK	81	495
Holland	25	380
Belgium	24	275
Denmark	16	230
Ireland	15	140
Luxembourg	6	34
Greece	24 (when they joined in 1981)	250

In this case it can be seen that Luxembourg, for example, is greatly over-represented especially compared with the 'big four'.

Figure 21.2 1979/84 European election results in Britain.

gesture against the amount spent on agriculture. This did not bring the EC to a halt because it was able to operate on emergency budgeting and a new Budget was agreed six months later. Parliament, again on a two-thirds majority, can sack the whole Commission but cannot dismiss an individual Commissioner – which might be a more sensible power. A great deal of the work of the European parliament is done through specialised committees which produce reports and form the basis of many debates.

The intention of the European parliament was to help to develop a more European political spirit. But it has really made little impact. There is not much coverage of its work in the media and, in most countries, ambitious politicians have seen it as far less important than membership of their national governments. Nor does it even have a permanent home. It sits in Strasbourg with committees meeting in Brussels and the secretariat is based in Luxembourg. The first requirement of an MEP is a stout suitcase.

The national interest

The Council of Ministers

This is the most powerful body in the EC. The ministers represent the national interest of each member state and this is where the conflict between national and Community interests must be reconciled. Which ministers form the Council depends on the issue being discussed, but the Council of Foreign Ministers is particularly important because it is the senior body and also helps to co-ordinate the work of the other councils. The Council's work is based on proposals from the Commission – it cannot put forward its own. But the critical issue is how the Council votes.

According to the Treaty of Rome, majority voting is possible but voting strength is not equal. The 'Big Five' states have four votes each,

A meeting of the European Council in 1984. These are the political heads of the members of the European Community.

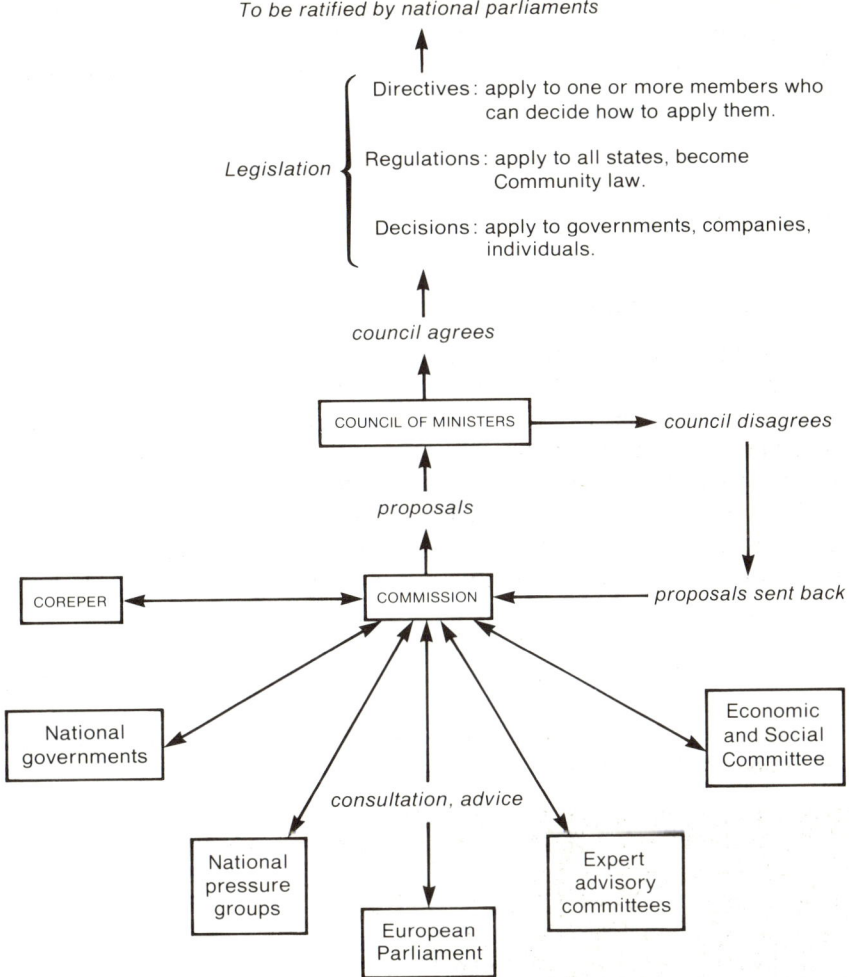

To be ratified by national parliaments

Legislation {
Directives: apply to one or more members who can decide how to apply them.

Regulations: apply to all states, become Community law.

Decisions: apply to governments, companies, individuals.
}

council agrees

COUNCIL OF MINISTERS → *council disagrees*

proposals

COREPER ⟷ COMMISSION ⟵ *proposals sent back*

National governments

Economic and Social Committee

consultation, advice

National pressure groups

European Parliament

Expert advisory committees

Note: Case law based on decisions by the European Court form a separate source of European law. Such decisions help to refine and explain EC legislation by showing how it works in practice. But the Court relies on the different governments to enforce its decisions.

Figure 21.3 European Community legislation.

the rest two each apart from Luxembourg with one. The smaller states are all protected by having more votes than the population size of their country would justify. The problem with majority voting is that a state in the minority on an issue may feel that its vital national interests have been overridden. Since 1965, the members have preferred to reach agreement unanimously. The result is that decisions can also be held up by any one country refusing to agree with the rest. By not agreeing they have a veto on the decision, and this means that agreement can be impossible, even on minor issues.

One result of the search for unanimity is the pressure to compromise. A great deal of 'trading' takes place before issues are settled so that agreement on one issue often depends on attitudes toward others.

Britain, for example, has held up price rises for farm products as a way of putting pressure on the other states to reform the EC Budget. However, in 1982, this tactic failed when the rest, impatient with the British government, voted to increase farm prices and overturned a veto for the first time in sixteen years. Does this mean that the 'unanimity rule' has disappeared? Probably not, because this was a rare case, although it does illustrate what can happen when members feel that the system is being abused.

Committee of Permanent Representatives (COREPER)

Each member state has a permanent representative in Brussels with the rank of ambassador. COREPER is therefore a permanent link between each national government and the EC. It prepares the agenda for meetings of the Council of Ministers and co-ordinates their work. Naturally it has an important role in discussions with the Commission over future policies but it is also a place where disagreements between national governments can be explored and perhaps settled.

Economic and Social Committee

This is a permanent advisory committee which is consulted by the Council of Ministers and the Commission. It has representatives from trade unions, employers, professional organisations and it is sometimes called the 'Economic Parliament'. Its members are there in a personal capacity but they are likely to report back to governments as well as to their own national pressure groups.

The European Council

The European Council is the place for meetings between heads of government. These 'summit' meetings take place three times a year and are a chance for private and informal exchange of views. But they can be used as well either to settle issues where there are disputes or, at least, to sort out the general guidelines for action. Naturally any decisions made at this level are virtually certain to be agreed, given that each leader carries enormous political weight in his or her own government.

Problems of agreement

The institutions described in the last few sections provide the framework of the EC and attempt to balance national and Community interests. But, in reality, national interests predominate. This is not surprising and it does not mean that the EC in its 'Community' sense is a failure. Individual membership of the EC itself must depend on whether governments see it as being to their advantage. But how do governments measure such advantages?

No government can expect to find that everything it wants will be accepted by the others. In national politics a government is in a dominant position, but still needs to compromise. In the EC, it has to negotiate with equals and search for unanimous agreement in the Council of Ministers. The interests of groups within each country can be very different. Ireland, for example, is still largely agricultural and speaking up for the 'farming interest' at the EC is a vital consideration for Irish governments. Britain, on the other hand, is mainly an industrialised country with such problems as declining regions and this is reflected in the British arguments puts to the various EC meetings. Even when people are involved in the same kind of activity across national frontiers there can be tensions. Wine growers in France, for example, are very hostile towards importing cheaper wines from Italy.

There are bound to be huge difficulties in putting policies together and then getting them agreed. The Commission has to consider the views of each national government, other EC institutions, pressure groups, as well as having its own views about the Community interest. This is just in forming the proposals which it then sends to the Council of Ministers. At this stage, and in the Council itself, there is a great deal of bargaining. But the only way that the system can work at all is if compromises are accepted. If protecting the national interest means believing that *every* decision must be favourable the EC would break down. Perhaps the real miracle is that it works at all.

The effect of EC membership on British politics

Political institutions

The EC is more than just some kind of trading association. EC law is binding on its members and this affects the way that laws are applied within each country. Where there is a conflict between national laws and EC laws, then EC laws take precedence. One result of this is that our traditional, and legal, view of the sovereignty of the British parliament must be modified, as was pointed out in Chapter 10. However, the real test of whether we have lost sovereignty depends on whether the EC could stop us carrying out policies which a British government thought *essential*. An example might be to stop, or tax, imports from other EC countries because we faced a severe economic crisis. This would be against EC law and if it was to be a permanent policy then continued membership would be impossible. If it was a temporary device, perhaps used only against selected imports, then it might be agreed, however reluctantly.

The work of government

The ability of governments to act on their own has changed. In key areas, such as agriculture, policies depend on agreement between the members of the EC. In this sense there are now limits on the freedom of action of British governments. The whole process of consultation has been widened considerably, so has the volume of work which ministers and civil servants have to cope with; Europe is now another arena where ministers have to perform and where reputations can be won or lost.

EC membership has added an extra layer of work through most parliamentary activities. Both the Commons and the Lords have set up new committees (see Chapters 10, 11) to scrutinise new proposals for EC laws and regulations, and comment on them, before they are accepted by the government. Debates on EC issues are held in both Houses and ministers involved in EC decisions must be prepared to take full political responsibility in the normal way – for example by answering written or oral questions.

Pressure groups

As many policy decisions have taken on a greater EC focus, so more pressure group activity has been directed towards Brussels. Farmers, for instance, constantly try to press for better EC arrangements for their produce. But many other groups are affected. One result is that pressure groups from different EC countries have come together to form European federations and have set up offices in Brussels. Others have a less formal organisation but still try and work together.

The need to establish links with the Commission has also been seen by local authorities who send delegations asking for help in developing their own areas.

Political parties

The 'European issue' has been a major factor in party politics since the early 1960s. Membership of the EC is strongly supported by the Liberal/Social Democratic Alliance, and the same is true of most Conservatives, although some right-wing Conservatives have never been entirely happy about membership.

The major split over the EC was found in the Labour Party. In fact Harold Wilson was prime minister when we applied in 1967 and, at that time, he was supported by Labour's NEC and the annual conference. But left-wing hostility to EC membership grew. The argument on the Left has been a mixture of dislike in becoming part of a 'club' of capitalist countries, with a fear that the loss of sovereignty would make it impossible to introduce socialist measures. Naturally some of the costs of membership, examined later, have given Labour powerful ammunition. Between entry in 1973 and 1975, the Labour Party refused to send MPs to the European parliament or representatives to the Economic and Social Committee. The party, and government, were then split over the 1975 referendum on EC membership. The issues died back until 1979, when Labour once again opposed direct elections to the European parliament. In 1980 the Labour Party's annual conference voted in favour of British withdrawal from the EC without a further referendum and this was one factor behind the formation of the

Social Democrats in 1981. Withdrawal became a firm promise in the Labour manifesto for the 1983 election, though Labour's heavy defeat in that election has since led the party to modify its position. In 1984 Labour took a full part in fighting for seats in the European parliament although a number of Labour MEP's remain in favour of pulling out.

The economic impact of the EC on Britain

When Britain joined the EC it was not expected that there would be advantages for every part of the economy. However, it was hoped that the gains would be greater than the losses. But some of the most important 'losses' were clear straight away and have become major issues in our relations with the EC and the debate over membership.

The Common Agricultural Policy (CAP) and food prices

The CAP is designed to encourage EC food producers and protect them from competition with cheaper food suppliers in the rest of the world. Britain protected its own farmers for years before it joined the EC but its way of doing this was different from the CAP. Before 1973 Britain used a system of deficiency payments. This meant that cheap food came in from abroad and helped consumers, but governments protected farmers by paying the difference between the cheap food and their own higher production costs.

The CAP works differently. Farmers are protected by tariffs being levied on food imports from outside the EC. This makes the price of imported food higher than the price of EC food. On top of this, there are no controls over the amount produced, because the Commission buys up any surpluses if the price falls below a certain level – the **intervention price** – so that food prices can be maintained. The result has been that 'mountains' of beef and butter, and 'lakes' of wine and edible oil have been created. These are stored, with the intention of releasing them when there are shortages and prices begin to rise. In 1984 a milk quota was introduced for each country to cut down milk surpluses but it is too early to decide whether it has been effective. It certainly annoyed dairy farmers.

The intervention prices of farm products, such as cereals, milk, beef, pork, wine, are decided by an annual meeting of agriculture ministers. Naturally those countries with a large farming population are anxious to squeeze out the highest price increase possible. Another major part of CAP spending is in the subsidies given to food exports from the EC to make up for the difference between higher EC prices and lower world prices. The result is that the EC now accounts for 60 per cent of world exports of butter and 40 per cent of cheese.

No one disputes that farmers need to be protected – the question is how it should be done. The CAP protects farmers' incomes and has encouraged the EC to be self-supporting in food, which is no bad thing. But countries such as Ireland and France with a large percentage of people engaged in farming and who export food, gain. Those such as

Britain with a smaller percentage, and who need to import food, lose. Thus the CAP has two effects on Britain. Firstly, we pay out a great deal of money because we buy food from other EC countries as well as from the rest of the world. Secondly, the shift from the old system of deficiency payments to CAP raised food prices anyway. But the problems of CAP are very much bound up with the issue of the EC Budget.

The EC budget

The EC raises its money from customs duties levied on imports from outside the EC and part of each country's VAT. This penalises Britain especially because we need to import food and because we have VAT on more products and services than some countries. Spending is dominated by CAP which, as we have seen, goes largely to countries which produce food. The result is that Britain is a net contributor to the EC budget because it imports more food, and other goods, from outside the EC than other member states, so it pays more in customs duties and food levies; and receives less because it has a smaller agricultural industry. The problem is not as great as in the past because our trade with EC states has increased but a substantial difference still remains.

The drop in 1981 was due to special refunds negotiated by the government. Its case was simply that Britain, as a member country with one of the lowest incomes per head of population, should not be expected to be one of the largest contributors. But these refunds were temporary and no permanent solution has been found. The fault lies with the CAP but changing it is almost impossible at present because powerful member countries like France benefit from it considerably. And the amount spent on the CAP means that there is less to spend on areas more vital for Britain – such as social and industrial projects.

UK's Net Contribution to EC Budget

(Payments minus £m receipts)

1977	369	1980	705
1978	804	1981	55
1979	947	1982	390
		1983	685

Figure 21.4 UK's net contribution to the EC budget.

Has membership been worthwhile for Britain?

When Britain joined the EC there was hope that a number of 'dynamic benefits' would work to our advantage. Being part of a huge trading area with a population of over 250 million and a total income second only to the United States would be a great opportunity for our industry. Certainly our exports to the EC have risen sharply; it now takes 43 per cent of the total. West Germany is now Britain's biggest single export market and *The Economist* magazine has argued that 2.5 million British jobs depend on access to the EC. But imports from the EC have risen even faster and now account for 44 per cent of the total figure. Some British industries, such as motor vehicles, have suffered in the face of competition from France and Germany and, in manufactured goods, Britain has a large deficit with the EC. This deficit is, however, cut back sharply if British oil exports are included. What we have found is that many of our industries needed to become much more competitive to take advantage of EC membership. Although oil exports have been very important, this benefit may not last much beyond the year 2000.

An advantage of membership is that countries outside the EC have found Britain attractive for investment, for building new factories and within the EC tariff barriers. In 1980, 59 per cent of all direct investment into the EC came to Britain, America and Japan being the major outside investors. However, this is offset by British companies investing in Europe.

There are three underlying problems which make it difficult to assess the economic arguments about our membership of the EC. Firstly the decision to join coincided with the beginning of a world-wide recession. Secondly, any calculation of benefits must depend on how the CAP and Budget issues are decided – in 1981, for example, we should have paid £1 billion to Brussels instead of the £55 million which was the result of rebates. Thirdly, there is no way of measuring what would have happened if we had not joined. We would not have faced the problems of the CAP and the Budget but there would not have been early access for our goods into EC countries. On top of this, our exports of

War. The traditional image of Europe. The members of the European Community may not always agree but at least wars between us are a thing of the past.

manufactured goods to non-EC countries, which were declining before we joined, would in any case have had to face tough competition from EC producers.

Being part of the EC has political as well as economic meaning. Some claim that Britain has never fully appreciated that the EC is more than a trading association and that the mistake has been to consider our membership solely in economic terms. In any case, political and economic issues are often difficult to separate. For example, EC policy towards cutting imports from Japan or dealing with large multinational companies is stronger collectively than with each state negotiating on its own. In foreign policy the EC states work closely together and have developed a joint approach to problems such as the Middle East. During the Falklands crisis of 1982 Britain received very strong support from most EC members and sanctions were imposed on Argentina.

To many British people the issue of the EC seems to boil down to the questions of whether or not we should belong. Others in Europe are more concerned with how far the EC should expand to include other countries, such as Turkey. Although this would increase the problems of the CAP and the Budget as well as adding new versions of national interest, it could add stability to these countries by tying them to states with stronger democratic traditions. Whether or not Britain stays in the EC it is certain to continue. In spite of difficulties, it is an achievement that a part of Europe with a long history of nationalism, protectionism and war has been brought closer together in a working partnership.

Discussion and essay questions

1. How does the EC attempt to balance the national interests with Community interests? Why do you think it is often argued that the EC could never develop unless national interests are protected? Does this make closer ties between member countries too difficult?

2. Why is the Council of Ministers the most powerful institution in the EC? Why shouldn't issues be decided on a majority vote?

3. What is meant by 'Community law'? How are Community laws passed? What effect does Community law have on Britain?

4. What are the main arguments in favour of, and against, British withdrawal from the EC?

5. What do you think are the most important effects of British membership of the EC?

6. 'In politics, economics, foreign policy, leisure, even sport, Britain has been drawn towards Europe.' Does this make British people more 'European minded'?

7. 'Britain can only become a real member of the EC when we stop talking about leaving.' Discuss.

8. Why is it claimed that membership of the EC means that Britain has lost sovereignty? Is this important?

Index